From Boys 2 Men

Yokahama Bay, Oahu

Library of Congress Cataloging-in-Publication Data

Lubin, Marshall B. (Marshall Burton), 1946-
From Boys 2 Men, an Adventure in Paradise

1. From Boys 2 Men, an Adventure in Paradise
Memoir--Non-fiction--Travel--Adventure   1. Title
Pending

Second edition 2013

ISBN-978-1-4507-1653-6

Manufactured in the United States of America

Book design and cover photo by
Marshall Lubin

Original photographs & newspaper articles
at www.FromBoys2Men.com

Acknowledgements

Special thanks to those who wrote at a time when 99% of the human race could not understand what they read: William Shakespeare, Hermann Melville, Jules Verne

And to those more modern authors that had the privilege of being both read and understood: Fredrick Nietzsche, Hermann Hesse, Aldous Huxley, James Michener

James Cook for the audacity to double the area of the known world without slipping off the edge.

The *family of man* for the instruction and guidance it provided us during our two year sojourn around the world.

Google Earth for its ability to locate islands and villages visited and for calculating the distances between them.

Captain Tom Tursi for lending his expertise in celestial navigation.

Time Magazine for its assistance in supplying information on piracy.

Jim Simmons-Castaway in Paradise for providing historical maritime information.

David Berg and Michael Duffy for proofreading & editing.

Courtney Lawver for graphic design.

And a beautiful woman who inspired me to write. She shall remain anonymous.

Sailing New Guinea

From Boys 2 Men

an

Adventure in Paradise

By

Marshall B. Lubin

An ancient Felucca

Contents

The Beast

I
Leavin' on a Jet Plane...

Our emancipation was the greatest gift completing high school could have bestowed on us that effervescent June afternoon. Years of State mandated education had come to an end; we were about to slip the restrictive shackles of parental guidance, leave behind the cumbersome rules of home, the fetters of citified adolescence and head into a summer of shameless bliss.

It was a warm, sunny day in June; the year: 1964. At 11:15 in the morning, the four of us met at the Pan American Airways terminal at Los Angeles International Airport, chauffeured to our destination by the folks. Our parents, not quite eager to see their adolescent children heading off on an unsupervised three month trip, noted the excitement of the foursome was peaking as they entered the airport parking lot. None of us had ever been away from home for more than two weeks, but now we were about to embark on a summer surfing safari to the Hawaiian Islands, the first step in search of the island's big waves.

✳✳✳✳✳

Unfortunately, the Islands' *big waves* usually arrive during the winter months, driven to the small Pacific islands by distant storms that have their origins in the Gulf of Alaska. Well, let's not spoil the boys' adventure before they get to the boarding gate.

The four teenage boys, Marshall, Charles, Tom and Gary, had just completed their senior year at high school; didn't yet have any definite college plans, but knew in their hearts that they could use some time away from home, away from the parents and away from the usual drab scenery of the Inland Empire.

✳✳✳✳✳

It was a long time dream to go to Hawaii; to ride big waves like we had seen in the surfing movies; experience what

9

contemporaries like: Doyle, Jacobs, Takayama and Noll, had surfed in the late fifties.

What two of us couldn't know was that a serendipitous turn of events would land us in the adventure of a lifetime, circumnavigating the planet at a time when the world was at relative peace. During the next two years, Charles and I would sail to places we'd never heard of, meet people on islands we did not know existed and hear numerous languages we could not understand.

At that time in our young lives, we had not yet heard the term circumnavigation, didn't know what a ketch was nor had we ever stepped foot on a sailboat. But hey, we were only seventeen! At the beginning of our unplanned walk-about, we may not have known how to crew a sailboat, but we would soon learn.

Our foursome had just completed high school; but unbeknownst to us, our real education was just beginning. At our tender ages we had no idea of the mean spirited people that existed in the world, the ends that good hearted people might search out in their desperation and the ferocious storms that nature could pummel us with. But we would soon encounter all of those and more.

Being the children of middle class parents from Los Angeles' Inland Empire, we were used to the high school student life; daytime classes, evening study sessions, school dances Friday nights with a girlfriend.

I had been dating Margaret for over a year; I think I was falling in love with her; surely puppy love at seventeen. She had soft brown hair, sparkling brown eyes, was of medium height and had a curvaceous body that held my attention. On weekends, she joined us on surfing jaunts to the coast. We had gone to the senior prom together; we were becoming inseparable. The impending surfing excursion to the islands did not sit well with her; it was only for three months, I argued. I would soon return to her sweet embrace.

The four of us worked on our cars when we could. More importantly, the weekend was reserved for a thirty mile trek to the coast in search of cresting waves on nearby Southern California beaches: Manhattan Beach, Trestles, Huntington

Beach or the Seal Beach Jetty.

The older cars that we could afford made a regular demand for maintenance. I had learned to remove the transmission from my '47 Ford sedan by myself. I could rebuild and replace it in under four hours. The aging sedan was teaching me to drive more conservatively; otherwise I was pulling that transmission out often.

In order to support our autos and pay for gas, we sought after-school employment. But when our interest suddenly turned to a summer sojourn to the distant islands, a far greater need for income became readily apparent.

The early sixties ushered in the era of the Surfer: surf movies, surf music, Surfer Magazine, Woodies, all a part of the new surf culture that we swiftly adopted. At the age of fifteen, we parted our hair on one side, pouring lemon juice on top to facilitate it bleaching a yellowish blonde during the winter months. We now had *the look*.

We attended shows at the Santa Monica Civic Auditorium, where we watched big wave movies shot in Hawaii and visited surf shows where Woodies and other surf paraphernalia were displayed. At one show there was a group of bleached blond surfer guys singing in the middle of the lobby. They stood on a dais while singing acappella; harmonizing well, they created a really nice sound. A new group, they called themselves The Beach Boys; perhaps you've heard of them? They were a nice accoutrement to the surf show, but the movies, the beach, the waves, was what it was all about; riding Hawaii's big waves was what young board riders dreamt of. It was the world series of surfing.

All four of us had significant surfing experience. The best wave riders, myself and Charles, had been surfing three years, episodically during the winter months, but we were in the water daily during the summers. We had an insatiable thirst to hone our surfing skills.

Tom had surfed two years. He was tall and strongly built. Gary was a novice; he was really skinny, tall, and lanky; he didn't appear very strong. We questioned him about going to Hawaii; not harboring sufficient confidence in his wave riding ability. When we went to the beach, he spent more time watching the swells than riding them. Believing we would be riding much bigger waves in the islands, we thought he might be spending his summer on the beach. Undaunted, he answered our challenge with a self-righteous, "I'm going!"

✶✶✶✶✶

Both Charles and my parents had lived through the Depression. It made them very conservative. They had experienced hunger, unemployment, and the degradation that poverty and uncertainty can provide. Both served in the Great War, although I don't know what was so great about it. In the early fifties, they were pretty tough guys; like others, thick skinned; a product of their early years.

Seeking the independence of a high school grad, I chafed at the restrictive nature of living with the folks. My father was from a very conservative Jewish upbringing, he believed in following all the rules, no deviations allowed. He was strict, unforgiving, and authoritarian; he felt that I needed to go directly to college, get a job and marry. It was the path to success in 1960's America; anything else was unacceptable to him. It was a path that, in my parent's household, accepted no challenges to its righteousness, its rectitude, its integrity. All the more reason to flee.

Charles found himself in a similar situation. His father was tough. A second generation Italian, he could be harsh towards Charles and his younger sister. Looking for some freedom and the ability to make his own decisions was a carrot that Charles eagerly sought. He took solace in the companionship of his budding sister; finishing school, he felt it a perfect time to seek a peaceful existence elsewhere. "Who knows what Hawaii will lead to?"

Tommy lived with an aunt in town. I never met her and learned nothing about his family life; he was very secretive in that aspect. But he was a really good guy, was becoming a good surfer and had a great girlfriend. He looked forward to the summer in the islands.

Gary, the tall, brown haired, lanky kid, lived with his nana. She was a nice old lady, somewhat bowed from her years, with wispy grey hair tied back in a bun. She was eager to see him go to Hawaii for the summer. Nana felt Gary needed to get out more; become more independent; kick up some sand, joust with the boys, maybe even some girls. She was a cool grandma.

✳✳✳✳✳

I suppose the first indication that I was not going to lead a normal life, if indeed there is a life that can be termed *normal,* was when I was expelled from high school for wearing the tails of my shirt outside my pants. Most of us would not see this as an egregious act; however, I had a difficult time complying with rules that made no sense. My rebellious attitude was beginning to make an early appearance.

From that time onward, I seemed always to be clashing with school authorities. Either my curly brown hair was too long, my shirt was worn outside my pants, or I wore tennis shoes in place of oxfords. They didn't complain about my deep-set, chameleon-like eyes that changed color with my clothes or that I was a gangly kid. With the reaction I received from those in charge, it appeared that the school authorities were interested in most things about me, except my education.

Their harassment reached a level that became frustrating; I dreaded going to school. However, I was fortunate to solve this dilemma by transferring to another campus. Luck brought me in contact with a sagacious administrator at district headquarters, one who could see beyond the bullshit; he understood the daily challenges I faced. His insightful suggestion to move my obstinate attitude to another location and to, "stay out of trouble" allowed me to finish my senior year at high school.

Surfing became my escape. I could jump on my board, paddle out into the waves and bond with nature. No authorities, no senseless rules, only the swells that allowed me to express myself in unlimited fashion; slashing, cutting, riding high and low while my soul melded with my surfboard; then the waves.

The ocean whispers its song, the porpoise that swim near shore communicate their message; either you do it right, or you swim. Hair length, shirt tails, styles, colors, nationality were all superfluous. The water was cool, clear, and blissful. For me, it became my secret hideout in the volcano; the place where I could seek refuge when others felt a need to harass, belittle or demean me.

✶✶✶✶✶

Saying goodbye to the families took some time, "After all Mom, I'll be home in a few months, and yes of course I'll write, and eat, and call if anything exciting happens." There were the gratuitous tears that bind a family, handshakes among the males--hugging wasn't cool in the sixty's--and a final wave as we made our way through the departure gate. Our excitement had reached a point where we virtually levitated up the boarding ramp; gently planting our butts into our assigned seats. Readied for departure, Pan Am's Flight 101 carried us aloft over the Pacific Ocean on our twenty six hundred mile odyssey to the island of Oahu in the Hawaiian Archipelago.

✶✶✶✶✶

The Hawaiian Islands are located just within the Tropic of Cancer, sandwiched between nineteen and twenty two degrees North latitude. Island mythology avows that the Hawaiian goddess Papahanaumoku gave birth to the numerous east Pacific islands long ago. However, modern day thought suggests the islands were created thousands of years ago by a tortuous birthing process that took place silently beneath the sea, beginning as subterranean volcanoes that had their origins as a rift in the ocean's floor. An uninterrupted flow of molten lava from the earth's blazing interior, over twelve hundred miles below, fed the submarine building process. The lava hardened in the much cooler temperature of the tropic's shallow waters and continued to build upon itself until the mass eventually emerged above the sea; it then cooled and solidified in the earth's atmosphere.

The persistent flood of lava formed a larger and larger land mass until it covered miles of ocean, coalescing into a hard porous rock incredibly rich with minerals ejected from the earth's core. The flow formed what is currently known as the

14

Hawaiian Ridge, with six small islands cresting above the ocean's surface. The lava-formed rock wore down over numerous millennia resulting in an iron-rich red soil yielding tropical flora that covered the islands in a green carpet of lush vegetation.

Plant seeds, having floated across thousands of miles of ocean, landed on the shores of the nascent islands or were dropped from birds on the wing. The germinating seeds produced a colorful bouquet studded with plants that would later become known as: plumeria, bird of paradise, Hawaiian ginger, hibiscus and many others, creating a breathtaking vista of rich plant-life. The garland of colorful flora added variety to the sumptuous feasts of guava, banana, taro, mango and other leguminous plants that greeted pelagic birds that landed and built their nests in the islands.

Over the years, more seabirds found their way to the islands and began to populate the land mass with their offspring, nesting among the hollow crags found on many of the island's soaring volcanic cliffs. Feeding on skipjack and yellowfin tuna, squid and small shoaling fish, the unpopulated islands became favorite nesting grounds of petrels, terns, shearwater and albatross.

It has been postulated that natives from the Tuamotu Archipelago traveled to the Hawaiian Islands in giant oceangoing canoes. Maintaining their stability with the aid of twin hulls, the canoes were propelled by rudimentary sails and large paddles manned by the strongest of their crew. The Tahitian Islands, located in what is today French Polynesia, are located approximately three thousand miles to the south of Hawaii.

Making this type of open ocean passage in a primitive sailing vessel was perilous for the early explorers, however, the Tahitians were known for their fine navigational skills. Learned teachers taught young students knowledge of guiding stars found in the darkened sky. They demonstrated where the stars could be found at various times during the year; all knowledge was passed by word of mouth. Employing those skills allowed primitive islanders to pass through thousands of miles of uncharted ocean while combating formidable currents and unpredictable winds. Following the evening stars landed them on the shores of the Hawaiian Islands sometime around 500 A.D.

Finding the islands abundantly populated with wild fruit and birds on land and the surrounding sea teeming with marine life; the early Tahitians left behind settlers that began to cultivate and populate the islands.

*****

After toasting our good fortune and the prospects of a summer of surfing in Hawaii, we drifted off into a light haze as our aircraft winged its way through the afternoon sky. Navigation was not a concern as we sped headlong towards our South Pacific goal at four hundred miles per hour. Rather, we slipped off into lala-land where dreams of finding the coolest waves in the world, meeting some beautiful whines and having the summer of our lives filled our semi-conscious thoughts. Our last piece of adolescent wisdom before dozing off was, "Thank God for summer."

*****

In the early sixty's this was the life of young surfer dudes: attending high school during the day, surfing on weekends, with nocturnal dreams of someday riding Hawaii's big waves.

Someday had become a reality for the four adventurous graduates, although landing at Oahu's Honolulu Int'l Airport was a shock from the moment the sleek Boeing 707's cabin door swung open. The open door allowed the ninety percent humidity and eighty five degree ambient temperature of late June to ravage the traveling neophytes. All four immediately began sweating as their bodies made rapid adjustments to a seeming descent into Dante's Inferno.

*****

It was 2:30 in the afternoon. Having our first taste of the tropics was a bit of a shock. We now knew it would be necessary to make some serious adjustments to our usual style, including increasing fluid intake and wearing less clothing. "Not a problem," we thought.

Dressed in the traveler's attire of the day, we all sported dark slacks, dress shoes and a Madras jacket over a white dress shirt with the collar buttoned. A pencil width tie bound tightly around our necks completed our adolescent flight apparel. While this outfit was fine for the mainland, it was definitely not island attire. Once assaulted by the heat, we found ourselves to be uncomfortably, awkwardly and conspicuously overdressed.

A forty five minute drive from the airport delivered us to our waiting rooms at the Ala Moana YMCA. Its cool air-conditioned interior was our first respite from the over-powering heat that confronted us at the airport. We found our rooms, dumped our gear and changed clothes; donning shorts, we headed across the highway. Strolling through a couple of parking lots that surrounded the Ala Wai Yacht Harbor, we finally arrived at Ala Moana's well-known surf beach.

Not to be disappointed, a set of six foot swells rolled in from a quarter mile off shore, breaking one hundred yards from the coarse, sandy beach. The four of us stood and stared at the continual line of swells with ear to ear grins on our faces. We had found the mother lode. We had just arrived in a foreign place that we had only before glimpsed in pictures; we were here and God Almighty, the surf was incredible! We could have all died at that moment in time; we would have gladly found our places in heaven with those same unrestrained grins on our faces.

We raced back to the Y and grabbed our surfboards; we had spent the year in after-school work to reach this point. The hours of evening and weekend toil allowed us to scrimp and save. We banked extra money for rent and food; we had purchased our round trip tickets and now we were in paradise. Heading for the beach, we delighted in riding some of the best waves we had ever seen. We surfed till the sun set and the darkening sky made it almost impossible to see the endless swells rolling towards shore.

The next day, after surfing away the morning hours at Ala

Moana, was spent parsing the local newspapers for used cars. We needed transportation that could ferry the four of us, with our surfboards, to the distant beaches found on both the north and south shore of Oahu. That meant a half hour or more driving to celebrated beaches with great tube-shaped waves.

A 1947 Pontiac was discovered sitting in the back of a used car lot. Surprised that we were interested in what the salesman viewed as an inveterate *junker*, we purchased the beast for seventy five dollars--hey, it was the sixty's! We had fallen in love; the Pontiac displayed a perverse beauty that we totally embraced. It had an oxidized gray exterior and bare tires; tired, gray, worn naugahyde upholstery, not so delicately covered the bench seats. A three speed manual transmission, that couldn't get rubber in any gear to save its life, sat coupled to the six cylinder, flathead engine. To add to its contrarian beauty, a body panel was missing from the right side. In front, where you would expect to find a grill, was an open space exposing the radiator to view; superior cooling we surmised. The opening gave the Pontiac a distinct look of disrepair, the perfect summer surf buggy.

The vertical portion of the rear seat was immediately removed; the cardboard backing that separated the rear seat from the trunk was torn out from the center opening. Thus, a space was created where the nose of the four surfboards could slide up to the back of the front seat with the tails protruding from the rear of the trunk, a perfect fit. The surfboards were anywhere from eight feet ten inches to nine feet two inches in length. Short boards did not exist in the mid-sixty's; hot doggers had to put a great deal more effort into moving the long board to do cutbacks and kick-outs. For safety, a red cloth was attached to the tail of the boards.

Fully equipped, we were now ready to conquer the island's beaches, both near and far. Understanding that we had made a gamble buying the seventeen year old Pontiac, the four of us said a prayer, hoping our $75 surf buggy would endure the coming trials of summer.

While surfing at different locations around the island by day: Ala Moana, Sand Island, Queens, and Yokahama Bay, night offered us the opportunity to search out alternative living arrangements. A review of our meager finances brought to light the fact that a move of this type, where we could pay a monthly rent, would prove to be financially astute. Currently, the four of us each paid the daily room rate at the Y; it was a serious drain on our budgets. We soon found and moved into a spacious apartment in the outskirts of Waikiki; occupied mostly by islanders, both Hawaiian and Samoan. It was a great location for meeting locals and gaining insight into their secret surf spots.

In the evenings, we listened to our neighbors spin stories from their families' past histories, including tales about far away Pacific islands like Samoa, a place that was currently unknown to us. We soon learned that Samoa consisted of a group of islands located twenty seven hundred miles to the southwest of Hawaii; it was peopled by tall, dark-skinned Polynesians similar in physical characteristics to the Hawaiians.

We were told the Samoans were great sailors and navigators, using the stars to guide them across the vast Pacific. Our new friends spun tales about how, "In ancient times both the Marquesas and Tonga were discovered and populated by our ancestors." The primitive natives, eager to explore and conquer, continued throughout the east Pacific, discovering most of the islands of Polynesia. Polynesia, a major division of the South Pacific Ocean, encompasses multiple island groups including: the Samoas, Cook Islands, Hawaii, the Marquesas and the Tahitian or Society Islands.

The evening history and geography lessons were spaced between diurnal surf trips to various parts of Oahu, some exploring, and always an eye out for the wahines, who vacationed on Oahu in equal or greater numbers than their male counterparts.

The beaches were full of young women lounging, tanning, and surveying the muscular Hawaiian beach boys. Getting a date was never a problem. Actually, hooking up with shapely young mainland ladies that had come to the islands to enjoy the summer, tan themselves on Waikiki's beautiful sand beaches and hopefully have a mid-year fling, seemed to happen without any effort.

It was a time that adolescents were morphing into young adults; both male and female eyes made inquiring tours as sun bathers lounged; the scent of hot bodies lathered with tanning lotion wafted across the sand floating on the afternoon's light ocean breezes; the heat of the tropics increased hormonal reaction rates; pheromones pinged off umbrellas, chairs, lounges and each other. Most young males, unable to control their testosterone surges, laid face down in the sand.

After surfing for a few hours in the morning, we would join those lounging at the beach, talk to girls we had met and make arrangements to meet for dinner. Arriving at the apartments of our newly made girlfriends after a day in the water and our afternoon sunning ritual, we learned about their lives as they spoke of the homes and families they had left behind for the summer.

We were young, but buying beer at the local market went unchallenged by store clerks. We would provide the liquid refreshment while the girls would supply the twilight meal making for a fun and relaxing evening.

Later, we would stroll along the shore; the star-soaked sand reflected the floodlights of beach-front hotels: the Outrigger, Royal Hawaiian, and the Hilton Hawaiian Village. It was incredibly romantic; the sound of the surf breaking just offshore, a sky filled celestial nightclub of dancing stars overhead and one of the most beautiful beaches in the world. It was difficult not to fall in love, even if it was only for the summer.

Displaying an interest in visiting other parts of the island, the girls were invited to come along on our daily surf trips, although it was not yet the time when women would become avid surfers. That time would arrive a few decades later. Still, it was always great to have the ladies along on those exploratory trips; they were very supportive of our surfing and usually had a different view of events and places, adding a feminine dimension to the day's activities.

Their influence was felt when the girls suggested we stop at Waimea Falls after viewing the famed Waimea Bay; a big wave beach in winter that was disappointingly devoid of surf during the summer months. From the parking lot, a short stroll up a dirt path through dense growth delivered us to the picturesque waterfall. The scenic and well-known falls, fed by cool mountain rainwater, cascaded gently over moss covered rocks falling sixty feet into a deep, clear, pool below. The rock rimmed pool was large enough to swim in or dive into from above; its placid surface reflecting the dense green foliage of the surrounding hillsides. The pool's unruffled, shaded waters tumbled downstream through a narrow creek where they emptied into the bay, almost a mile away.

Needing to show off our adolescent bravado, as young boys do, we climbed half way up the falls, leaping into the clear waters of the pool below. I, being the wildest of the four, climbed the entire sixty feet to the top of the falls and then dove into the air, making an impressive swan dive before crashing into the waiting pool below.

Unfortunately, I landed half on my back and legs rather than hands and head first. Somewhat stunned, I was a bit pale as I slowly surfaced to the laughter of those waiting. "Good dive, Marshall!" they yelled as the color slowly returned to the blanched, stinging skin of my back and shoulders. I lay quietly on the water's surface, waiting for the stinging to diminish while sensation returned to my traumatized shoulders. In a moment, the discomfort subsided; I joined the others on the pool's rock rim.

✳✳✳✳✳

With a disappointing frown showing our displeasure, the four of us discussed the fact that the surf seemed to diminish each day. We could only enjoy so much touring. True, the girls enjoyed visiting different beaches around the island, but we had come thousands of miles to ride waves, and riding waves was, almost, the only thing that would make us happy.

In our nocturnal deliberations with the Samoan neighbors, and without trying to depreciate the great beaches we visited, discussion turned to other places to surf. The neighbors spoke lovingly of their homeland and the beautiful beaches, the great waves, and the families they had left behind in Samoa. They suggested going to Pago Pago--pronounced Pango Pango and simply Pango by locals--located on the island of Tutuila, to search out more and perhaps better surfing spots where we could ride uncontested tube-shaped swells, all day long, every day.

Reaching back through decades of dust covered observations, thoughts, and sounds; they unearthed the heart warming familial memories of years gone by. The neighbors verbally painted vivid pictures that told of the enchanting seaside villages populated by beach houses floored with local hardwoods. The walls were made of woven palm fronds that could be lowered to protect the inhabitants from rain and wind, and raised to allow the mild ocean breezes to cool the indoors. The foundations of the houses were built on palm stumps, two feet above ground, protecting the homes from rushing water during the heavy rains of the monsoon season.

Food was procured by fishing with a net near shore or from a boat during the day. At night they slept on hand-woven mats piled high to insulate a warm body from the cool, firm floor. Only a cotton sheet was needed to ward off the light dew of morning and warm a sleeping soul. They spoke of picking breadfruit from nearby trees. Mango, papaya and guava also grew wild on the island, and goat cheese could be bought or traded for fish from a neighbor. The cheese came wrapped in a banana leaf fastened with a cord improvised from a native vine.

We listened in awe. It sounded too good to be true; it sounded like an Alexander Selkirk fantasy. In the early 18th century, Selkirk was a real-life castaway who lived four years on a deserted island in the Juan Fernandez Archipelago, located near the southwest coast of South America. Years later, Daniel Defoe created the fictional Robinson Crusoe novel based on Selkirk's adventures. We thought, "How could someplace be so cool?" Coming from the asphalt confines of Los Angeles, it sounded more like a fantasy island; someplace that might be viewed in a movie or read in a book, rather than a genuine island.

Enraptured with the thought, we discussed a possible

extension to our trip. Should we venture to the south, to a new land we had never before heard of? Should we be, at age seventeen, adventurers that could actually find a tropical paradise where we could live on the beach, meet beautiful native women, spend our days surfing the island's uncontested waves while living off the land? In our youthful ignorance and unbridled optimism, we could think of no reason why not.

Seeing the lights of discovery flashing in our eyes, the neighbors understood we were interested in venturing farther into the South Pacific; they offered to write a letter of introduction to their family members still living in Samoa. They told us that the family would meet us at the airport, take us home and give us a place to live until we could find our own way. The hospitality of the islands would be extended to us unconditionally and for as long as necessary.

Suddenly, we were being exposed to an opportunity to venture into a life that was so incredible, so out of the ordinary that we had not even dared to dream it.

Displaying our adolescent caution when considering a new and foreign idea; we discussed the possibility of extending our trip on several evenings. Not wanting to be capricious in our decision making, we reviewed the trip's pros, its cons.

After contacting the airlines, we found that only Pan American flew to Tutuila, but there was a brand new airport in Pango. In addition, travelers were required to purchase a round trip ticket when flying to Samoa, as it was an American protectorate. The government didn't want any young kids getting stranded on the island without an exit strategy. We looked at finances, finding we barely had enough money to buy a return ticket to Samoa.

Having ruminated on the idea of extending our nascent trip; of cutting the umbilical cord that connected us to our friends and families, our homes, our security, the limited world we were familiar with; we realized an adventure doesn't begin until you take that first step. We made the final decision to, "Go for it!"

It was agreed that Charles and I would make a reconnaissance trip to Pango; we purchased two round trip tickets. After paying for the airline tickets, Charles had thirteen dollars, I had seven. That gave us a total of twenty dollars to begin our evolving adventure, not an overwhelming sum.

The idea sent our heads spinning; conjecture only encouraged our unknowing minds to wander: if we met up with a family in Samoa and were cared for until we could build a beach house from driftwoods and palm fronds, than all would be well. Surely the locals had the knowledge and would help us with the construction. The neighbors stated that things were pretty cheap in Samoa and our twenty dollars would go far. Actually, we were told that we wouldn't need any money that the hospitality of the islands would care for us.

✶✶✶✶✶

At this point, any sane person might think the boys were delusional, but hey it was the sixties, they were only seventeen and had no pressing appointments on their calendars.

Hittin' the surf

II

Where in the World is Pago Pago?

Having purchased two round trip tickets to the island of Tutuila, Charles and I were dutifully chauffeured to the airport in the beast. Tom and Gary sat in the front seat while we secured our surfboards in the back; rushing to the airport, we didn't want to be late for our mid-morning flight. At 11:00 A.M., we said our goodbyes. Tom prodded us, "Write and let us know what you find in Samoa." I replied, "We'll write as soon as we know something definite." Not quite sure what to expect, we held on tenaciously to the letter that was written by our neighbors to their Samoan relatives.

With our minds focused on an unknown future and being very excited about this extension to our surfing safari, we never did look very closely at the letter. It was written on one of those inexpensive, blue, single page, fold-up sheets that double as international letters. Being the only connection we had to anyone at the other end of our flight, it was carried securely in a front pocket by Charles.

What made the trip interesting from the outset was the fact that we were the only two non-islanders on the flight. Everyone else was Samoan. The other passengers were either flying home to see family or were returning home from a vacation in Hawaii.

Being somewhat self-conscious, we felt as though we were the main topic of discussion by the other passengers. We overheard them speaking in hushed tones with an occasional giggle as they spied on us through the cracks between the forward seats. The other passengers were very friendly, greeting us as they walked past our seats on the way to the lavatory. They were obviously curious about the haole's presence in what is usually a totally native environment.

Hours later, the Pan Am 707, the luxury liner of the day, dropped out of the cool clear skies, and blasted through some drifting cumulus clouds. It deployed its ailerons as it rolled first left, then right, turning its nose into the wind while making a decelerating approach to Pango's new airport. The landing itself was uneventful; after taxiing to the edge of the runway the plane spun around with its tail facing the end of the tarmac. It dropped its rear ramp for the passengers to disembark.

Upon alighting from the aircraft we noted there were no buildings around the new airport, no hangars, not even a control tower. We did see a wind sock waving lazily on one side of the airfield. "Odd," we thought. That was our first clue of just how primitive this island nation was in the 1960's. Soon the baggage was unloaded from the belly of the aircraft and was lined up on the edge of the runway; the surfboards along side. Once everything was cleared from the aircraft, the pilot raised the rear loading ramp, throttled up the engines and taxied down the runway for takeoff. The returning flight was soon airborne leaving everyone behind on the ground in the very peaceful, quiet and deserted *airport*. And at 2 p.m., it was blazing hot under the unrelenting rays of the Samoan sun.

The locals gazed our way as we stood separately with our single bags and two surfboards lying on the ramp. The heat started the surface wax melting; gravity caused it to migrate towards the boards' rails, we flipped them over allowing the wax to cool on the boards' underside. Curiosity overcame the Samoans; they walked over to check if someone was coming for us. I replied, "Yes, someone is supposed to pick us up."

People began arriving to meet relatives, loaded up their baggage and departed for the town a few miles away. More locals arrived, kissed and chatted with relatives, looked at the two haoles standing and waiting alone on the tarmac; soon they were all gone. Everyone had been picked up; only the two of us remained standing there in the ninety degree heat of summer at two thirty in the afternoon, waiting. We stared at the road leading to the airfield, hoping to hear the sound of an approaching vehicle, see someone drive up, jump out, hand extended to shake ours, but no one did.

Fifteen minutes passed very slowly and then we thought we heard the straining sound of an engine as it powered an approaching vehicle uphill to the quiet plateau where the airfield was perched. We knew it had to be for us; no one else was in sight. A stranger in an old green military Jeep had returned to the airport to check on us. He stopped his Jeep directly in front of us; turning his gaze towards Charles and I, he said, "Hi" and asked who was picking us up. Glad to see his interest, we eagerly replied to the stranger, "We don't know the name of the person coming for us." That was his first clue to our own ignorance. "They are a relative of our neighbors in Hawaii." We explained that we had a letter of introduction to give to our new, and as yet, unmet, unnamed, and unknown host.

Asking to see the letter, the stranger introduced himself as Sam. Sam was duly handed the postal sheet. He inspected the addressee's name and street address and could not decipher the scribble. We looked at the front of the letter and couldn't read a legible name or address, either. We all had a good laugh. At Sam's insistence, we loaded our bags and surfboards into our new friend's Jeep. He suggested taking the two of us into town to try to find someone who could interpret the letter; hopefully, he could locate the family who was supposed to meet our plane.

We drove the few miles into town where we encountered the village of Pago Pago. Pango, as it was called by the Samoans, consisted of a few buildings spaced infrequently around the harbor. There were no hotels in Pango at that time, guest houses sufficed for the rare traveler that passed through the islands.

✳✳✳✳✳

Actually, the only non-islanders passing this way were usually from cruising yachts. Leaving Australia and heading east while meandering between fifteen and twenty one degrees of latitude south of the Equator, a sailboat could island hop across the Pacific, visiting places like New Caledonia, Vanuatu, Fiji, Samoa, then head north to Hawaii and finally the west coast of the U.S. The opposite heading was followed by Americans traveling west through the South

Pacific. An alternate route consisted of sailing south from California to the Galapagos Islands and then turning west towards Tahiti, Samoa and so on.

✻✻✻✻✻

Few businesses existed in Pango. There was a general store, an open air market and a couple of small restaurants. Homes were scattered randomly around the shore. There was the town pub, the Islander. It looked to us as an as yet undiscovered piece of the planet inhabited by some of the friendliest people on earth. "Maybe we really are in paradise," we thought. At the top of the bay were a couple of square concrete buildings that were part of a government compound.

Our new friend Sam dropped us off at a restaurant that was an extension of the proprietor's home. Sam said he would try to locate someone that could interpret the letter, hopefully discovering who our hosts might be. We entered and sat down at a table in the empty dining room. In a few minutes the owner walked in and made a face like he had seen a ghost. The last thing he ever expected to see in his humble establishment was two young boys from the mainland. Tourists just didn't come to Pango. There was nothing to do there, nothing to see. Blinded by the beauty of everyday living in a tropical paradise, its commonality caused its inhabitants to see it as banal.

But we saw just the opposite, stunned by the intoxicating beauty of our surroundings; we stared out the windows that lined the walls of the dining room. To one side we could see the entire bay with small fishing boats that lay passively at anchor. The far shore was surrounded by tall hills sparsely populated with native homes. The homes were surrounded with bright green vegetation and colorful flowers. Everywhere we looked we were awed by the abundant beauty of prolific vegetation that seemed to cover every inch of nutrient rich soil.

Returning a few hours later, Sam had found a family that would be honored to have us stay in their home. Sam drove around to the opposite side of the inlet that formed the deep-

28

pocketed bay known as Pago Pago harbor. The bay had a dogleg shape to it, providing adequate protection to mariners seeking refuge from the powerful storms that frequented the South Pacific.

Within the bay was a small U.S. Coast Guard Base with one eighty-foot patrol vessel and a small contingent of personnel. The harbor had a few medium-sized fishing vessels scattered around a small boatyard and some old wooden boats that might have carried copra in their youth. They had obviously seen better days, long ago. Wharves filled in the near side of the harbor that culminated in the small Coast Guard base.

The base was developed by the American government to create a safety net for shipping in a thousand mile radius from Pango. Frequent Pacific storms arrive during the monsoon season, creating a hazard for maritime vessels transiting the area. However, the services of the Coast Guard were rarely needed as Pango was not in line with any major shipping routes. Only small fishing boats and inter-island cargo ships plied these mostly tranquil waters.

The Samoan islands are located in the midst of the tropics, fourteen degrees south of the Equator. They are cooled daily by the trade winds that blow around the world from east to west. *The Trades,* as they're known, have carried sailors around the world for centuries. They have given inspiration to explorers looking for new lands, carrying traders far and wide with cargoes from newly discovered lands to old. In recent decades, yachtsmen have used the trades for around the world cruising, as the wealthy and the retired have frittered away their leisure time circumnavigating the world by sail. It's not a bad life.

We took in the sights as Sam drove us around the bay, stopping at a concrete walled house where we were introduced to our new family. Three generations lived together under the roof of the patriarch, William. His wife and their three sons, who had all married, shared the six bedrooms of the concrete home with their three grandchildren. William had done well for his family, they were considered wealthy for the area, hence the home built from concrete rather than traditional native materials. The home was built on a plateau one hundred feet up the side of a hill, above the harbor, where it had a commanding view of the deep-water bay and surrounding mountains. Surrounded by various species of palms, bird of paradise, purple mangosteen, purple and rose colored bougainvillea, the house's landscaping added color to the somewhat drab appearance of concrete in paradise.

The home was sparsely furnished, making Charles and I feel as though we might be imposing. But our host was more than gracious, stating we were welcome to stay as long as we wished. There was a sideboard in the family room where dining and serving dishes were stored. Cupboards in the kitchen held cooking utensils, pots and pans; a table for preparing meals and a small four burner stove fueled by bottled propane filled out the kitchen. Meals were taken in the family room where there were no tables or chairs; custom was that everyone sat cross-legged on the floor during meals. A large woven mat supplied a thin barrier between the family's bottoms and the cool, solid concrete floor.

All family members slept on hand-woven mats piled high according to rank. Charles and I were given six mats each, creating a density we found to be quite comfortable, with a top sheet to ward off the morning dampness. The married children of William had their own rooms where they slept with the grandchildren.

Meals were a community affair with everyone participating. The women cooked and cleaned up after dinner while the men were responsible for providing the meals and the home environment. After dinner the men spoke about their day and discussed community affairs. The women were mostly silent during the meals, but listened attentively to stories being spun by their mates. As the elders were not fluent in English, most mealtime discussions were conducted in Samoan leaving the two of us in suspense as to their content.

Speaking with the sons, we learned that William, a humble fisherman, learned the fishing trade from his father. He owned a small fishing boat that was manned by his three sons. They would cruise to different parts of the island employing nets to catch surgeonfish, parrotfish, goatfish, skipjack tuna and an occasional shark. In deeper waters, they line-fished for swordfish and dorado. They brought their catch into a central market and sold it to villagers not only in Pango, but in other communities around the island. Fortunately, they were very good fishermen; the warm clear waters around Tutuila supplied bountiful feasts of both deep sea and reef fish, affording them a nice living for their multi-generational family.

The women cultivated a small plot of land behind the house. They planted vegetable seeds or cuttings; carrots, lettuce, tomato and cucumber all grew well. Melons grew large in the hot climate; all maturing rapidly in the mineral rich red soil. The garden was watered by the profuse rainfall of the tropics creating a colorful accoutrement to the fresh fish served at the evening meal. Dessert was supplied by the wild fruit that grew all over the island, with an occasional scoop of homemade ice cream added as a special delight.

The native dress was well suited to the hot tropical weather. The common garb was a piece of cloth, printed with a bright floral pattern worn around the body. The men tied the garment, called a Lava Lava, or Lava for short, around their waist; it extended to their ankles.

The ladies would place the cloth behind them, bringing first the right and then the left side forward, wrapping the Lava around their bodies; they pulled the ends over their shoulders, knotting the material behind their neck; an outfit that was light, cool and airy for the warm, humid climate. When going into town, the men would add a shirt to their Lava, making them respectfully dressed to visit friends in public or at home.

There was a slow, but obvious, change taking place in both of us. When we had arrived in Honolulu, we left behind the custom of wearing long pants and substituted shorts as our main form of dress in the tropical heat. Now, we took another step towards going native by adopting the island's Lava rap. It was very comfortable and, in a short time, we actually felt and looked out of place when not wearing it. When working or trying to keep cool, the long length of the Lava could be doubled up and tucked into the waistband, making the wrap function like well-ventilated shorts.

William's three young sons, who had learned some English in school, gave us a tour of the village, introducing us to friends and acquaintances. We learned about island life, its trials and its conflicts. Seems all was not well among the Pacific islanders: petty jealousies existed, name-calling took place and when arguments got out of hand, rock throwing became the main form of combat. Fortunately, they had no modern weapons or things could have been really messy. When Charles asked what an argument was about, some unintelligible answer was mumbled in a mix of Samoan and English; he was left none the wiser, their way of saying, "Don't worry about it."

William's sons also introduced us to the Islander, the lone pub in Pango. Refreshing ourselves with a cool beer one afternoon, we met some of the sailors' in transit through the Pacific. Three small sailboats sat in the serenely peaceful waters of the bay; the owners and crew enjoyed refreshing themselves during the late afternoon with a cool, native brew at the Islander. The main point of interest, however, was the native girls that hung out there. Beautiful women with long black hair, bright eyes and soft brown skin tanned by the radiant sunlight of the tropical afternoons; wrapped in a vibrantly colored Lava, they made any sailor's day.

Due to our youth and bright smiles, Charles and I made a hit with the local ladies. After imbibing a few beers one night, we were invited to join two honeys at their place. Not wishing to disappoint the ladies, we headed out into the darkness; striding up a foot path to a native home where we were introduced to the island's greatest pleasures. The next morning, we returned home without any comment from the family; they knew we could take care of ourselves.

A few nights later, Jeff, the eldest son, said a friend of his was eager to meet the young visitors from America. Being curious and wanting to explore everything that came our way, we looked forward to meeting another inhabitant of this unspoiled paradise. We followed Jeff, climbing high up on a hill that surrounded the harbor. Had it not been for the dark of night we would have enjoyed a magnificent view of the surrounding panorama. The unseen vista was highlighted by the Rainmaker, a tall, soaring mountain that rose high into the wind driven clouds. Those clouds bombarded the mountain with sheets of rain on a daily basis. It seemed to be in the storm path of every ocean squall headed to the area; appropriately named, the Rainmaker was the wettest spot in the islands.

A fifteen minute walk through the hills on dirt paths, worn bare by years of foot traffic, brought us to our destination. The home of the sightless Joseph was perched on a plateau high on the hillside. After entering, we were introduced to a white haired, sixty year old man who explained that his blindness was due to an aberration of the birthing process. It was a heads up that the medical care that existed in this area was primitive, at best.

Joseph's home was made of native materials, wooden walls and floors hewn from the hardwood Ipil tree. It was covered with a thatched roof woven from the fronds of coconut palms. The windows were rectangular spaces covered by wooden shutters that prevented storm hardened wind and rain from assaulting the interior. Joseph had an outhouse a short distance from the main house; he used kerosene lamps to light the interior when he had guests. Joseph lived alone in his cozy hillside nest, enjoying the tranquility of his hermit-like solitude.

We exchanged pleasantries; Jeff interpreting back and forth between Samoan and English. Joseph told a story of seeing, in his mind's eye, a terrifying, intensely bright flash that he could only imagine to be an atomic explosion. He wondered if this was a real and current possibility. Charles reassured him that since the end of WW II no nuclear blasts had taken place and with God's good grace there would not be any more. He seemed to have a great fear for the planet and its inhabitants; he felt relieved when Charles told him of the current peaceful nature of the world. It was touching to hear Joseph's sincere concern for the well being of the world population; especially from a gentleman who lived high on a hill, on a remote island, far from any teeming metropolis. On Tutuila, no television existed. Information was often passed by word of mouth. For someone without eyesight, Joseph seemed to have a profound understanding of the perilous nature of our planet; it appeared he had a great deal more insight than his young guests who came to visit that night.

The next day, feeling we had been out of the water much too long, I approached William, asking if he knew of anyone with a vehicle who might take us surfing. There was a dearth of swells in the protected waters of the harbor; we were getting itchy to ride some waves. William said he would speak to a friend about finding us a ride. He assured us that we would find good beaches with lots of waves.

A few days later, a cousin arrived in a jeep. We loaded the surfboards and together drove west, out of Pango. We rode on a primitive paved road that didn't appear to see much traffic. Actually, none that day. After driving thirty minutes along a gorgeous palm lined coast we came to the village of Fagaitua; its sea-loving inhabitants living in twenty or thirty homes scattered throughout the tree lined shore. Looking out from the beach, we could see waves breaking two hundred yards out. Jeff and his cousin sat on the beach watching while Charles and I hit the surf. Paddling out from a white sand beach, we found a shallow reef submerged two feet below the surface. Three foot swells made their way from the open ocean to the reef where they acquired a tubular shape, crashing noisily on the reef's outer edge. Later, the villagers told us to be careful; the reef was covered with a unique type of *fire coral* that burns if it gets under the skin. We were told that, "Given a chance, the coral would begin to grow in the moist sub-dermal layers of an open wound." Completing our afternoon of surfing, we returned home as the sun fell toward the western horizon and the sky filled with elongated, wispy, cirrus clouds; their undersides softly lit with the crimson glow of sunset.

Having been in Pango for only seven days, we were still in the exploring stage. We were walking down by the bay when a car drove up. Surprisingly, it stopped beside us. Charles thought this was strange, since we were told there were very few vehicles on the island. It was stranger still, because we didn't know anyone there. However, it seemed everyone knew who the new visitors were and so did the Governor of the island. With only twenty Caucasians on Tutuila, we were conspicuous simply by our presence.

American Samoa is a protectorate of its big brother to the northeast, and an American Governor ruled the island, with an iron fist. He knew what was going on everywhere and allowed things to happen or not, depending on his mood that day. He was exactly the type of authoritarian figure that I had acquired a distaste for in my youth. His messengers bore an invitation to visit with his majesty; we knew he wasn't inviting us to the Governor's Ball. I decided we should ignore his summons, explaining to his courier that we were busy today. We told his envoys we would confer with him on another, future day. The messengers seemed stunned by my response; they drove off muttering to themselves. The Samoans couldn't quite understand why these young visitors wouldn't want to meet the Governor. After all, he did rule the island.

Charles and I shared a subconscious feeling that meeting the island's authorities could have unexpected and unwanted results. Thinking of my earlier experiences with authorities, I did my best to give them a wide berth. However, having given the idea some thought, we did question why the Governor wanted to see us?

Unfortunately, our refusal to respond to the Governor's summons didn't go over well with his majesty; a few days later, again while walking along the bay, his emissaries returned with orders to deliver the two of us to his office, immediately.

We were whisked away in an official vehicle. Deposited in front of a large concrete building at the foot of the bay, I could feel the small hairs on the back of my neck begin to rise. With some trepidation, we entered the glass windowed building.

The Governor himself seemed a pleasant enough man, a pedantic gent of unquestionable character. At least we thought so, until he began quizzing us about our intentions in Samoa. Trying to avoid a straight answer, we responded that we had none that would interest him; not the response he had expected to hear. He queried us about what we were doing in Pango. Charles explained that we had found Hawaii to be disappointing; as the surf continued to deteriorate from the time we had arrived. We had purchased an airplane ticket and traveled another two thousand miles looking for the surf of our dreams. It had occurred to us to build a small hut on the beach, perhaps marry Samoan girls and in essence *go native*. The Governor, not at all enjoying the narrative, responded, "Do your mothers know what you're doing?"

Thinking it best to be in the good graces of the Governor, Charles explained how friends in Honolulu had introduced us to our host family. He mentioned the introductory letter, explaining we had only recently arrived on the island. The Governor, not wishing us to even temporarily live off the graciousness of our host family, decided to play the stern father figure. He stated, "Fine, either get a job or get out of town; you have thirty days and my men will be watching."

Unfortunately, the husky Samoans that were employed on the police force looked like they could flatten a car simply by sitting on it. We decided it was in our best interest to behave.

Upon departing the government building we allowed our adolescent thoughts to surface, "Hmm, sounds just like home; get a job! Do people actually work in paradise? Somehow, there seems to be an inconsistency here. What happened to the beachcomber's life: surfing in the morning, fishing in the afternoon, living out the dream in our self-built hut on the beach with a beautiful native girl? Get a Job! Woo! Paradise lost!" Our premonition about meeting with the authorities had been dead on; a sense of disappointment and disillusion enveloped us.

While we were trying to decide what action to take, we distracted ourselves by paddling our surfboards around the harbor; we took in the sights of our new, perhaps temporary, Pacific Island home. Hearing someone hailing us from a boat tied up at the pier; we paddled over to see who was making all the noise. As we approached an old dilapidated copra boat, a crewman onboard waved. He asked, "What are you guys doing paddling surfboards around the harbor?" Apparently, no one had ever brought surfboards to Pango; the sight of two guys paddling around the harbor was a bit of a surprise. We were invited aboard the aging derelict where we introduced ourselves to Frank. We told him about our ill-fated adventure that seemed to run aground before it had started. Reiterating the Governor's ultimatum, we mentioned our need for a job or the alternative, "get outta town" message.

Tom and Me

III

Enter the *Isabel Rose*

Curious about our new friend, we inquired into what Frank was doing in Samoa; couldn't have been too good we thought, he didn't even own a surfboard. Frank related that he had been hired to work on this small inter-island cargo boat, the *Isabel Rose*. The boat was recently purchased by a collection of businessmen from the Pan Pacific Lines, in Honolulu. She was being organized to carry cargo around the islands. Frank explained that he had been hired on as the cook on the *Isabel Rose* since the first of the month and at the time he was the only crewman on the boat.

A month earlier, Frank had arrived in Samoa on a trimaran from the Fiji Islands. The Kiwi, a three hulled sailboat, was crewed by Frank and two New Zealanders, who had originated their trip in Auckland. Heading for the states, they had sailed off leaving Frank in Pango, by his choice. There weren't a whole lot of job offers in the area or much to do in Pango, but as we later found, Frank wasn't really trying to go anywhere.

Looking at the *Isabel Rose*, it appeared to have been rescued from a floating junkyard. The metal railings were rusted; brown spots marked the dirty white topsides; if you looked at the hull-planks from the level of the water you could see through the dried out wood into the boat's hold where ill-fated cargo might be stowed. The caulking that would normally fill the space between the wooden planks had long ago fallen away, leaving behind a small gap sufficiently wide to allow water to flow into the vessel when she was loaded with cargo. The added weight would submerge more dried out planks inviting an ever increasing amount of ocean to seep into the boat causing it to slowly, imperceptibly, sink.

The boat's forward cargo hold had a hatch cover that measured ten by ten feet. Its age and rotten wood caused it to sag in the center. It could be seen that trying to lift the hatch cover off its stops would probably result in the cover disintegrating; which of course it did.

We later found that the boat's motor didn't run, that the *Isabel Rose* had been sitting in Pango harbor as a derelict for over a decade; she was not considered seaworthy. In her first incarnation, the diesel powered boat was used for ferrying copra from the surrounding islands to Pango. In its current guise, it seemed to be practicing magic as it made an illusion of being a floating, functional, cargo boat.

Since we couldn't find anything else to do and the clock was ticking down on our thirty day ultimatum, we considered a job offer that came through Frank. Discussing the paucity of possibilities that had presented themselves; we had decided that returning home was not an option; we had embarked on an unanticipated adventure and we were eager to see it play out, however that might happen.

After talking to the boat's captain, we decided to sign on as crew. The offer was fifty dollars per month, plus all the food and drink we could consume. In return we would be instructed in how to maintain the vessel; chip rust off metal railings, paint the topsides, learn some boat handling skills and manage cargo when the boat could find jobs hauling something to somewhere. We would also be required to stand watch when the boat was in transit; meaning we would need to learn how to steer the boat, and stay awake doing it, for hours at a time. "Not a problem," we thought.

It seemed some ambitious businessmen in Honolulu had given Jerry, a red headed, fair skinned, venal man of thirty five years, some money to buy a boat. He planned to earn a fortune hauling cargo throughout the South Pacific. This idea somewhat confused us. "How do you take a boat that barely floats and turn it into a gold mine?" we asked. Perhaps their idea was a bit of a stretch? So, the silver tongued Jerry bought this eighty seven ton piece of floating junk for eighty six hundred dollars, with a motor that didn't run. The boat was essentially a floating rust bucket that had a crew with no ocean going experience and was going to make a fortune? Hmmm…we thought.

What we later found was that Jerry had absolutely no

knowledge of work of this sort and it showed in his lack of thought for both the boat and the crew. That fact became all too evident as time passed. In our youthful innocence, what we hadn't anticipated: there might be ulterior motives in play.

*****

In the far away recesses of the South Pacific, there are places where no law exists, where there are no time-outs and no penalties are awarded for bad behavior. There, those with a proclivity towards aberrant behavior: the dysfunctional, the disturbed, the psychosocial, the homosexual and the just plain delusional can be found roaming unrestrained, unobserved, and unknown.

*****

In a few months time the surreptitious thoughts that can pervert an honest man began to show themselves in Jerry's actions. Like many, avaricious thoughts of gold had infected his mind as he became psychologically inebriated with toxic images of easy money. Unfortunately, he had lost all thought of decency, of common sense, of morality. He had relinquished the restraints that a law abiding conscience would exert to guide his thoughts, his plans and his actions...

*****

A crew of six was soon signed on to the *Isabel Rose*; except for the captain, all young, inexperienced, empty-headed kids, looking for adventure. The boat was to be skippered by a hard of hearing American sailor in his late twenties. Tony had traveled around the Pacific on various small vessels. He was short for a man, about five feet eight inches, had thinning light-brown hair and a thin frame. He wore hearing aids in both ears; he walked around sporting sandals with calf-high white socks, and wore thick black rimmed glasses that made him look like a toad. Tony wore a white captain's hat and, due to his inability to hear well, often mispronounced words, adding to his comic appearance.

41

Getting to know Tony led us to believe he would have been comfortably at home on Gilligan's Island. And while we had a soft spot in our hearts for Tony, we realized it was best to check everything he did.

Then there was Frank, a twenty something year young man from New York with an accent that said he had just stepped off a trolley in the Bronx. He was aimlessly wandering the South Pacific in search of his own demise. Frank needed to find some way of freeing himself from the torturing guilt that constantly shadowed him after the car-crash death of his best friend Bill.

Frank and Bill had been driving home from a party late one night in New York; they had consumed enough alcohol to be declared legally drunk; they shouldn't have been driving that night. Bill had discussed leaving the party with Frank, making the argument that they needed to get home for work the next morning. They left the party and soon Frank was too tired to keep his eyes open. He fell asleep at the wheel of his Ford sedan. Crossing the highway's center line, the resulting head-on crash into another vehicle was horrendous. Twisted metal, fractured glass, broken bodies; no seat-belts, nor air-bags prevented death and destruction from visiting that night.

While seriously injuring Frank, the collision killed the unsecured Bill; the force of the impact propelled him through the passenger side of the windshield. Frank's skull was fractured in the accident; it was a miracle he survived. He escaped death by a slim margin thanks to the refined skills of the emergency room physician. In order to relieve pressure on his traumatized brain, further surgery was required to remove a piece of Frank's skull. When the edema subsided he had a metal plate inserted into the bones covering the right parietal portion of his brain; a souvenir of that night's juvenile foolishness.

Frank spent months in hospital recuperating from his injuries, first in a coma; later going through a rehabilitation protocol to relearn the delicate art of walking and talking. His resultant injuries appeared similar to those of a stroke victim. He had difficulty with ambulation, forming words was challenging; he had lost the use of his left hand, arm and leg.

Frank carried the stroke victim's souvenir, a small rubber ball to compress in his fist in an effort at muscular re-education. No matter what Frank did, and even though he didn't care, he still needed his hand to function. However, Frank felt just the opposite. His best friend had died. It was Frank's fault, he couldn't deny it; it was very difficult for him to live with the blame.

It seemed Frank's soul had been sucked into a black hole of doom and despair. He could no longer focus on things that mattered: he could not see the beautiful cloud speckled blue sky above him; he could no longer hear the songbirds chirping away in the trees; he could not feel the warmth of the sun on his bare arms. Nothing filled his mind except one word: GUILT.

Not being able to face the reality of his current situation, or Bill's parents, Frank descended into a numbing depression from which he could not escape. His only regret was that he didn't die in place of Bill.

*****

Frank desperately needed to escape. He decided to journey to the farthest recesses of the South Pacific, become a phantom; lose himself. He was crushed by the death of his best friend. In his mind, he had no reason, no right to continue living. And so... he had traveled around the South Seas, mainly keeping his secret to himself; he eventually signed on to the *Isabel Rose*, not knowing, or caring, where she might carry him. Too bad he ran into Charles and Marshall.

*****

Dick Fa atsu was a nineteen year old Pacific Islander with a gift for mechanics. He was intelligent, good-natured, somewhat immature, as most twenty-something islanders were, but a good guy who could be counted on in an emergency. Dick had a stocky build and dark short hair that he wore in a crew cut. His haircut gave him a distinctive look among his Samoan brothers. As was local custom, until married he lived with his mother and took her good counsel.

43

He had a lovely native girlfriend whom he wanted to marry, but finances held him back from proposing. Getting a good job on an inter-island boat hauling cargo throughout the isles of the South Pacific was a step in the right direction. Dick looked forward to getting to work and more importantly, to a life with his future bride.

Jimmy was a tall wiry Samoan with curly hair who had an air of superiority about him, an air he used to hide his ignorance. He was a simple lad of twenty one without much education; it was mandatory in the islands, but easily ignored. He was looking for a sea-going job to begin earning a greater income and to provide more experience than he could encounter at home. He was strong and would be an asset to the crew during the loading and unloading of cargo; he would also provide manpower for the upcoming adventures we would all experience on the *Isabel Rose*. For Jimmy this could be a ride off the island of his ancestors. He had lived here all his life, had seen the world through the lens of a newspaper, books and stories told by passing yachtsmen; he was very curious and cautiously ambitious. He didn't know much of what lay beyond the boundaries of his island homeland, but he was highly motivated to find out. Being superstitious, Jimmy always gave the haoles a wide berth and some deference during discussions. Like any smart young guy, when others with greater knowledge were around he was quiet and listened intently.

The Samoans were innately imbued with a native charm taken from their rudimentary education, their honesty, their simple lifestyle and the fact that they liked to have fun. They were more interested in singing, drinking and dancing than complicating their lives with higher education, succeeding in the corporate world or world travel. Their ancestors had done well; wasn't all their family: parents, cousins, aunts and uncles doing just fine? Wasn't the island a tropical paradise that God had planted them in to enjoy? Would it be wise to fool with God's perfect plan? That all sounded fine until they interacted with travelers from other countries. They heard stories of modern cars, television and the advancing civilization of the industrialized world that existed beyond the confines of their tiny island. And they wondered…

I took my honey for a canoe ride,
Away ha hey hey.
The canoe tippy
and she grabbed my ulee,
Away ha hey hey.

The *Isabel Rose* was originally an inter-island cargo trader some seventy eight feet in length that plied the waters between Pango, capital of American Samoa, and the surrounding islands including Apia, the capital of Western Samoa. In her early years she was well dressed, powered by a 12-cylinder supercharged diesel engine putting out five hundred horsepower. She could easily plow through the sea at a steady twelve knots.

However, the years had not been kind to the *Isabel Rose*. She was dried out from sitting for more than a decade under the blazing tropical sun of the South Pacific. Her hull planks had long ago surrendered the caulking that creates a barrier between her and the ocean. Her main engine didn't run; she was infested with the seaman's mortal enemy, the cockroach. Her electronics, which were primitive to begin with, had not functioned in years; she had no pumps. The metal lifeline, a rail that surrounded her aft decking was so rusted that rather than save a life as it was meant to, it would more likely break and fall into the ocean with a man overboard. To add to the ignobility of this impoverished vessel, she had a head that hung over the stern allowing untreated waste to fall directly into the ocean.

The *Isabel Rose* had wooden bunks that cried out for a soft mattress, yet none were to be found on board. Surely, they had been commandeered for service elsewhere, long ago. After signing on and finding the accommodations less than attractive, most of the crew elected to live at home until the Isabel Rose was ready to sail. Impoverished by her lack of resources, her disintegrating condition, the boys silently questioned her ability to cross long stretches of open ocean.

As was normal in the tropics, work began late in the morning and at a leisurely pace. The six-man crew would report to work at ten in the morning. Captain Tony, with his clipboard in hand, would delegate work tasks to the men. He began by asking, "Who knows how to chip rust?" Nobody would raise their hand. He asked me. Not completely understanding the question and having absolutely no knowledge of the sea, I replied, "Why would anyone chip rust?" It sounded like a fool's task. Tony explained that when you rid metal of superficial rust, you could then paint the remaining solid metal found beneath; fresh paint would prevent it from corroding into useless metal.

Tony issued chipping hammers to the crew; we eagerly went to work banging at the rust on the safety rail. Only it was not possible to find any solid metal underneath; the rail had sat for years on a boat six feet above salt water, it was corroded completely through; it was worthless. Since we lacked the funding to replace the disintegrating railing, Captain Tony ordered, with a slight smirk, "All right, stop chipping and start painting the railing."

When that order was given, the crew began to understand just what type of operation we had signed onto. We began to make mental notes for future comparison with a focus on our own safety; the captain didn't seem to give much thought to the appropriate care and maintenance of his boat nor the protection of his crew. So...we had some very nice looking railing that you really didn't want to lean against.

We next moved to the task of inspecting the forward cargo hold. It was time to remove the cover and inspect the interior. We attached lines to the hold cover's four corners; we tried to hoist it with a block and tackle rigged on the forward cargo boom. As the hatch cover began to lift by its frame, the center of the cover gave way, falling into the forward hold with a wood snapping crash. We still had the frame attached to the lifting lines, so we raised it to clear the rim of the cargo hold and put it aside on the deck.

Peering into the hold for the first time, we could see four

feet of water partially filling the darkened space below. With the appearance of a black hole, no one volunteered to wade in to clear the debris. Only God knew what lurked beneath those seemingly tranquil, but foul smelling waters.

After procuring a pump from the local boatyard, we cleared the forward hold of its foul water and later cleaned the rubble from the bottom of the boat. Things didn't look too bad inside, after all, it was an empty space designed to hold cargo to be transported to another location. What we couldn't see, of course, was the wood rot that had infested the timbers of the boat, weakening its infrastructure.

In addition to many other things, the *Isabel Rose* was in dire need of a paint job. After ten years of rotting in the tropical sun she looked like local road kill. As they say, it was time to put some lipstick on that pig. The crew spent days, first cleaning the hull, scraping off old paint and then rolling fresh paint onto the topsides. Interestingly, she didn't look half bad with a fresh paint job. Of course, no one could tell from looking at her from a hundred yards away that nothing onboard actually worked.

Jerry, the representative of the company that owned the boat, finally arrived one day, was introduced and addressed the crew. He let us know that we would be carrying cargo around the South Pacific. But the chimera that dwelled within his psyche was about to let loose: with a dramatic flair he rose to his feet, slowly looked around the crew, staring each of us in the eye; he then confessed his real intentions were to make *big money* carrying gold to those who needed it. His next fantasy was to, "Ferry guns to Sukarno in Indonesia." Excited by doing something we had only read before in fictional stories, the crew was ready to get to work and begin moving gold around the South Pacific. However, some thought sarcastically, "Are you kidding?"

Shame on Frank, who innocently suggested that those tasks might be made a little easier if the *Isabel Rose* had a functioning engine. We all laughed...obviously you could put lipstick on this pig, but how to make her fly?

Jerry was up to the challenge; he arranged with mechanics at the Coast Guard base to overhaul the engine. The crew commandeered a small boat to tow her to the Coast Guard base. We understood that Jerry slipped the engineer some money, a common tactic in the South Pacific, in exchange for a promise that they would make this ancient, rusty, dysfunctional engine run again. Afterward, the crew discussed Jerry's remarks; it sounded like he too had been spending idle time on Gilligan's Island. We decided the best idea was to wait and see what might actually materialize.

In a week's time the engine was repaired and, surprisingly, ran. Smoke exited the ships funnel atop the pilothouse; pumps were attached to the engine and the generator sprang to life, providing light to the main salon and electricity to the boat's gauges.

The crew was soon told that the boat had picked up a job carrying cargo from Apia, the capital of Western Samoa, back to Pango. Apia was located on the north coast of the island of Upolu, which, with its sister island Savai'i, made up an island nation known as Western Samoa. The islands lay about one hundred miles west of Pango and were under the sway of the nation of New Zealand.

Scheduled to leave, the crew all moved aboard in anticipation of shipping out to Apia. However, the newly repaired engine ran only a short time and soon gave notice it really didn't want to go to sea. We had to delay the first voyage on the *Isabel Rose* for further repairs. When the crew did ask when we would leave, the answer that we rapidly came to expect, *soon,* was received by all.

Well, *soon* did finally come to pass. A number of days later the crew pulled in the dock lines, Captain Tony put the engine telegraph in slow ahead, the engineer answered in the engine room turning up the throttle on the engine while engaging the propeller; the Isabel Rose slowly pulled away from the dock on its first ocean voyage in over a decade. The sea was calm, the air warm and the sky clear as we departed the safety of Pango harbor. We headed northwest towards Apia, a short journey that we would cover in eight to twelve hours of cruising.

The next day, after an unremarkable journey, we arrived at Apia. The harbor a calm bay with a few fishing boats scattered about. For once, all seemed well with the *Isabel Rose.* Her engine ran well, lights shown bright. The stove warmed nicely to allow Frank to cook the crew's meals and the ship-to-shore radio both sent and received messages. The crew felt good about the boat and attitudes improved considerably with our first open ocean trip behind us.

Upon arriving in Western Samoa, we tied up to a buoy in fourteen feet of water; the *Isabel Rose* had no anchor. Interestingly, Apia felt even hotter and more humid than Pango. The crew waited while Captain Tony went ashore to check on the waiting cargo. He didn't return. We waited; sitting on deck trying to cool ourselves from the blazing sun and unforgiving humidity. It became crystal clear why people in tropical climes seemed to lack motivation. The hot air forces its way into your lungs and when exhaled a person's energy slips away with the expelled air. The only respite came from drinking cold beer of which we carried a sizable stock. We tried diving into the bay to cool off; the water was like a bath, it offered no relief whatsoever. Exiting the water to the deck of the boat, we would be dry in three minutes, covered with a fine mist of sweat again in seven.

The crew waited for three days; nothing happened. Captain Tony had evaporated. We went into town and encountered a one street downtown area reminiscent of an old west town. The main road was unpaved, a light wind blew eddies of soil from building to building, rambling bushes blew through town. The main street was lined with wood and metal buildings; the town was practically deserted. Except for the wind, life seemed to be at a standstill in Apia. Some of the buildings were constructed of corrugated metal, rusted from their proximity to the sea. Paint wasn't something that was found in excess; the community appeared as though nothing had changed here in a long, long time.

Questioning a local we met passing by, we were shocked to learn that almost everything on this island had to be shipped here; nothing was manufactured in Apia. Only food was grown on the land and fish caught in the seemingly infinite sea that surrounded this scenic island. At home, we had never questioned the shelves full of food and dry goods available in every store. It was always there; anything that was needed was made in America in 1964, at least as far as we knew. It seems for the first time in our young lives we were actually opening our eyes to the reality of the world in which we lived. *Our* world was expanding rapidly; it was becoming more interesting each day.

As all parents can attest, teenagers easily become restless. With no word from the captain or anyone else, Charles and I decided it was time to go surfing. Charles decided to find out where the island's best surf spots were. Walking along the main street we found some locals loitering in town, trying to keep cool under the unfiltered light of the tropical sun. He asked one of the Samoans about places to surf. The question surprised the Apian; no one had ever inquired about where to surf on Upolu. We found it surprising that a sport that was so popular in Hawaii, a relatively short distance to the north, was unknown here. We asked where the best waves broke on the island; we were told the other side of the island was home to the largest waves.

The town's only form of transport was a rain-rusted, creaky, antiquated bus that traveled from one side, over a mid-island ridge, to the opposite side of the island. We found the bus station where we were told the buses departure time. Returning to the boat, plans were hatched to catch the next bus over the mid-island pass.

In the interim, Capt. Tony had returned to the boat. He had no idea what had happened to our cargo. There was nothing for us to deliver to Pango, no explanation of where he had been for three days. Since no work had presented itself, Charles and I decided to go ahead with the planned surf safari. Tony asked if he could accompany us, we couldn't think of a reason to say no. We untied the surfboards from where they had been secured on the boat. Rowing to shore, the trio arrived at the bus station on Tuesday morning, surfboards in hand; another surfing safari was under way.

What we didn't realize was there were no highways on the island; roads were few and all unpaved. The forty year old bus, that carried livestock as well as human cargo, cruised at twenty miles per hour; there was no rush hour to avoid, no schedules to maintain, not even a return trip on the bus's itinerary. But we didn't know that. The bus, its aging shock absorbers exhausted long ago, bounced over every rock and crevice in the road. It reached the high point on the island and began to descend towards the distant shore that was still hours away. The bus never exceeded twenty five miles per hour. Charles prayed the driver would go faster, but he maintained his current, unhurried pace. We gave up all hope of getting in some waves that day in exchange for arriving unharmed at the other end of our journey.

The evening's falling sun welcomed us to the sea-side village of Matautu on the far shore of Upolu. Upon arriving at our destination, we inquired of the bus driver, "When will you return to Apia." Lots of hand gestures were employed as the driver spoke no English. The driver began his pantomime, holding up two fingers indicating, "In two days." That was Thursday, but no one really cared what day it was, every day was pretty much the same here, heavenly. Feeling a little embarrassed and concerned that we didn't have much money to pay for lodging, we inquired about a place to stay for the night. Charles folded his hands together and placed his head on top, eyes closed. The bus driver looked at us quizzically.

We had landed in a small village of perhaps one hundred people. There was no commercial lodging in the village. No one, ever, came to Matautu unless they lived here. There were only small, modest homes numbering perhaps thirty, protecting the villagers from the blazing daytime sun and the monsoon rains. The torrential rains were responsible for keeping this tiny island abundantly flourishing with native vegetation and wild fruit. It appeared that we were starting a new trend, tourism in Matautu.

"O.K." we thought, "So where are we going to sleep tonight?" Perhaps it should have been a clue when the bus driver continued sneaking looks at us in the rear view mirror. Obviously, we weren't locals, but we were the travelers who should have known where we were going. After all, we were the educated ones; we had come from some far away land and we were the ones looking for surf with those odd looking boards that had been packed onto the roof of the bus.

Apparently, the islanders thought we knew what we were doing, or at least should have. Obviously not, another oops! And more laughter, much more.

Signaling for us to wait, the bus driver excused himself and strode off to talk to the villagers. Twenty minutes later he returned, explaining in Samoan, with considerable hand gesturing and an illustrative pantomime that he had procured places for the three of us to eat and sleep. We would stay with local residents who had spare rooms. Apparently, some offspring of the villagers had departed their isolated coastal paradise with thoughts of finding their way in the world; they left behind vacant beds for visiting surf emissaries. God only knows why anyone would want to leave this tropical paradise. There were no cars, no paved roads, actually only the one road leading to the opposite side of the island. No industry existed; no development found its way to Matautu, no noise except the crashing of waves on the reef, the singing of birds in the trees, the wind as it ruffled the ubiquitous vegetation. No pollution existed in this tiny village on the coast of nowhere. There was no need for heat, maybe some cooling would have been nice; but really, this was heaven.

Island women washed clothes by hand, spreading them on a bush to dry in the sun. They picked wild fruit during the day while the men fished in the ocean for food to feed their families. Small vegetable gardens were tended to by the ladies. Fowl were allowed to roam free so long as they left a regular gift of eggs in their nests. The children were taught in a small room that was reserved for classes, the education being as rudimentary as the schoolroom.

It was the ideal location to settle down and have a life. We had already tried that but were greeted by American Samoa's island government with less than open arms. Now, we were in a foreign country and any greeting by the native government could be even less hospitable. Can you imagine a country being invaded by six foot surfers carrying nine foot surfboards to slay the islanders and ravage their villages? Perhaps not.

The next day, Charles and I searched the shore; we found the best waves only one hundred yards up the beach.

Walking the distance to where we could enter the water near the break; we paddled out towards the waves while the inhabitants of the village watched inquisitively from shore. We rode two to four foot waves all morning, replenishing our souls with the surf and sun that seemed to electrify our days; our time in the water helped wash away the boredom of waiting for the *Isabel Rose* to do something. The only negative was that the waves broke on a shallow barrier reef, which made falling precarious. After this discovery, we decided to be more careful, doing our best to put on a good show for the villagers.

After exhausting ourselves with an exhilarating morning, we paddled to the beach, put our boards aside and attempted to communicate with the villagers. We found ourselves in a community of strangers who didn't speak English; Charles and I didn't speak Samoan. Communication was slow and difficult, but was interspersed with lots of laughter. The laughter broke the tension, allowing everyone to relax. We exchanged ideas, told stories of America and had a spirited conversation that lasted the afternoon; meantime, the evening meal was being prepared.

While exchanging stories, the villagers listened politely gave an Aah or Umm every so often, but we hadn't a clue if anyone understood a word we spoke. The villagers would speak in their native tongue; we listened intently, we echoed the speaker, trying to verbalize what we thought we heard. When communication failed, we began laughing again. Little was learned, but everyone seemed to enjoy the attempted exchange.

The islanders were awed by the appearance of these strapping young boys, riding waves like never before seen in their village. They spoke with us as though attempting to communicate ideas with cousins who had returned home after years of living in a foreign land. We were welcomed like family into this tiny village of humble islanders. The extended hospitality warmed our hearts as the dinner of sautéed fish and home grown vegetables warmed our stomachs.

After dinner we retired for the night in a private room on sun-bleached white sheets; they were the crispest we had seen in months. Awaking in the morning, we devoured a breakfast of eggs and fresh fruit. We inquired of our hosts, when the bus might be leaving for the return trip to the other side of the island. The driver came and rounded us up; he wanted to make sure we didn't miss the return bus to Apia.

Sadness filled us as we left this gorgeous village on the coast of nowhere. Primitive yes, It was decidedly enchanting. Naturally simple, beautiful people in a beautiful place with seemingly nothing to care about except putting food on the table each day; not a bad place to hang out.

Our thoughts returned to our own unpredictable life. Never knowing what would happen the next day made us rise each morning with a feeling of suspense and intrigue. We had a great time surfing and spending time with the villagers of Matautu and it was a relief to get away from the *Isabel Rose* for a couple of days.

The return bus ride was equally fraught with discomfort as the ride to Matautu. The word that Tony received when we returned to Apia was the same, *soon*. As we gazed into the harbor from shore, we were delighted to note the old wooden copra boat still afloat and moored to her buoy. The three of us rowed out to the boat and related to the crew that there was no change in our sailing orders. None! Again, we were waiting for *soon* to arrive.

During these days, we swam in the ocean and read books to pass the time. Almost no work was done on the boat, as there was no money to pay for any supplies or equipment that was needed. The restlessness went on for another full week and then Captain Tony received orders to return to Pango.

In the time we had spent in Apia, no cargo had been procured; we made no money, smuggled no gold and carried no weapons. While the crew really had nowhere to go, we did feel a bit cross at the fact that we had spent three weeks waiting for nothing to happen. We were beginning to feel a bit uneasy and significantly less confident about our bespectacled leader. This would have been a good time for creative suggestions, however, like fish out of water, the crew found themselves at a loss for direction. And so...we untied from the mooring.

Happily, the return trip made for some lasting memories.

The *Isabel Rose* had departed the protection of Apia's harbor in the late afternoon; she was cruising east along the north coast of Western Samoa. The boat was motoring well with her speed at eight to nine knots; twilight approached. The wind was calm, a moderate swell rolled by, and the sea surface like glass. We watched as the color faded from an incredible sunset; blending shades of orange and red that reflected off the underside of bulbous cumulus clouds that mottled the late afternoon sky.

I was on duty steering the boat on what seemed a beautifully calm night. Surrounded by the darkness of the unlit coast; the ships radio was tuned to the emergency frequency. Suddenly, I heard a transmission that focused my thoughts. It was rare to hear anything on the radio; I paid attention when a static filled transmission rang out from the tiny speaker attached to a bulkhead above me. It was a, "May Day," an emergency call to anyone who could hear the radio transmission. I was receiving a message from a Kiwi aircraft, flying somewhere in the night's sky. The radio operator called out, "Unidentified boat, unidentified boat, if you can hear me, you are on fire!"

I was shocked by the message. My eyes opened wide as I gazed forward, over the boat's steering wheel, through the pilot house windows, scanning the horizon for a vessel on fire. As I heard the message I could only wonder whom the unfortunate crew on what ridiculous boat, was being called. I couldn't imagine a boat being on fire without the crew being aware of their plight. I was about to burst out laughing when I heard a plane flying low overhead. "Oh my God!"

I looked out the side door of the pilothouse and watched the Kiwi aircraft dipping its wings in greeting. As the plane passed, I noted the insignia of the New Zealand Air Force on the side of the silver fuselage. At that moment a shiver ran down my spine as I realized the speeding aircraft was calling its warning to the *Isabel Rose*!

As the color rose in my cheeks, I questioned myself, "how could the boat be on fire?" I yelled for Captain Tony; telling him of the radio message. The captain rounded up the crew and had them start probing for the fire. All we had to do was look up. The funnel above the pilothouse had flames shooting fifteen feet into the air. The flaming boat must have been easy to spot against the darkened canvas of the sea. From the bird's eye view of the aircraft, it probably looked quite striking.

The engineer throttled back the engine, stopping the boat in mid-ocean. Having no functioning fire hoses, the crew scrambled to find buckets; we began a bucket brigade going from sea to funnel. Soon the fire was under control, but the crew was in shock to find the boat had been burning with no one noticing.

Dim-witted may have been the appropriate term to describe our current mental state; we were embarrassed by our inability to even notice that the boat was in flames. We made a note to improve our observational skills. We tried to find the source of the fire; the next half hour was spent searching for its origin, but we discovered nothing. The fire was out; we didn't feel that the boat or crew were in imminent danger. The episode was discussed by all, we decided to continue the journey to Pango while keeping a sharp eye focused on the ship's funnel.

After another hour of cruising some eight or nine miles, Charles, now on duty at the wheel, looked up at the funnel; he found it beginning to blaze again. He alerted the crew, the boat was stopped again. The bucket brigade was successful at extinguishing the fire a second time.

A more thorough search of the area around the funnel was carried out. We found that the engine's exhaust pipe ran up from the engine room, through the crew deck to the steering deck and up through the center of the funnel where it released its super-heated exhaust. The advanced age of the metal pipe in combination with the sea's salt air had caused rust to form, eventually producing holes in the pipe. The holes allowed sparks from the engine to escape the confines of the metal pipe and lodge in the sun-dried walls of the wooden funnel. It was a short wait for the funnel to again burst into glaring red-yellow flames that lit the darkened evening sky. No doubt it made the day for the pilots who had first spotted the flaming boat from the air.

To prevent the fire from reigniting the funnel, Captain Tony ordered whoever was on duty to continue wetting it down for the rest of the trip. Our buckets filled with sea water were lined up behind the helmsman, ready for use. The smoldering fire created a hazy grey halo that surrounded the oval funnel, while a light trail of grey smoke followed us the rest of the way home.

Upon returning to the protected bay at Pango, we docked the *Isabel Rose* next to the Coast Guard base. The well trained mechanics were enlisted to do additional repairs to the recently rebuilt engine and the Swiss cheese exhaust pipe. The return trip from Apia had over-taxed the boat's engine requiring further servicing to maintain the power plant in a functioning state. God forbid that it should have to run for more than one day; we could have a real disaster.

The Isabel Rose

IV

Viti Levu, Sounds Like a Disease to Me

A couple of weeks drifted slowly by while the final phase of the engine overhaul was being completed. We were reunited with our Samoan brothers; commandeering an idle Jeep, we headed off along the coast, in search of the endless wave.

Bright, blue-sky days spent in blissful surfing, evenings reading sea stories by the dim light of a bare bulb and an occasional visit to the Islander. Simply gazing at the hillsides, smelling the fragrantly scented air wafting from the blooms of gardenias, frangipani and roses, watching the white billowing clouds scurrying silently overhead consumed our days.

Life in paradise was certainly different from the life Charles and I had lived during our first seventeen years. The tall buildings of metropolis were gone, the sinuous concrete ribbons of freeways had not yet arrived and the cacophony of sounds produced by the bustle of civilization were not found in proximity to this utopian isle.

Captain Tony picked up wind of a job for the *Isabel Rose* in the Fiji Islands. Up to that time, we had never heard of Fiji. None of the crew knew where the Fiji Islands were, but with a group consisting of three hundred plus islands, we figured even Captain Tony could find them.

On the morning of the day the *Isabel Rose* was scheduled to depart, Dick Fa atsu returned to the boat; his face displaying the fear of deep, tortured thoughts. He found me on the dock where I was waiting for the others to return with provisions for the trip. Dick had just returned from his family home; he related that his Grandmother had had a premonition. She told him that, "In a dream I saw this voyage was going to be very dangerous and I fear for your life."

As much as Dick wanted to earn enough money to marry his sweetheart, he wasn't interested in dying during the effort.

59

Unhappily, he was ready to quit the crew at that moment and head home, putting as much distance as possible between him and the derelict vessel. This would have been a problem for the crew as there were only six of us; Dick was an important part of the group. To allay his fears, I told him that he needn't worry, that I would protect him. How I would protect him, I had no idea, but it sounded good. Dick saw and heard the sincerity of my promise, was calmed and decided to stay with the boat.

Truth being we really needed Dick to manage the dysfunctional engine while on our eight hundred mile voyage to Viti Levu in the Fijian Archipelago. Without him the whole trip could founder. Besides, someone might find out that Charles or I knew something about engines and we'd be damned if we were going to spend time in an engine room where the temperature was one hundred twenty degrees and the humidity was pushing ninety five percent. With those thoughts in mind, this trip through paradise was on the cusp of losing its appeal.

The rest of the crew arrived from town with the boat's provisions. After loading on food, fuel and the all-important beer, we departed the serene limpid blue waters of the inner harbor and headed for open ocean and the next leg of our serendipitous adventure. Taking one last look at the steep, lush, vegetation covered hills that surrounded Pango's harbor, we left with a sense of loss for the place that had been our home for the past six weeks; a warm spot in our hearts remembered William, his sons and the caring family that had adopted us.

The day we sailed, the ocean was relatively calm. Unruffled by the presence of a breeze; the air was quiet and peaceful, leaving a smooth glaze on the sea's surface. Heading slightly north of due west, a moderate five to six foot swell kept the *Isabel Rose* slowly rising and falling with the passing of each wave; she did her slow, easy, ocean dance as she traversed endless miles of sparkling sea that welcomed her from every direction.

All went well until on the second day out, while I was on duty steering the boat; I noticed a gong sounding. My first thought was that I was hallucinating; a gong in the middle of the ocean? It didn't make sense. Later, as it continued, I thought it was perhaps caused by the beer that I was consuming to keep cool. Surely, if others heard the gong sounding, someone would say something? Gong! Gong!.....Gong!...The sound did come irregularly, making it even more bewildering. When it stopped for a period of time, I thought, and hoped, it was gone. But soon the gong sound returned; I realized it was not my imagination and began to wonder what its origin might be.

The gong's report returned my attention to focus on the boat; momentarily, I let go daydreams of dancing native girls, their brown skin glistening in the sun as beads of sweat silently cascaded down their gently curving sides; the tiny drops of warmed water gathered by their grass skirts that hung lazily on their hips as they swayed in rhythm to the sounds of island ukuleles strumming in the distance.

While looking over the boat and out into the sea, I noticed the *Isabel Rose* seemed to be moving at a surprisingly slow speed. I contacted Dick to see if he had throttled back the engine, slowing the boat. Dick replied that we were motoring at standard ahead; we should have been making eight to nine knots. But I could see that the boat was moving much slower.

Finally, I could no longer stifle my curiosity. I woke up Captain Tony, explaining about the episodic gong sounding. Tony wouldn't have heard the sound, as he was partially deaf; he often turned his hearing aids down to a low level while at sea. He turned his hearing aids up and replied, "Yes, I can hear a sound." Gong... Gong.....Gong...

We decided to make a methodical search of the boat in an attempt to localize the source of the sound. Moving aft of the pilothouse the gong was audible but much weaker. Moving forward the sound grew slightly in intensity. We put our ears to the deck and the gong was magnified. We decided to hoist the forward hold hatch cover; a precarious maneuver, as the boat rolled and pitched with the passing swells.

Once the hatch cover was set aside, we peered inside the dark, empty cargo space. Tony and I heard the sound of splashing water and then the Gong rang out again. As our eyes adjusted to the interior darkness we noticed a wooden pallet floating on the surface of the six foot deep water. As the pallet surfed into a steel support stanchion it let out with its Gong report; it then floated off into the darkened recesses of the hold. As it floated back again, striking the metal support, it would repeat the bass sounding Gong! I descended a wooden ladder into the hold and moved the pallet to dry ground; a simple maneuver that resulted in extinguishing the irritating sound.

We then turned our attention to the sea water splashing inside the hold. The water in the forward cargo space explained the decreased boat speed; the area was more than a quarter full of seawater. We were transporting a significant portion of the Pacific Ocean and it was creating a burdensome drag on the engine. The weight of the water slowed the *Isabel Rose* to a crawl while producing a significant waste of fuel.

Again, we stopped the boat mid-ocean, rigged a recently procured pump in the engine room, connected some commandeered hoses and started pumping the unwanted cargo overboard. Apparently, no one had realized that the seams between the hull's planks, having lost their tar covered caulking long ago, would no longer maintain the integrity of the boat's hull. As we traversed the Pacific, water simply flowed into the boat through the open spaces with no buffer to prevent it.

Pumping out the hold took hours; we decided to float in place until the seawater was removed from the boat's interior. There was no sense burning all our fuel if the boat wasn't moving at cruising speed. That could exhaust the fuel supply before we reached our destination, making this voyage more problematic than necessary.

Eventually we emptied the hold of water, throttled up the engine and were off. Without our supplementary cargo, the *Isabel Rose* cut nicely through the water. We realized that we would need to check the hold every so often. In a few hours time, water was again seen swirling around the boat's Cedar ribs; we decided to turn on the pumps intermittently, throughout the day and night. At least this way we had a chance of reaching the Fiji Islands.

Continuing on course with an eye on the water level in the forward hold, in a few days the *Isabel Rose* cruised into the harbor at Suva, the capital of Fiji. The harbor was surrounded with sloping hills climbing skyward on the south side of the harbor while the opposite shore was flat and barren, the result of impending development. The hills were pleasantly green, the sky a vibrant blue with wispy cotton clouds moving rapidly across the aerial panorama. Homes had been built on the hill; overlooking the harbor, they took advantage of the extraordinary view and the afternoon winds that gently cooled the heights.

The *Isabel Rose* tied up at King's Wharf, named for the monarch; Fiji was a British Colony. There, the crew waited to be inspected by Customs and have the boat's papers checked by immigration. Soon, government officials arrived and reviewed the ship's manifest that stated we carried nothing. They checked the crew list and granted us access to the town, but requested we anchor the boat out in the bay away from the small dock. The dock was occupied with large native boats and small ships loading and unloading cargo, busying themselves with the hardy lives of working ships and the men that man them.

Once again, the crew entered waiting mode. We were supposed to have a job carrying something to somewhere, but, as we had come to expect, nothing was ready. We enjoyed the town even though it was small, hot and humid. In late August, walking in the shade almost made it bearable. And then there was the odor. Someone explained it was the scent of copra being cooked to extract the oil. It permeated the air, adhered to your clothing, stuck in your nostrils like 18th century snuff.

We went to the movies often; it was cheap and thankfully air-conditioned. Each show began with the audience rising to sing "God Save the Queen" and then the newsreel, its presentation a grainy black and white, would begin. The dreary colorless films illustrated a dramatic dichotomy from the overwhelming beauty and voluptuous color of our surroundings. The news was from a world that no one seemed to be markedly interested in. In the middle of the

South Pacific, the newsreels gave us the feeling that we were on another planet.

During one evening's show, the newsreel presented a film of three American naval vessels. They were steaming around the Cape of Good Hope at the southern tip of Africa, an area well known for torturing passing ships and their hardtack crew. The wind was blowing a moderate sixty knots, the swell a not unreasonable twelve feet. As the ships continued, the wind increased to eighty knots and the small fleet began to watch their bows submerge into the frigid swells. The narrator explained, "The ships reduced speed to maintain their bows above water as the wind increased to a Force 3 hurricane of one hundred knots." The ships slowed their speed again while watching aluminum plates being ripped from their gun mount by the rampaging wind and foam covered seas. We watched with wide eyes in awe of the unbridled power of nature in all her fury. Sailing on a small wooden ship that had a problem staying afloat in the best of times, it frightened us to imagine being caught in storm wracked weather. A hurricane force storm like what we were witnessing could have nothing but a pernicious ending for the *Isabel Rose*.

✻✻✻✻✻

You have to understand that in the sixties, Fiji was not yet a well known location. It was more like the ends of the earth. Movies that were shown there were very old, displayed many scratches, broke often and were not very interesting. Seemed no one really cared what happened in Suva. Hell, most people had never heard of it.

✻✻✻✻✻

We were told that fifteen years ago there were cannibals on these islands. It was there the term *long pig* was coined, the indigenous people's phrase for cooked humans. After a battle, the barbie was the reward for those warriors that didn't carry the day. When we saw how some of the natives looked longingly at us, we believed the rumors.

Everything was very different there. Fijian police stood on a

64

pedestal in the middle of an intersection; they directed traffic with hand signals; traffic lights did not exist. The police wore native dress that added a certain uniqueness to their daily appearance in the street. Their uniforms consisted of starched blue shirts with black ties on top, white gloves with a white skirt below. The skirts had a zigzag pattern at the bottom. They sported black boots with white, knee high socks that were partially covered by their skirts. It was odd seeing men in skirts; it was noticeably different from policemen in Los Angeles.

✳✳✳✳✳

A week after arriving in Suva, the crew received word that the boat was hired to tow some barges to another island. A plantation owner needed the barges to transport sugar cane to the capital; there it would be processed and shipped to overseas markets.

The crew had never towed anything before, we didn't have the proper gear to tow the barges and so, being the flexible boys we were, shifted rapidly into learning mode. Dick asked how we would tow the barges, since the *Isabel Rose* was not a tugboat. Captain Tony told the crew that we would make a harness from a thick wire cable. We would then attach the ends to both the barges and the Isabel Rose. No one had done this type of work before; we had a great excuse when nothing worked properly.

A Fijian pilot was put on board; an expert in the local waters, he would guide the boat, with its cargo riding astern, to our destination through the island's surrounding reef. He was our insurance the *Isabel Rose* didn't end up on the reef.

The barrier reefs surrounding the Fijian Islands had been created by tiny marine invertebrates known as polyps during the Pleistocene period. The tiny creatures, with an internal composition of calcium carbonate, would eventually die, leaving behind their calcium hardened skeleton. In a hermatypic process, other polyps would then grow on top of the skeletal remains and the process would repeat itself thousands of times; slowly building up the abrasive, crevice-filled, calcium based reefs. Coralline algae secreted natural glue, a limestone substance that functioned to cement the cast-off skeletal structures together, and, after a few eons, a coral reef was born.

The crew was really happy to have someone on board who knew the local waters. Considering the problems the boat had had to date, his presence added a measure of safety that had formerly eluded the neophyte crew on our nascent sail-about.

We were given a heavy coil of steel cable. Rusted, thin, approximately three eights inch diameter, we were to make a harness from this slender cable. It didn't look like it was strong enough to pull the heavy steel barges, and then there was the rust factor. Having no other options, Captain Tony, in a slightly demoralized tone stated, "Let's make do with what we have."

On Friday, Charles maneuvered the boat to where we were picking up the barges. Viewing the two steel barges side by side, it was difficult to discern which was worse; the forty foot barges exhibited heavy rust from bow to stern. Then there was the slim towing cable we were going to tow them with, also encased in rust. The crew just looked at each other with the usual, *oh no!* looks on our faces; we continued with the work. At least we would be relatively safe within the barrier reef; no open ocean, no rough seas. Sinking would not be an issue on this brief, overnight trip.

The twin barges were rafted side by side. Then the metal cable was run from the *Isabel Rose* to the mid-point between the two rusty steel hulks. Looking at the weight of the two vessels and the diameter of the tow cable, much doubt existed in the minds of the crew. We weren't terribly surprised when the cable broke fifteen minutes after getting under way. After noticing the barges were falling behind, Charles stopped the boat, circling around in front of the two free-floating craft. We picked up the broken cable to see how to best reconnect it. It seemed that the cable was simply too thin. Having a good length of the thin cable onboard, I suggested we double it, hoping that each strand would take a portion of the load, easing the strain on both strands.

Charles gave over the helm to Tony. Charles and I, being half amphibian, jumped into the crystal clear, lukewarm sea to retrieve the cable end that was still attached to the barges; it now hung slack under the sea.

The pilot strolled out of the pilothouse and saw us swimming in the water. He started screaming something to the crew. The crew then starting screaming at the two of us swimmers, "Get out of the water!" They looked like a bunch of idiots on the stern of the boat, yelling, whistling, and gesturing wildly with their hands. Of course this was all completely unintelligible to the two of us; we continued to dive for the cable.

Finding the end lying on the ocean bottom, we brought it alongside the boat. We passed the end of the broken cable to Jimmy and climbed aboard. My first question was, "What was all the yelling about?" Captain Tony replied that the pilot had said, "These waters were full of man-eating sharks and you shouldn't be swimming around here like you were in someone's backyard pool." The pilot thought we were crazy and appeared to be near a nervous breakdown. Seeing us back on board, he began to relax.

With the cable reconnected the boat resumed her journey. Fifteen minutes later, the hulls broke away a second time. The crew questioned if the cable had broken again, but this time it was a bollard on the barge that gave way. The bollards were very old; the salt air had created pervasive corrosion causing the metals strength to markedly weaken, just enough for the strain of towing to allow the bollard to shear off. It parted at the level of the barge's deck, slipping the towing cable.

Charles and I were, at times, more comfortable in the water than out. Another swim in the ocean brought the three vessels together again. Jimmy occupied the pilot with conversation so he wouldn't have a heart attack when he saw the two of us swimming in the ocean a second time.

The water was too beautiful, refreshing, invigorating not to swim in. It was warm, full of colorful tropical fish, crystal clear and only thirty feet deep. The sandy bottom was easy to see in the clear water and the myriad fish species, curious at the interlopers in their domain, filled the water surrounding us. The cable was reattached to a cleat on the barges and the

Isabel Rose started off towards our destination, the village of Nambouwalu.

Half an hour later the cable snapped again. This was getting old; the entire crew was becoming frustrated with the continuing equipment failure. We seemed to be spending more time repairing and reattaching the cable than under way. While no one was in a hurry, we still wanted this task to go a little more smoothly. Not surprisingly, we were looking just like the inexperienced ship of fools we were.

After reconnecting the two ends of the cable for the second time, it was decided the boat was going too fast, putting an excess strain on the under-sized, weakened, cable. After considerable debate it was agreed, by consensus that we would proceed at a much slower speed. When forty five minutes passed without the tow cable separating, we were delighted to settle back, relax and allow the *Isabel Rose* to do her job, just a little bit less rapidly.

The next morning, under the direction of the pilot, the *Isabel Rose* arrived at Nambouwalu; we deposited the barges on a buoy that was awaiting their arrival. The crew viewed the shore and saw it to be completely undeveloped, no dock, and no signs of life. Once again we had entered paradise. It was so incredibly beautiful; we became statues, muted by the overwhelming magnificence; we stood on deck, staring at the shore. The rich green foliage glistened in the morning mist, growing to the water's edge where it kissed the shaded water of the bay. The shallow water was a crystal clear emerald green; we could see fish swimming lazily as they cruised the undersea searching for food. Birds could be heard singing their morning song to their mates; listening for a response that would guide them back to their nests with the morning meal.

Someone spotted a footpath and Captain Tony said he needed to take care of paperwork for the barges with whomever was receiving them. Not being shy, and not wanting to stay onboard the boat, the entire crew, including the pilot, volunteered to go ashore with Tony.

It was Dick and Jimmy's turn to row the dinghy ashore with everyone on board. We stowed the dinghy under the shade of a large mango tree; its huge canopy heavily laden with fruit.

It was a short walk through the shade of the overgrown native vegetation to a native home; there Captain Tony met the plantation manager and completed his paperwork. Farther inland, but unseen, lay fields of sugar cane that grew without irrigation thanks to the copious tropical rainfall. The rich soil, with a strong iron content, made crop growing possible without the need for additional nutrients. Farther inland were acres of banana, also naturally grown for both domestic use and the export market.

The fields were manned by local natives who lived in a small village built alongside the cultivated fields. All travel undertaken on the island was by foot or on horseback. Their primitive homes were lit by kerosene lantern; no electricity existed here. The cutting of ripened cane, the gathering of full grown but still green bananas was done at a leisurely pace. Machetes were the tool of choice on this island farm where all produce was harvested by hand.

Fascinated by the beauty of the surroundings, I decided to go for a walk on this fantasy island; it seemed to be almost untouched by human hands. I followed a footpath worn through the woods. After walking thirty minutes, as I gazed at the double canopy of tall and taller trees growing overhead, I heard the sound of a cantering horse. Seconds later a rider came into view. The rider stopped his horse short and looked at me with surprise, eyes wide. The rider said something in Fijian, I said something in English. It was obvious from our expressions that neither side had a clue what the other was saying.

My mind went into overdrive as I was suddenly overcome with an uncontrollable urge to ride the stranger's horse. Knowing that I couldn't communicate with the rider verbally, I began my Marcel Marceau impression, a pantomime to explain my desire to the stranger. I pointed at myself, then at the horse. I made a riding motion like I was holding the bridle's twin reins in my hands. The rider looked at me somewhat suspiciously, perhaps he thought I wanted to steal his horse; but then, realizing there was no place for me to go, he acquiesced. The rider easily slid off the horse. I, with a great deal less dignity, jumped onto the horse's blanketed posterior. Not being used to riding horses, it took me two tries to successfully reach the animal's back while the horses owner looked on in amusement. Holding the reins, I turned the horse and rode off the way the rider had come. Riding for five minutes, I enjoyed the beauty of the virgin forest that surrounded me. Filled with palms, ferns, ficus and mahogany, its vibrant, multihued, century's old growth had the feeling of a wise elder, cool and refreshing in its demeanor. Bindweed vines fell from the heights, lounging lazily as though they were waiting for the ape man to swing by. In a few moments my thoughts returned to my generous new friend and the fact that he was awaiting my return. I turned the borrowed horse, returning slowly to our meeting place.

I slid off the horse's back and returned the reins to its owner. He smiled, said something in Fijian; I smiled, said, "Thank you." The rider rode off to complete his temporarily interrupted journey. My head spun. In my wildest dreams, I never thought I would be riding a horse, bareback, on a small island in the middle of the South Pacific through some of the most beautiful forest I had ever seen. I pinched myself to make sure I was awake.

I retraced my route on foot, returning to the native home. There, I met up with the other crew members; we were all fed, hydrated and soon began to tire from the tropical heat. In mid afternoon we headed back to the *Isabel Rose* to get some rest; sighting the boat, we were distressed to find her upper deck in the midst of flames shooting into the air. Fire had, once again, surrounded the ships funnel above the pilothouse. The strangest of sights; this seventy eight foot boat sitting in a sheltered lagoon, quietly, passively, awaiting the return of its crew, surrounded by paradise, burning.

By this time calamity was becoming commonplace; it no longer alarmed the crew. We took our time, rowed out to the boat, grabbed buckets and slowly extinguished the fire. Luckily, we were young; these episodic brushes with danger were part of the adventure for us. We had no fear of anything; we now began to see the humor of the situations where we found ourselves to be the innocent victims.

At times, we felt as though we were being tested, each day

another challenge; were we tough enough to deal with these ongoing incidents of sporadic adversity? Like most, our previous lives were completely devoid of this type of unexpected adventure; every time an incident of this sort ensued we were exposed to unanticipated, unwanted and unknown needs; we learned as we went. Nothing surprised us any longer and we could never complain of our days being dull.

The fire had damaged the deck above the pilot house and the first mate's bunk room. While this was a distressing situation, it was not a serious problem since the boat didn't have a first mate; the cabin lay empty. The origin of the fire turned out to be the auxiliary generator. Hey, we thought, who needs electricity, anyway? Considering the age and disrepair of the *Isabel Rose*, we realized our mistake in leaving a mechanical device running with no one on board. The generator was shut down; the entire crew sacked out for a couple of hours rest before returning to Suva, later that evening.

With the pilot guiding the boat, the return voyage to Suva was uneventful, which in itself was a surprise. We had become accustomed to sleeping with our Lavas on and one eye open, never knowing when the next disaster would strike. This short trip was fraught with danger, with the problematic barges, the fire and simply keeping the *Isabel Rose* afloat. The boat's ongoing state of disrepair was responsible for creating a distortion of the *Adventures in Paradise* theme that continued to fill our thoughts.

Returning to Suva resulted in the same doldrums we had previously experienced. Now we had one paying job under our belts; for some reason the next job did not come quickly. As always, when queried about our next trip, the response the captain offered the crew was: *soon*. At least for the moment, the *Isabel Rose* was tied up at the main dock where rowing a quarter mile into shore was unnecessary.

✲✲✲✲✲

One day, Frank invited Charles and I to visit the

guesthouse where he had lived for six months prior to sailing farther east. We walked half way up the hill that backed Suva Bay; the scene from up there was majestic. With an eagle's eye view of the bay and beyond, Frank pointed out that we could see for twenty miles. The barren hills on the opposite side of the harbor gave way to mountains rising into the clouds that brought rain to the hillsides nourishing the thick, untamed growth.

Charles and I were introduced to the family that owned the house. Frank showed us his room; he spoke about his stay here before he sailed on towards Samoa and our encounter in Pango harbor. Prior to arriving in Samoa, Frank and the crew of the trimaran had sailed to Tin Can Island, a small island named for its capacity to stockpile fifty five gallon fuel drums during the war effort. Another piece of paradise in the middle of a vast body of water, sprinkled with mini paradises.

After Frank's accident in the states, he had flown to Fiji, thinking this was a fine place to lose himself. He had never heard of these islands, but believed it was a place where he could somehow shed his guilt or perhaps die trying; at that time he didn't care which. After arriving, he rented a room from this family of gentle Fijians and tried to determine what would be the best way to dispose of himself. Having not found an answer to his quest, he joined the crew of the Kiwi thinking perhaps he would drown on the voyage to Samoa. But that didn't work, either.

✶✶✶✶✶

During the crossing from Samoa, the crew discovered an interesting thing about Frank; he always slept with his eyes open. Walking into the bunk room after finishing a watch, Charles noticed Frank in his bunk, laying face up, staring at the ceiling. He had never experienced seeing someone sound asleep with their eyes wide open. The next day Charles questioned Frank about his unusual sleeping habits and Frank replied it was the result of his auto accident in New York, "Some sort of neurological sequela to my brain injury," he explained. Frank did enjoy demonstrating the metal plate in his head; occasionally knocking on it with his knuckles to entertain the ladies. Fortunately, it was covered by skin and hair.

Whenever the crew was together, while partying or working on the boat, someone always reminded Frank about the importance of squeezing his rubber ball. At first, Frank denied its value, not really caring if his hand worked or not. But as things progressed on the *Isabel Rose,* it became evident that Frank's duties consisted of more than just cooking, a task he begrudgingly endured. He was an important part of our small group, we needed his strength and both of his hands; he began using the ball.

Considering his reluctance to participate, Frank was sometimes the hit of our parties. The guys would invite girls onto the boat, listen to music, drink beer and dance on deck. Frank would usually retire early; his distressed attitude would not allow him to have any relations with women or much enjoyment of any kind. Being the rascals that we were, we would lead the ladies into the sleeping quarters and show off Frank sleeping with his eyes open. At first no one believed he was asleep, but Charles would talk to him...no response. He would pass a hand in front of Frank's eyes...again, no response; he never blinked.

By this time the entire crew had adopted the native style of dress; it was especially comfortable. Called a sarong in Fiji, a rectangular piece of cloth that was tied at the waist covered the bottom half of the body on males. It was a similar piece of material to that worn in Samoa, although imprinted with a colorful pattern indigenous to Fiji. Women also wore the sarong but tied them around their neck so that only the men went bare-chested, usually.

We had been in Fiji for six weeks at this time; we had not been paid since signing on to the boat in Samoa. Captain Tony tried to contact the boat's owners in Honolulu; he requested they forward money to pay the crew and to purchase provisions for the boat. Hearing nothing from the company, Tony was forced to sell the boat's anchor and chain that he had recently acquired, the chronograph and our only search light. The money was used to buy food and beer to keep the crew nourished until something further could be worked out. The *Isabel Rose* remained tied up at the Kings Wharf to fill her water tanks, load beer and other needed provisions.

When that money ran out, Tony extended his financial requests to the crew; he borrowed all the money we had. He gave us each a note, saying that, in time, we would be repaid by the company. Obviously, the money was needed to feed us; he was difficult to refuse. But where was the Pan Pacific Lines?

Contemplating Australia

V

A Black-Tip Came to Dinner

One late afternoon, a thirty eight year old Fijian walked by the boat, begging for food. At first, we told him to move along, and then noticed the man was physically challenged; he had no arms. He carried a laminated card in his shirt pocket explaining his plight. He motioned to the pocket so we could read of the attack that took his arms, his future and his ability to care for himself.

The card told the story of his near brush with death. In his youth, the islander had been swimming in the ocean, near his village on the far side of the island, when he appeared to be prey for a vicious, twelve foot, black tipped, reef shark. It attacked, tearing both his arms off. The horrified adolescent's screams brought help from his fellow villagers; they ran off the hungry shark that left the bleeding, armless, young man near death. Rushed to the primitive island hospital, the shark man's life was saved, but with his arms gone, he was left helpless to fend for himself. None of the crew had the stomach to turn away someone in his condition. It was a tragedy, the likes of which none of us had ever had to deal with; it touched our hearts to think how difficult this man's mangled life had become, through no fault of his own.

We helped him aboard and shared our food and drink with the armless man. He told us stories of his attack and how challenging his daily life had become. Depression seemed to follow, always a short step behind him. After dinner, he thanked us for the hospitality and headed off to his home. The crew, thinking we had done a good deed, was surprised to see the shark man on the next day, and the day after that. He had looked into our hearts; finding mush there, he was willing to take advantage of it without a second thought.

Island women always came to visit the crew on the boat, sharing food, drink and occasionally themselves. At first, they had a kind word for the shark man. But soon he became a chore that no one wished to deal with. He needed to be hand fed, his mouth and his behind wiped and helped everywhere he moved on the boat; he had a foul mouth and spoke disparagingly of the girls. Tired of his attitude, we shared our last supper with him and sent him home with the order, "Not to return." The crew had done our duty; it was time for someone else to care for the limbless wretch.

✳✳✳✳✳

Happily, *soon* had finally come. The boat had been commissioned to carry a load of cargo to the Marshall Islands. Another unknown group of islands, they were located two thousand miles to the north of Fiji, in the Mid-Pacific basin. The cargo was loaded by stevedores; the boat's crew headed to town, our assistance unneeded. The goods consisted of general cargo: linens and cloth for manufacturing and canned foodstuff. The deck was loaded with fifty-five gallon drums of aviation fuel. The *Isabel Rose* was now a floating bomb.

Returning to the boat later in the afternoon, we spotted the drums secured on deck. Wondering what they contained, the answer was supplied by the white stenciled letters painted on the side of the cans: AVIATION FUEL. Knowing of the boat's poor condition, we were shocked to see the volatile fuel secured on deck. At first, baffled by the senselessness of carrying a highly explosive cargo, soon a sense of anxiety wove its way through the six of us.

With the cargo loaded on board, the problem that had plagued the boat from the beginning began to reassert itself. Seawater began to seep into the hold; as each ton of cargo was added; more seams were exposed to the unfettered flow of the sea.

For some reason, during this misadventure around the South Seas, no one had ever paid any attention to the lack of caulking between the hull planks. The boat had experienced flooding from the start, had overcome the problem with periodically running pumps, yet no one had the slightest inclination to repair the hull. True, with our occasional multi-day trips, the desiccated hull planks had become swollen from their immersion in sea water. However, the planks still had open seams that should have been filled with caulk. Seeing the boat fully loaded with cargo, plus the drum-cluttered deck, apprehensive glances were shared among the crew.

Due to the explosive nature of the cargo now lining the deck of the old wooden boat, the Harbor Master ordered her away from the dock. Powering up the engine, Captain Tony steered the boat away from the Kings Wharf, securing the slowly sinking boat to a mooring buoy in the bay for the night.

Early the next morning, after rising and breaking fast, the crew had a meeting to discuss the impending voyage of the *Isabel Rose*. She was riding low in the water from the excess cargo that had been loaded, both below and above deck. During the night she had taken on more water. The patina of seaworthiness fell slack from the face of this tired old lady of the sea; she had more hull planks and their open seams exposed to the sea than ever before.

She also had an explosive cargo on deck. We were hesitant; questioning if she would ever reach her destination, far to the north.

The men of the *Isabel Rose* were greatly disadvantaged by her lack of equipment: she had one small dingy, no motor and no emergency provisions. She had no safety gear, no life jackets; rather she was barely afloat and would most likely founder at sea on this far-flung journey. It was becoming readily apparent that this was an ill-fated trip; one that was planned by the management for the sole benefit of the management. The fact that the crew would be lost at sea during this voyage hung heavy during our meeting, but that idea didn't appear to bother anyone from the company.

The tired old copra trader had problems from the day she was purchased in Samoa, and with full knowledge of her faults, no money was ever advanced to repair the leaky hull; nor had the crew ever been paid. Then, there was Jerry, the red haired wheeler-dealer who would return to Honolulu with a sad story of the *Isabel Rose*, vanished at sea with the loss of all hands.

But there would be a nice insurance payment for the sinking of the boat and the cargo. Jerry would be sitting pretty, making a tidy profit for himself and the owners of the Pan Pacific Line, the group of investors that had funded Jerry's South Pacific folly.

Realizing that we had nothing to gain from this trip, and a great deal to lose, the crew decided to leave the boat where it was. "Let it sink in place if necessary," a thought we verbalized; it was time to abandon ship. The American flag was removed; we packed it with our few belongings, grabbed the surfboards and rowed ashore.

Captain Tony, aware of a duplex Jerry had rented for his personal use in Suva, led the crew to the house, where we settled in.

Named Hibiscus House, the native home was a charming cottage with four small bedrooms, double beds affording us ample sleeping quarters. Multicolored flowering hibiscus shrubs surrounded the home that was located one half mile from the harbor. The house sat high on a hill where it had a commanding view of the bay; it received the afternoon's cooling ocean breezes as the trade winds brushed the hillside with their caressing balm. The walls were constructed of painted plywood with floors of native mahogany, worn smooth by years of bare feet walking upon the planks; the windows were covered with wooden shutters that could be held open with a short stick allowing the cool afternoon breeze to enter, and lowered during the torrential rains that pounded Fiji during the monsoon season. No glass interrupted the flow of air through the rectangular windows. Nor was glass necessary in Suva as the ambient temperature never fell below seventy degrees Fahrenheit.

✳✳✳✳✳

Up to now, the escapades of the *Isabel Rose* had been accepted as part of an unforeseen adventure that was greeted with both laughter and surprise by the crew. At times, we showed our dismay at the boats ongoing problems while demonstrating a youthful ability to react to adversity while escaping injury. However, this most recent enterprise had a pernicious taint to it; things had suddenly become quite serious.

When Jerry returned from his business in town, he was shocked to find the crew on shore, in his rented bungalow. Jerry, a tall man, well over six feet, with fiery red hair and a goatee to match, had the look of a deer caught in the headlights. The veil of honesty that Jerry wore during his communications with the crew had fallen from his face and shattered on the floor like a glass vase. Nefarious thoughts sat comfortably in the cradle of his distorted mind and now they were visible for all to see. He felt no guilt, no shame; he had no challenges from his conscience concerning these six young men and their potential loss at sea. He was obviously guilty of what could have become premeditated murder. He had counted on the crew being drunk and following his instructions to sail off into the sunset. If it weren't for the young crew having some modicum of knowledge and an alcohol clouded grasp of the obvious, we all would have drowned soon after departing the safety of Suva harbor.

Meeting with Jerry, we questioned him, "How could you have overloaded a boat like the *Isabel Rose*, with her leaking hull, her dearth of equipment and expect her to make a long distance ocean voyage? The ship would have sunk, the crew drowned!" His answer was severely lacking in sincerity, "Hey, you guys are the best, you can do anything!" While this statement was almost true, no heroics could have created a successful conclusion to this voyage.

Unfortunately for Jerry, that response struck a chord in Frank, who rushed forward, forcefully swinging his right arm; he landed a punch on Jerry's left cheek. As Jerry fell over backwards from Frank's assault, Frank jumped on top, smacking him with both fists; it appeared as though he wished to share with Jerry the fate that he had planned for the crew. After watching Jerry being thumped sufficiently, Dick and Charles pulled Frank off. His assault was seen as counter-productive, even though the two of them agreed with Frank. The others, myself included, watched in disbelief, jaws dropped open in shock at Frank's vigorous offense; stunned, we didn't know how to react.

Having some concerns for his safety, and seeing he didn't

have a chance of winning what had turned into an acrimonious encounter, Jerry left in a huff; he stayed at a guesthouse in town until he could get a flight back to Honolulu, the next day.

The entire crew settled in to the half of Hibiscus House that the company had rented. There, we awaited instruction from Captain Tony or better yet, hoped divine intervention would give us some direction.

After Jerry had left, Charles, Dick, Jimmy, Captain Tony and I discussed Frank's assault on Jerry. Laughing, we all congratulated Frank while patting him on the back; we agreed he had done the right thing; we also sensed that something new was emerging from within Frank's long-depressed persona.

A renaissance was taking place. For the first time in months, possibly years, Frank cared. The potential for loss of the entire crew, for those that Frank had come to care about during our short time together, created a spark in him. That spark ignited his explosive outburst that was properly directed towards Jerry. The entire crew was overjoyed with the new Frank.

In the meantime, the port authorities noted that the *Isabel Rose* had not departed the harbor. They observed her to be riding lower and lower in the water; she no longer flew the American flag and appeared to have lost her crew. Being concerned for the boat and its explosive cargo, they hired a tug to tow her into the main wharf. A fire truck was dispatched to pump out the forward hold which was slowly flooding. A security perimeter was set up around the boat due to the explosive nature of the cargo; yet hundreds of people from the area crowded around to witness the sad fate of the *Isabel Rose*.

The cargo was off loaded, the fifty-five gallon drums removed from the deck. The government took possession of the boat, awaiting reimbursement for services provided to keep the boat from sinking.

The crew did not dispute this. Actually we were happy to see the boat go. We had done our best to keep the boat afloat and functioning for the past few months. She had become a floating death trap that was not fit to leave Suva's harbor. Another point for the crew: six lives saved.

*****

With no work to occupy us, we began to roam the island; it was time again to quell our thirst for waves. Taking in some nice surf spots, we rode some hollow swells at nearby beaches. By this time, however, we had almost no money and could not do the island justice in the touring department.

One day, we met up with some guys from a transpacific telephone cable-repair ship; their ship home ported in Suva. We invited our new friends to the house. Native girls were invited and the partying began. Surprisingly, for the lack of funds the crew possessed, there always seemed to be plenty of liquor around. During one of our celebrations, a new liquor named Absinthe was introduced to those at the house. The light green translucent liquor was poured into a glass, water was added causing the clear liquid to turn white. Interested in the unusual liquid, we were warned that Absinthe could be a dangerous substance. Seeing it in a normal liquor bottle, we wondered why it would be produced if it was dangerous? Further discussion brought to light that the liquid was flavored with wormwood, a toxic substance.

In time, the partying slowed down and it appeared that a few of the women had been adopted by the crew. The native girls were now sharing quarters in Hibiscus House. As the boredom grew the inhabitants of the house would pass the time playing card games. At that time in Fiji, it was custom for the women, while relaxing at home, to wear their sarongs around their hips. This they did, while playing cards in the house with the adolescent guys; not a good idea.

*****

To cool ourselves in the daytime we drank kava, a native brew produced by crushing the root of the kava plant in a bowl with water. Kava, known locally as an intoxicant, had a depressant effect on the central nervous system. On us teenage boys it worked to loosen the inhibitions that normally kept us civil.

*****

Charles and I were seventeen year old boys. We sat on the floor, cross legged, while playing cards with bare breasted women while marinating in our own testosterone. Raging hormones coursed through our teenage bodies, an androgynous mist emanated from the pores of our skin enveloping the room in a cloud of corpulent lust. The card game didn't last long, as we soon ran off to the bedrooms with the native women. Gin Rummy simply wasn't that interesting.

The parties went on, music blaring, liquor flowing; we were becoming candidates for the Guinness Book of World Lechers. One evening, neighbors from the other side of the duplex came over to complain about the noise. Seeing that they were also very young, we invited them in to see what they were about. John and Jeanie Foster explained they were recently married in Tahiti. They were now enjoying a few years of their lives sailing around the world on their fifty six foot yacht. John related to the group that he and his bride were heading to New Guinea to collect butterflies for a museum. That statement led to a complete silence from everyone in the room. No one wanted to doubt John's word, but collecting butterflies in New Guinea?

*****

John, at the age of twenty three, was eligible for the military draft. In the mid sixties, America's conflict in Southeast Asia was just beginning to percolate. He had recently graduated college on the East Coast and if not for his dispatch from the Carnegie Museum, would have been dispatched himself to Vietnam; with a rifle, and not on a yacht. So...thanks to parental connections, John was given the dubious job of collecting butterflies in the outback of Papua, another area that was suspected of harboring cannibals in the mid sixties. Let's see, possible cannibals in New Guinea vs. certain Viet Cong in distant Southeast Asia; capturing butterflies in Papua vs. possibly being captured in the Mekong Delta; not a difficult choice. So, there they were, making a leisurely journey through the South Pacific on their way to the largest island in the world to collect butterflies; the men silently questioned, "How would that qualify as a draft deferment?"

✼✼✼✼✼

John and Jeanie, seeing the good cheer of their neighbors, joined in the partying and soon were part of the crowd. During some lulls in the activity John explained that their boat was having work done at a repair facility; that because they were in Suva for three months their crew had moved on. They needed some time yet to get the boat ready for the next leg of their round the world adventure.

John, a tall, brown haired guy, 6'2" and weighing about two hundred forty pounds, had begun his journey by sailing down the east coast of the United States. He headed west through the Caribbean, transited the Panama Canal; continued westward to the Marquesas and finally Tahiti, a somewhat circuitous route to New Guinea. After meeting Jeanie in Tahiti, John took a time out for a year. The two had dated and fallen in love, which was not a difficult thing to do in French Polynesia. Michener regarded that area as the epicenter of the *erotic mist* that permeated the South Pacific isles. There they had married.

The film, Mutiny on the Bounty was being filmed in the Society Islands and Jeanie had a small part in the movie, starring Marlon Brando. In early 1964, needing to show some progress on his search for the elusive Papuan butterfly, the Fosters had departed Papeete. Heading west to the Fijian Islands, they found a competent boat yard to do the needed maintenance on John's sailboat.

Not being in a hurry to move on, John's boat repairs dragged on month after month. Still enjoying their honeymoon, John and Jeanie took pleasure in touring around Viti Levu and Vanua Levu, much as we enjoyed touring local beaches with our surfboards.

✼✼✼✼✼

Knowing we were practically penniless, John advanced Charles and me some money; we resumed our days of discovery of the islands best beaches and surf spots. Using native transportation, we searched the island looking for breaks in the barrier reef that protected the islands from the ocean's pounding waves. Where there was a gap in the reef, the waves would build from the rolling swells that had traveled thousands of miles to reach the islands, cresting into a breaking wave. We would catch the hollowed out swells riding to our hearts content. We surfed away the hours as the afternoon sun reached its zenith and then began to fall away towards the distant western horizon. Dusk would find us paddling for the safety of shore, leaving the crashing waves behind as darkness enveloped the surf zone.

Day after day we would search the island for the best surf spots, disappointed occasionally, but welcomed by the locals to new spots with an enthusiasm never experienced at home. The Fijians had never seen anyone surf on their beaches, the excitement built as we paddled out into the water; the kids screamed and laughed as we began riding the face of breaking waves. For the locals it was like movie stars having arrived in their private part of the world; they were having a ball watching the seaborne action.

✳✳✳✳✳

For Marshall and Charles, it was a return to their dream. They had again found paradise, left the negative parts of their trip behind and were now experiencing the blissful dream they had come in search of. Surf, sun and an occasional encounter with a native wahine made life worth living for the now eighteen year old guys from Los Angeles.

✳✳✳✳✳

How strange the name Los Angeles sounded; as though from a foreign language. We had become accustomed to names like Viti Levu, Vanua Levu, Suva, Papeete, Papua, Pango. Nothing like the names we had grown up with. Each new name, each new place was like another adventure waiting to happen. Where would the next place be? What would it look like? At times we looked at each other and wondered how we had arrived here?

It seemed we were the perfect age for this whole mind-boggling journey to be taking place. We were young and resilient, barely had the insight to see any danger that we might encounter and when we did, didn't care. Any obstacles that confronted us turned into challenges that were to be overcome in the quickest and easiest manner. With our open minds, fresh spirits and adolescent strength we made short time of any problems that soon came to be discussed in the past tense.

Our fantasy filled days ran into erotic nights that ran into endless days. We drank incessantly, surfed each wave like it was the last and collapsed into our woven mat beds at night like the dead. It was a good life, and of course, one that was soon to come to an end.

*****

One day in November, Hibiscus House was visited by a messenger from the American Consulate in Suva. The islands were too small, out of the way and unimportant to warrant a full embassy. Remember, at this time, most Americans had not yet heard of Fiji. The messenger requested that Charles and I visit the consular offices at our earliest convenience. In a few days, exhausted from long hours of surfing, we walked the short distance to the government offices.

In mid-afternoon, we arrived to inquire what business required our attention. It seems that while the crew lived on board the American flagged *Isabel Rose*, we were considered to be living on American soil. We were listed on the boat's crew manifest; all was well. However, with the act of abandoning ship, we had come ashore in Suva without visas. The government stated, "You have entered the country illegally." They went on to explain, "You are now trespassing." Following protocol, deportation notices for all the crew members had been issued by the Fijian authorities; fortunately, the consulate had interceded on our behalf. The consular officers issued temporary passports to Charles and me; they requested the Fijian government give us time to find passage out of the islands. The government understood the plight of all the crew and acknowledging that we harbored no Machiavellian motives to overthrow government rule, gave the members of the crew fifteen days to find our way off the island.

✳✳✳✳✳

Soon afterward, John invited Charles and me to come see his sailboat. She had a brilliant white hull with blue trim, was fifty six feet in length, and had two tall wooden masts making her technically a ketch. Her two foresails added the term *cutter* to her designation. The boat's sails were manually hoisted up the masts. She had a four cylinder engine for back-up power; an auxiliary generator charged the boat's batteries. The foresails ran up stainless steel stays that were attached to the front of the main mast, giving stability to the sailing rig and allowing the boat to point higher towards the wind.

John explained that the boatyard had hauled the boat and after cleaning the bottom, applied a new coat of anti-fouling paint. Having returned the boat to the water, John was concentrating on some woodwork that needed to be painted; he would spend a few hours a day working on assorted tasks. Looking forward to a break from our daily surf trips, we volunteered to help; our assistance being readily accepted.

We began to go to work with John each day beginning about ten in the morning; sanding, varnishing and painting where needed. John said that he wanted to take the boat out for a sail on the following Sunday; he invited the two of us to come along. Charles protested, explaining that we had never crewed on a sailboat; we would be more trouble than help. John replied, with cleverly concealed motives in mind, "not to worry, I'll show you what to do."

Sunday arrived and with other guests from town joining the group, John motored the yacht away from the boatyard dock and out into the open waters of Suva Bay.

Earlier in the morning, he had given instruction on how to hoist sails, trim sheets and steer the boat. John put the boat into the wind while Charles and I hoisted the main, jib, forestaysail and mizzen. Once the sails were set, he turned the boat, steering towards the open ocean. Looking up, we watched the sails as they filled with the mildly scented air of the tropics.

The billowing white sails powered the boat forward. The engine was turned off. We were dazzled by the thrill of a boat moving gently, silently under sail; it was the most incredible experience we had to-date. The sails were trimmed following instruction from John; she was a beautiful, sparkling, white yacht under full sail, smoothly, almost eagerly, cutting through the sublime blue tropical water. Having had so many negative experiences on the *Isabel Rose*, we waited for something to go wrong, but nothing did. "Wow, paradise is on an up slope again," a thought Charles and I shared.

In a few days, word arrived from the Hawaiian company that owned the *Isabel Rose*. An agent for the company, a man named Ray, came to Suva to clear up any business that needed attention. Being in a rush to leave the island, Ray deposited the funds he had brought for the crew with the American Consulate.

He deposited money for back wages, remember we had never been paid for our work on the *Isabel Rose*. He left money to repay what was borrowed from the crew, some extra to feed us and paid for our lodging. He left a written statement saying, "As of that time the men were released from their *obligations* as crew to the *Isabel Rose*." Our obligations? Not surprisingly, the agent both flew into and out of Suva the same day, while he still had his skin.

After settling up all the bills but before the crew disbanded, all six gathered for a farewell dinner. We verbally reviewed the trials and tribulations of the *Isabel Rose*. From the days of boredom, highlighted by inactivity, to the fires, the chronic sinking problem and the near tragedy of sailing an overloaded, leaking vessel, two thousand miles across the Pacific Ocean. We had worked hard together, had supported each other in our times of trial and in a very short period had become a cohesive group of young men that functioned as one. We did not lament the poverty of our recent adventures on the old wooden boat, but rather eagerly looked forward to the richness of our unlimited futures. There was sadness as we finished our meal; we proceeded out into the night to continue our lives, all heading in separate directions.

The Samoan contingent of the crew, Dick and Jimmy, who now seemed like brothers to the rest, returned to their island paradise home, a short distance to the east. Captain Tony, now known as Crazy Tony, went in search of another boat to sail around the South Seas. The entire crew had tried their best to get Frank to accept that, "Accidents happen and neither his death nor his meanderings around the South Pacific would benefit anyone." To everyone's relief, Frank, after many evenings of discussion about life, his folks who sorely missed him, and his future, had decided to return to the home of his parents; he was New York bound. Charles and I were invited to join John and Jeanie on their fantastic voyage in search of the elusive Papuan butterfly.

Sails Trimmed

VI

And along came *Paisano*?

Having been informed that the Fijian authorities had served Charles and I with a deportation notice, John thought it best to sign us onto *Paisano's* crew list. That ended the problem created by our paperless invasion of the island. He then invited us to move on board the boat, where we could eat, sleep and work. It appeared that divine intervention was at play in the oceans of the world; we were both relieved and thankful. Without John's invitation we would have had to leave the island at a time when we were at a loss for which way to turn. It also released the Fijian authorities from what could have been an unpleasant bit of work, the deportation of teenage American boys, one that was, while completely legal, truly unnecessary.

It also was a relief for John; he now had two strong young men to crew his sailboat. He could continue his extended honeymoon while contemplating thoughts on his mandate to seek out the little known butterflies of Papua. The three of us made an agreement: Charles and I would care for the ketch; sail it, maintain its paint, its varnished woodwork; we would patch sails and scrape the decks when required. In return, John would take care of the two of us: feed us, provide a place to sleep and anything else we needed while we accompanied him on his round-the-world adventure. He would also supply spending money on the occasions when it was warranted.

Getting *Paisano* ready for the next leg of our trip was an undertaking with which we could find no fault. Waking at eight, we ate a hearty breakfast and then turned to for work. Once again, we were slowly, ever so gently, becoming spoiled by this delightful paradise thing. Working two to three hours a day, while trying to keep cool in the hot tropical sun, made short work of the items needing addressing on the ketch. During this time we became acquainted with the special qualities of a wooden sailboat, its complexities, its needs; we began learning a bit about the art of sailing.

✳✳✳✳✳

Archeologists suggest that man first ventured into the Pacific during the Holocene Epoch, around seven thousand years ago. It has been postulated that famine or rising waters provided the motivation for Chinese nationals, living in the littoral regions of the southeast portion of the mainland, to begin oceanic travel. The seafarers of antiquity continued in an easterly direction, spreading their seed from island group to island group during thousands of years of marine exploration; they eventually populated most of the multitudinous islands of the Pacific Basin.

According to current carbon-dated evidence, the first settlements of the South Pacific were on the Samoan Islands. Later, mariners in their twin-hulled canoes sailed to Tonga, the Marquesas, Tahiti and eventually Hawaii.

The introduction of sails to maritime travel gave islanders, explorers and invaders the ability to cross great distances on the water. Norsemen, after ravaging a good part of Scandinavia at the end of the first millennium, set their sights across the North Atlantic, adding Canada to the lands under their dominion. Thor Heyerdahl demonstrated with his narrative description of Kon Tiki in 1947, the ability of ancient mariners to make a blue water transit from the West Coast of South America to French Polynesia, crossing over four thousand miles of open ocean on a raft constructed solely of reeds. The Dutch, Spanish, French and British all cruised west in hopes of discovering new lands and expanding their empires. They were all aided by sail. Leaving behind their oars and the need for large numbers of men to power them, primitive boats became much more efficient, lighter and faster.

Sails themselves changed dramatically over the centuries, as did the types of rigs found on sailing vessels. In the millennium preceding Christ, an Egyptian river boat called a *Felucca* hoisted a triangular sail up its sole mast, fastened to a mostly vertical spar. Later, square sails on a single mast were found to be more efficient. In the early 15th century, a single square sail evolved into multiple square sails and then numerous masts with each setting three to five sails. The square sails on a Dutch East Indiaman were efficient at pushing the boat downwind, but were ineffectual in sailing the boat to windward. A *lateen* rig, consisting of triangular headsails and often times the mizzen, were set on a forward/aft axis resulting in later 17th , 18th and 19th century vessels having the ability to sail upwind. The sails: flying jibs, jibs and forestaysils appreciably shortened the distance traveled and time needed to reach many destinations.

As private sailing yachts came into being in the mid 20th century, square sails were left behind as triangular mainsails became *de rigueur*. Known as a Bermuda rig, a single triangular sail was hoisted to the masthead, appreciably improving sail efficiency. A modern sailing vessel like *Paisano* had a rig named Marconi due to its resemblance to a radio tower. With a Marconi configured rig, a contemporary sailboat, circa 1960, was able to cruise at an average speed of six knots and cover one hundred fifty miles a day.

Certainly *cruising* was not an endeavor of A-type personalities; rather, it was the rarified playground of those not in a hurry, or in many cases, those with no place to go. They savored the elements: sun, sea, unspoiled air and the beauty of a small vessel tenderly, quietly, plowing through the indefatigable waters of the far reaching sea, in what some might consider slow motion. Few had the privilege of making an open ocean crossing. With no land in sight, cruising was a perfect time for day-dreaming, for meditation or contemplation while leaving the cares of a tumultuous world behind.

After all preparations for departing Fiji were in place, the date of November twenty-fifth was set to depart for our next destination.

Noumea, the capital of New Caledonia was to be the first port of call for the new crew of *Paisano*. A passage spanning six or seven days and nine hundred miles across open ocean; we began salivating at the thought of another adventure, this one under sail. No motors broke the holy silence of this journey, only the sound of the trade winds as they caressed the bulging sails giving the boat a slowly rolling, forward motion. We heard the sound of her lines stretching as the sails grabbed at the boat, pulling her forward. The old ketch creaked as she lovingly parted the ocean; the boat pitching higher as it crested small swells, then fell gently into the troughs that followed.

Charles and I felt like graduates. The gulf between the horrors of the *Isabel Rose* and the pleasures of *Paisano* were immense. It was as though we had left one world behind and, crossing through the looking glass, had entered another. While the malignant misadventures of the *Isabel Rose* were both foreign and full of danger; the joy of traveling on board the ketch was both peaceful and safe. Life had taken a dramatic turn; one that was far more positive than that to which we had become accustomed.

While sailing through the open ocean, it was necessary to man watch at the helm twenty four hours a day; boats do not stop at sea for naps during the day nor to sleep at night. With the three of us on board, and in order not to overtax us on our first oceanic voyage, John suggested that we man the wheel in three-hour watches, allowing for six hours of leisure to each off duty person. During the six hours off watch, we would need to sleep, prepare meals, navigate, make sail adjustments and see to any other needs that might arise.

The boat, which rose and fell with each passing swell, made a motion that at first was foreign. It made falling to sleep problematic. As gentle as the boat's movement was, it was distinctly different from the static accommodations normally found on land; it took some time getting used to; it was very different from the *Isabel Rose,* even more distinct than our stationary accommodations at Hibiscus House. After lying awake in our bunks, with the constant motion of the boat and the whispering sound of the sea as it glanced off the outer hull, fatigue rapidly took over and we fell asleep as our heads hit the gently rising and falling pillow.

I often woke with my back against the inner surface of the boat's hull. Heading to windward *Paisano* heeled over twenty to thirty degrees, causing me to sleep on the boat's interior wall rather than my mattress; it was incredibly comfortable.

As I felt the gentle surging motion of the boat, I dreamt I was being embraced by a supple, velvety, swaying cloud that rocked me to sleep; my cloud hovered slowly over a murmuring brook that ran whispering beneath. I felt *Paisano* cuddling me in the cloacal warmth of her womb; wrapping me, hugging me, warming me within her embrace. It was incredibly peaceful. When my eyes opened I could still hear the sound of the flowing water passing by the outside of the boat, but it was obvious that *Paisano* was my dream cloud. I contemplated my feelings, my emotions at that moment and whispered to myself, "How heavenly this trip is, how absolutely heavenly!"

Having researched the nautical charts, the skipper noted that the main island of New Caledonia was protected from the south by an extensive barrier reef located in relatively shallow water. In order to make a safe passage through the guardian reef it was decided to stop for the night and pitch camp on one of the many sandy atolls to the south of Grande Terre. As we approached a relatively large atoll that appeared to provide sufficient protection from wind and surf, the sails were dropped and Charles was sent up the mast to the first spreaders. From there he could view the underlying reef from a superior vantage point while John motored the boat in close to shore. Given the word, I dropped *Pasiano's* anchor fifty yards from the beach. Once the boat's anchor had been set, the clutter on deck was cleared and we were ready to go exploring.

Charles and I unloaded the dinghy and paddled ashore to scout the small isle. It was a low-lying sand island that would shelter us from the light evening breeze while providing a peaceful and safe place to sleep. You see, there were no inhabitants on this tiny, isolated piece of heaven. It sat in the middle of the South Pacific exposing itself to passing sailors, daring them to come ashore and bask in its virgin glory. Surrounded by crystal clear eighty two degree water filled with exotic fish, clams and lobster, a seafood feast awaited those who dared to peek beneath the surface of her watery skirt. But these intrepid sailors had other thoughts; dried driftwood was gathered from the beach for a fire and shipboard food was prepared for our evening meal.

John had brought a portable radio ashore; he tried to tune in a station for current news or music. Luck was with him that evening as his small radio tuned in a station playing Elvis Presley singing Blue Hawaii. John was surprised to pick up a station and we all were comforted to hear a familiar voice. John explained that he had picked up an American station on a skip. Not having heard the term before, I asked, "What does that mean?" John explained it occurs, "When a radio wave transmitted out into the atmosphere bounces off the ionosphere, just short of space, and caroms back to earth." It can be a long or short skip, sending its transmission near or to the far corners of the planet. We were really thankful to have intercepted the atmospheric anomaly, the familiar music making us feel at home.

The trip from Fiji was discussed. John made fun of our poor steering skills that seemed to deteriorate the longer we had been on watch. I had even fallen asleep one night, falling off the helmsman's seat in my slumber. I was rudely awakened as my head struck the unyielding hardwood deck. At the same time the boat, without a helmsman, pulled up into the wind, causing John and Charles to leap from their bunks and run on deck to see what had happened. I lay semi-conscious on the deck, my head in a daze, not knowing how I had arrived there. Once I cleared my head, I returned to the helm with a strict admonishment from John, "Stay awake!"

Being the assiduously detailed person he was, John decided to inspect the rigging to insure that the boat's unintended broaching caused no serious harm. Slowly inspecting the running backstay, which was under pressure, allowed him to see that the slider that held the metal stay had peeled open and was no longer a functional part of the boat's rig. The backstays, as their name implies, support the mast from the rear, preventing it from falling forward. A dysfunctional backstay could easily lead to a broken mast, not a good thing. Running back stays have to be moved each time the boat is tacked, preventing the mainsail boom from hitting the stay and damaging it; exactly what happened when I fell asleep. John jury-rigged the stay to a block on the deck;

the mast now had the needed support. *Paisano* was then steered onto her charted course, continuing on her way with only minimal disruption.

Laughs circulated throughout the group as we decided to call it a night. Crawling into our sleeping bags, we stared up at the incredible obsidian sky; it had the appearance of a smooth, dark canvas pin-pricked with a million points of light. Shooting stars ran across the vast void of space. We observed the endless mass of stars, constellations and planets as we lay on our backs searching the heavens; they added to the enjoyment while dispelling any thoughts of solitude or loneliness on our private beach-front camp.

We stargazed into the celestial cathedral of heavenly bodies suspended in the inexorable darkness overhead; all highlighted by the stars of the magnificent Southern Cross. We gazed in awe at the constellations: Corvus, Virgo and the Crab Nebula. It was breathtakingly spectacular, more stars were visible than in any sky we had ever seen. It was difficult to lie there, on that sandy beach and not be in complete wonderment of the planet we inhabited; its vastness, its complexity and its motherly attitude towards the children that play upon its surface.

After enjoying the rare view that kept our eyes wide open in astonishment at its infinite beauty, we fell off to an undisturbed slumber on the soft white sand while serenaded by the small waves that broke, not quite silently, on the nearby shore of our host isle.

Upon arising the next morning, the three of us decided to enjoy a bath in the crystal clear waters of *our* atoll. Swimming in the shallows near shore allowed us to view a few tropical fish swimming nearby. We had brought dive masks ashore; keeping still near rocks would cause the water movement to slow. After a short interval, small vibrant fish would cautiously emerge from two to four foot rocks submerged in ten feet of water; they began swimming around us on their usual feeding route. Soon, there were hundreds of the two to three inch multihued angel, clown, cardinal and damsel fish swarming around. It was an extraordinary sight. On the rocks could be seen crustaceans, limpets, anemones, and mollusks of fugitive tints with seaweed swaying about them in the slowly moving current.

Needing to head on, we returned to shore and dried ourselves in the maternal warmth of the morning sun. Gathering our sleeping bags and shore-gear, we loaded the dinghy and launched from shore. A short paddle brought us to the side of *Paisano*; she had been patiently awaiting our return in the calm sheltered waters of the small bay. She welcomed the crew aboard; we unshipped the oars, stowing the dinghy in its resting place. Raising her sails, we winched up the anchor and headed off into the day with a brisk breeze powering us on to our next destination.

The rest of the first leg of the trip went well. Navigating slowly through the barrier reef to the south of the main island, we dropped the sails and continued under power to easier avoid the shallows; finally reaching the port town of Noumea, capital of New Caledonia. The ketch arrived at noon to our first port of call, on the southwest coast of the main island, Grande Terre. Entering the small bay surrounded by lush vegetation, we anchored one hundred yards in front of the Noumea Yacht Club. After furling the sails, attaching their protective covers and putting away gear that was no longer needed; we placed the six foot fiberglass dinghy in the water, set the oars in their locks and rowed over to the small floating dock supplied by the yacht club. We had landed in New Caledonia.

Entering a lovely single story, white washed building with polished wooden floors; we were introduced to the club's general manager and welcomed to their country. The management invited the men of *Paisano* to use the club, where reciprocal privileges were extended to cruising yachts from foreign countries. We were invited to take meals at the club and use the facilities as our own.

However, the locals soon found that our *style* was not exactly their style. After coming to dinner barefoot, John was approached by the management; they requested the kids wear shoes to dinner. Ah paradise, or not! Wearing shoes was not such a terrible sacrifice considering where we were and what we were doing. So, in these circumstances we called John *Dad*; we told *Dad* his poor kids, "Have no shoes, won't you take us shopping to satisfy the request of our stylish new hosts?"

The next day we ventured into town, discovering a modern developed community like we had not seen since leaving the west coast of California. The modernity of the community shocked Charles and I back to reality; we had to revert to the customs of a twentieth century society, something we had not thought about for some months.

Simply going into a shoe store, seeing shoes displayed like they would have been at home seemed so odd. Everything was ready-made in Noumea; nothing was made to fit like in Fiji and Samoa, where actually little was made at all. We did find some ugly black shoes that we could slide our spreading bare feet into; John purchased them.

We strolled around the center of town to see how the locals lived. Noumea was more like any community you would visit in California except that everything stopped between twelve and four in the afternoon. It was so blazingly hot at that time that all stores and businesses closed at noon. Later in the day, activity again resumed when the heat was less oppressive.

✳✳✳✳✳

New Caledonia was first populated around 1500 B.C. It received its current name from James Cook as he sailed west touching on many of the South Pacific Isles. In the mid 19th century, these islands were colonized by the French government and used as a penal colony.

In the fertile waters surrounding the islands of New Caledonia lives the nautilus, a small cephalopod with a colorfully striped and uniquely coiled shell. The multi-chambered invertebrate raises and lowers itself through the nutrient rich layers of the sea by pumping air into and out of its segmented chambers. It is the descendant of the prehistoric ammonite, from the class *Cephalopoda* that lived as many as one hundred forty million years ago. Its unique shape and rich history make it a sought after specimen found in the libraries of many collectors.

✳✳✳✳✳

The crew returned to the club the next evening with our spanking new black leather shoes below our dress shorts, sans socks. We were eyed askance by the yacht club members dining that evening; only hushed comments could be heard from a distance. Imagine snobs in paradise! Viva La Françoise!

The rest of New Caledonia turned out to be another piece of the paradise puzzle, a puzzle with so many incredible facets. One day, Charles and I went to the beach to see if we could meet some of the local ladies. Amazed at the beauty of the young women lying on beach towels in their lovely bikinis, our now eighteen year old hormones, again, began to rage. Many of the island's women were a mixture of French and Vietnamese, a truly godly mix. They had jet black hair, almond shaped eyes and golden skin that glistened in the tropical sun. Others were a mix of French and native islanders that created another exceedingly beautiful group of women. We had never seen estrogen packaged so nicely.

Unfortunately, we found the girls to be very shy; we had a difficult time hooking up with them. The other problem was that they spoke French and we didn't, which was perhaps responsible for the first problem. English was not taught in the schools there; students had enough to deal with learning French and the language of the native population.

We introduced ourselves as visiting Americans traveling through the Pacific on a fifty six foot sailboat. This seemed to make no impression on the young ladies; they maintained their skittish demeanor. Charles pointed out that the sunbathing beauties didn't seem to understand English. The next day we tried wearing our new black leather shoes, unfortunately to no avail. This completely confused us; we were used to being the center of attention in most places we visited. Being from out of town, we were always a novelty. With our juvenile good looks and semi-buff bodies, we had always found meeting women both easy and rewarding, irrespective of language barriers.

98

Soon our attention returned to the ocean. Removed from the water for too long, we began to experience withdrawal from our dream; we needed to get our weekly surf fix. No one had ever seen surfboards and the locals could not envision riding waves on those funny looking, fusiform shaped boards. Again, we could not find anyone who knew of well regarded surf spots on the island. Everyone seemed to be busy either studying, working or participating in the activities of daily living that fill most lives. Like other island paradises we had visited, no interest in surfing had yet reached the remote Pacific islands of New Caledonia.

Not to be deterred, Charles and I set out again on a bus ride that would transport us to the opposite side of the island, where a surfing safari could be undertaken. During the ride, a conversation ensued with the always curious islanders; we had found some that spoke English. Communicating with the locals gave us the opportunity of learning about the land they called home. The locals explained that this area was being mined for its massive nickel mineral deposits that, once extracted from the ground, were exported to Europe. We learned that one quarter of the entire world's nickel accumulation was found on their small group of islands.

Once outside the boundaries of Noumea, we realized we had found another isolated, unspoiled, pure part of the world that seemed to be doing just fine without the meddling influence of a modern, developed city.

After a couple of hours travel we arrived at the village of Tula. Walking the short distance to the beach, we found a great break with waves two to four feet in height. A set of three waves was lined up seventy five yards from the beach. Paddling out into the surf, we seemed to be the main attraction in this modest island village, a scenario we were becoming familiar with. After spending a few hours riding waves, we returned to shore where the locals quizzed us about this unique sport of surfing. We spent the afternoon sharing information about riding waves in different countries and our own origins in the States. Islanders shared some of their history with us, making for a fair exchange and some very interesting conversation. Like most South Pacific islands,

Grande Terre was surrounded by a barrier reef that only allowed waves to break near shore where there were gaps in the reef formation or on the outer edge of the reef itself. With a mildly sloping bottom the swells would rise up before peaking near shore, forming mid-sized hollow waves that could be easily ridden; a true surfer's paradise.

At the end of the day, we retraced our steps to Noumea and the bay where the yacht club was located. Loading our gear in the dinghy and untying the painter; we rowed out to *Paisano* where she lounged at anchor in her pristine bay on the outskirts of the capital. Surrounded by a dense tropical landscape with numerous varieties of palm, ferns, orchids and Marquis Scrub, our little bay looked good enough to idle away a few years time. However, that was not John's plan. It was getting late in the year; John and Jeanie were planning on spending the holidays with her parents in Tahiti. John wanted to sail the boat to Australia, get *Paisano* settled in and then fly off to Tahiti, where Jeanie was waiting at the home of her parents.

After checking the weather report and finding a fair wind and no storms forecast, *Paisano*, after breaking fast on a Thursday morning, departed Noumea. It was early December; John expected the nine hundred mile blue water voyage to Brisbane to be short and uneventful. The trade winds blew strong and steady making the trip a delight. Our course took us a full week out of sight of any enchanted landfalls. We sailed into the higher latitudes of the southern hemisphere, crossing the Tropic of Capricorn, through the crystal clear waters of the Coral Sea and the tranquil Southwest Pacific.

On the afternoon of day three on our southerly course, we were graced with the arrival of a mammoth school of porpoise. The playful vertebrates spoke to us as they lunged out of the water; some gracefully pirouetting on their tails. The three of us were impressed, laughing openly at the antics of the humorous cetaceans. We had never seen porpoise *dance* on the surface of the ocean.

Confusing us with their other pod members, they made a clicking sound that was commonly used to communicate with each other. Seeing the smile on the face of the bottlenose porpoise, we felt as if they were a genial advance reception party sent to welcome us to Australia. Scanning the horizon, Charles noticed there were porpoise completely encircling the boat from a few feet away to as far as the eye could see, and in every direction. Lightheartedly, they would swim as close to the bow of the boat as they could, their smooth, grey skin coming within inches of the wooden hull. Never having seen such a large gathering of porpoise, it was a stirring sight.

Paisano had two small glass portholes in the forepeak. When the boat was heeled over from a strong wind, the portholes slipped underwater. We took turns looking through the ports to see the sleek porpoise swimming as they darted within inches of the boat. With their enduring grin, they seemed to be totally enjoying playtime with their new swimming companion.

The tropical sun shone bright as we slowly crossed the temperate Pacific. The sun's intensity was so great that by the time *Paisano* reached Brisbane, bubbles had formed in the white paint on the boat's topsides. Fortunately, the cooling breeze of the trade winds helped make the trip a great deal more comfortable for the crew, while allowing us to maintain our tans and bleached out hair, i.e., our surfer look.

Once we had overcome the sleep deprivation that began each trip, Charles and I had plenty of time to read. Unless you've been on an oceanic voyage, it's difficult to know that there's not a great deal to occupy your time when you're limited to walking around a fifty six foot sailboat. We'd find a shady nook to crawl into, perhaps pad it with a pillow and spend a few hours relaxing with a good book. When fatigued from reading for hours, we could often be seen gazing into the distance; our curious minds wondering what the next place would be like, or what God, in his ultimate vision, had in store for us tenderfoot seafarers.

One night, while still far out at sea, all three of us were on deck discussing how the trip was going; our conversation was interrupted by the sound of wings trying unsuccessfully to flap; we heard a low chirping voice, then silence. We would hear the flapping again, then nothing. Five minutes later the sound returned, causing us to go searching for its origin.

Grabbing a flashlight to illuminate the dark boat, we searched the deck and the boat's rigging until we found a Gooney bird stuck in the lifelines near the boat's stern. There, the lifelines came together forming a wedge that the bird had flown into. The night was very dark, moonless, and the gooney's poor eye sight often caused them to fly into boats, entangling themselves in the rigging. John pulled the bird free, set out some food and water; liberty was granted to our visitor to rest on deck. When the bird's appetite was sated and he was well rested, the gooney spread his wings, lifting off into the night, he left behind his temporary landing pad.

With fair and steady winds and a few good books, *Paisano* crossed the short distance between the two island nations in seven days. We looked forward to reaching Australia. After our difficulty communicating with the beautiful women of New Caledonia, we were comforted with the knowledge that there would be no barrier to speaking with the citizens of Australia. We knew that English was the spoken language in the world's Down Under continent, or so we thought.

✳✳✳✳✳

In retrospect the islands of the Pacific were a place onto themselves. A unique part of the world where each grouping of islands had its own language, the people their own customs; all of the islands were created with consummate beauty. The lack of development coupled with the verdant foliage of the tropics contributed to an awe inspiring vision of heaven on earth. We were overjoyed to have spent six months touring this area of incredible splendor.

Completing the final leg of our unplanned transit through the South Pacific, a six month odyssey that would remain in our memories forever; we had passed through the throne room of the sea gods; we found it to be without equal.

VII

A View Down Under

From the swaying deck of *Paisano*, searching long and hard towards the horizon, the impatient Charles was the first to pick up the silhouette of the continent's east coast. Land trailed off in both directions until it became a ghostly outline of the colossal land mass called Australia; its long arms stretching toward the horizon. It was our first indication of just how large a mass this continent encompassed.

Thanks to John's fine navigational skills, *Paisano* arrived on the coast at the northern tip of Moreton Island, an island that received its name from Captain Cook in the late eighteenth century. Having departed England, Cook sailed south past the Falkland Islands, rounded Tierra del Fuego and entered the Pacific Ocean. He continued west and north, discovering half of the islands of the South Pacific, Australia and New Zealand. In the late 1700's, his hard earned discoveries doubled the area of the known world.

Equally important and more prescient in nature was the discovery of Wort & Rob. Wort: a concoction of malt, vinegar, sauerkraut and fresh veggies; Rob: a mixture of lime, orange and lemon juices. Initially researched by the German naturalist Steller, who sailed the frigid northern seas with Bering in the mid eighteenth century, Lund refined it and Cook later employed the mix proving its efficacy. Cook, in the 1760's managed to circumnavigate the planet without the loss of one seaman to disease. Prior to the use of Wort & Rob, fully one-third of all seamen on multi-year voyages, on any vessel, in any ocean, perished at sea from the inexorable scurvy. Unfortunately, it was not adopted by the Royal Navy until the 1790's.

Oblivious to the dangers and disease that Cook dealt with two hundred years before, *Paisano* skirted the island heading southwest towards the entrance to the Brisbane River.

Viewing the river on a chart illuminated a serpentine

pathway that led upstream towards the city center and our destination. Due to the constant tacking that would be required to sail up river, it was decided the safest and least arduous passage would be achieved under power. The sails were lowered, flaked and wrapped in their covers while the ketch motored up stream at five knots. A few hours later, we finally arrived at Norm Wright's Boat Yard, close to the city center.

*****

Unbeknownst to us, Norm Wright had been a boat builder and sailor all his life. Learning from his father, Norm found the ways of the sea to his liking. Starting as an apprentice wood worker, he eventually learned every aspect of boat building, boat handling and eventually navigation that would allow him to participate in America's Cup challenges in later years. It is every serious sailor's dream to represent his, or her, country in the famed America's Cup competition that was held in the waters off of Newport, Rhode Island. As Norm had learned his skills from his father, he was currently teaching them to his twenty two year old son, Norm junior.

*****

Brisbane, however, was a return to the modern developed world with which we were more familiar. A well developed city of one hundred thousand citizens; the most utilized form of transportation was the automobile.

A small ferry landing, marking a gateway to the suburbs, was located fifty yards upriver from where *Paisano* was docked. The ferry, powered by its one cylinder engine, had a length of 30 feet, the interior of which was filled with bench seats for commuters. Overhead, a canvas canopy protected passengers from sun and rain. The small boat ferried workers who had left their homes in the morning's early hours. From the landing, they crossed the river where they could catch public transportation to offices located on the city side of the gently flowing, brown-water, Brisbane River.

Once the boat had been settled in, John made arrangements with the boatyard's proprietor to keep an eye on the ketch in his absence. He wished us a, "Merry Christmas" and headed to the airport to catch the next flight to Tahiti where he would join his beautiful wife Jeanie. Together they would spend the holidays celebrating with family in Papeete.

Tying up *Paisano* at the boatyard had the dual purpose of allowing us to do the needed maintenance on the boat while being located near transport to the downtown area. John also employed the boatyard to clean and repaint the boat's bottom, a task that needed to be done every twelve to twenty four months and required the ketch to be hauled out from the water on a submersible carriage.

The boat's decks were teak, giving her the majestic look of a fine old seagoing yacht. The wood needed to be washed down daily with salt water to keep it from drying out in the tropical heat; occasionally it needed to be scraped. Paint, especially dark colors like that on the boat's cap rail, would easily blister in the tropics' intense sunshine. So strong were the sun's rays in those climes that even white topside paint, that was designed to reflect the heat of the sun, often bubbled when exposed to its glaring rays. The bubbles in her topsides had to be scraped down to the bare wooden planking, then sealed and recovered with numerous coats of paint. Protecting the wood underneath from sun, sea and salt air is a priority on a cruising sailboat.

She also needed her woodwork to have fresh varnish applied every three months, as the blazing sun burned through the old layers of epoxy shredding them from the underlying wood like the peel from a banana. The main and mizzen mast, the two booms and the three hatch covers were varnished with three or four coats of the best material we could find. Sanding between each coat with wet and dry sandpaper added to her polished glow and protected the wood from the weather; it resulted in a beautiful finish that added to the pristine look of the old wooden sailboat.

Interacting with the very friendly Aussies was more of a challenge than Charles and I had anticipated. In conversation, the Aussies would respond with terms like: *Fair dinkum.* We responded with, huh? They called the guys, *blokes.* The women were known as *birds*, and all the males called us *mate*. At that time in history, at least in America, a *mate* was someone you might marry and have children with. Since we weren't interested in marrying any Aussie blokes, we were initially a bit uncomfortable with the greeting. At first it gave us the feeling all Aussies were homosexual, which we knew couldn't be true; but we never returned the greeting, "Hey mate." Rather, we felt very odd with the salutation and looked penetratingly at those that greeted us as *mate*. We were very confused until one day we mentioned it to a friend at the boatyard. He explained it was simply a greeting, similar to *buddy* in America. Wow, what a relief, and lots more laughter. It can be incredibly funny when miscommunication like that takes place. It really affects attitudes and personal interaction until the misunderstanding is clarified. We were unabashedly allowing our youthful ignorance to surface for others to see.

Some of the young guys, while checking out *Paisano*, had spotted the surfboards strapped onto the ketch's lifelines. They came to talk to us; making quick friends with guys their own age. They had questions about the surfboards and where we had used them. Our new friends wanted to know every detail about our recent adventures in paradise.

We were soon invited to take a weekend surf vacation, which required a ferry ride, to one of the islands located outside the mouth of the Brisbane River. Bob and Jeff, our newly made friends, explained that good surf was to be found on the windward side of Moreton Island and lots of birds hung out there watching the guys surf. It was essentially a place where guys and gals went to hang out, surf and party on the weekend.

The following weekend, the group found a ride to the ferry landing on the coast. We loaded our surfboards onto the commuter with some clothing for the weekend. The ride out to Moreton Island, about twenty kilometers offshore, was uneventful. In a change of positions, we had become passengers, an attitude we found very comfortable. No sails to set, no course to steer, we could just sit, relax and enjoy the ride.

New places always created awe in the two of us; we had passed this way on our first landing in Australia a couple of weeks ago. Seeing a place twice was unusual, not our normal itinerary. This whole trip was turning into a magical mystery tour that became more interesting every day.

We were just outside the geographic tropics, having passed the Tropic of Capricorn as the boat sailed south toward Brisbane. The scenery reflected the warm temps, the abundant rainfall and the high humidity with profuse growths of a variety of palms, acacia, hibiscus, incredibly colored and shaped orchids, ferns and many cycads.

Disembarking the ferry on Moreton Island exposed the four of us to a not small island where walking was the main mode of transport. It was a nice change from the noise of the city. After six months away from the rancor and rush of developed communities, all the city sounds now seemed magnified.

A short walk from the ferry found the foursome at the small two bedroom bungalow that had been reserved for the weekend. We dropped off our belongings, grabbed the surfboards and headed for the beach on the weather side of the island. Not to be disappointed, a four foot break was entertaining a dozen surfers in the water. The Aussies were tearing up the waves, making sharp kickbacks and swift kick-outs. The waves broke from right to left and made a beautiful mid-length ride in very warm water that we were later to find was shark infested. Again, we found ourselves ignorant of the endemic dangers created by a working whaling station located on the lee side of the island.

After Charles and I came back from riding waves, a group of birds standing on shore asked if we didn't hear them shouting at us. The girls explained that while we were riding on a wave, sharks could be seen surfing the translucent four foot waves breaking behind us. Those watching from shore were afraid that if we wiped out, we could end up as shark-bait; the beachgoers were trying to alert us to the looming danger. When asked if we had spotted the sharks in the water, we replied, "No, and thank goodness we didn't. It would have scared us to death." As for the people on the beach waving and shouting, Charles thought it was an impromptu cheering section.

Walking through the sand as we approached the water, we

were surprised to hear a squeaking sound that we chose to temporarily ignore as our focus was fixed on the surf. Afterward, curiosity overcame Charles as he began walking through the sand along the beach. Never before had we experienced walking on sand that squeaked. At first, Charles didn't believe that it was the sand. He took a couple of steps, each time a squeaking sound was produced. He stopped and stood in place; of course, nothing happened. He began to walk again and the squeaking returned. Jeff explained that the beach sand had a high silica content that caused the squeaking sound as you walked through it. It was really different.

Leaving his board on the beach, Charles had walked through the squeaky sand up onto a small knoll hoping to find a good view of the over twenty mile long island. He stood looking at the mildly undulating coast line when he suddenly noticed a slight movement to his right. He turned his head and spied a large monitor lizard standing a few feet to his side. Including its tail, the lizard was about four feet in length and had an eighteen inch tongue that was thrusting about to pick up nearby scents. Its deeply creased skin adhered to muscular, articulated, arms that allowed the lizard to carry its body only a foot off the ground. The giant lizard, head held high for a better view, seemed to be enjoying the coastal vista as much as Charles.

After enjoying the view, the lizard slowly walked off, apparently looking for something to eat that was smaller than the almost six foot Charles. Bite size is important to feral animals; Charles was a good two times the size of the wrinkly lizard. Later, we were told the monitors were herbivores and wouldn't bother visitors on the island. Looking at them, they had the visage of a prehistoric creature, fortunately in miniature. We were later informed that the animals were a protected species and not to be messed with, although Charles couldn't imagine anyone wanting to mess with a creature that big or that ugly.

Having surfed throughout the morning hours and then investigated the island's unique sand, we turned our attention to the beautiful women on the beach. We had a difficult time keeping our eyes off the honeys sunning themselves. Bikinis were the style of bathing suit the girls wore and they were delightfully skimpy, thin and adhered to their trim bodies like a second skin.

The Aussie women were fun, open to meeting new guys and interested in the journey that Charles and I were currently immersed in. They impressed us as intelligent, very fit and beautiful. They were a nice addition to any surf trip and would have been a delight to make a life with. But at eighteen, we were not quite ready to settle down. We did, however, make the acquaintance of some of the birds on the beach; making arrangements to meet-up later in the evening.

After surfing most of the afternoon hours we cleaned up, went to the store and bought food and drink for dinner. The four of us discussed the great wave riding we had found on the island and made preparations to meet the ladies in the early evening.

Heading back to the beach; driftwood was gathered and placed in a fire pit where a roaring fire was readied to cook the evening meal. The ladies brought crudities; hot dogs were barbecued over the open fire while copious amounts of the local brew were supplied for everyone.

Music was piped through a small portable radio that carried tunes from the mainland and the party began. After dinner everyone paired up and danced by the glow of the firelight. As the night wore on, fatigue seized us; we walked the birds to their cabins and returned to our bungalow to get a good night's rest. We all looked forward to a hot day of surfing on Sunday.

Sunday dawned bright and warm. Moreton Island was located three degrees south of the Tropic of Capricorn and the weather was very warm, even though it was early January. Our companions explained that the seasons were reversed south of the Equator; the northern hemisphere's winter was the southern hemisphere's summer and vice versa. We became acquainted with the term declination, the earth's physical relation to the sun and the sun's global effect on the continually changing seasons.

Overnight the surf had increased another two feet in height

and the shape was perfect. Sets of three or four waves silently rolled toward shore with a two minute lull between. Our group headed for the water and paddled out. Sitting on our boards between sets while searching the horizon for approaching swells, we noticed swordfish leaping high out of the water one hundred yards beyond the break. It seemed bizarre; the large fish appeared to be participating in an off-shore soaring concours. The pelagic high jumpers appeared to be bounding for joy as they streaked skyward, kicking their tails above the surface of the water. After spending a few hours riding the perfect left breaking, medium velocity waves, we paddled to shore and questioned others about the soaring swordfish we had seen.

The locals explained that when porpoise come inshore, they chase sharks out of the area; sometimes harassing the swordfish, as well. That was their motivation for becoming air-borne. That was a relief; we felt much more comfortable knowing that the porpoise would protect us by chasing the sharks away. Until then, we had no idea that the fun-loving cetaceans could be so protective. It added both a physical and psychological barrier between us and the potentially lethal sharks.

After surfing the morning hours, we laid down on the beach to take a short nap; we then made ready to return to the mainland. Gear was packed, surfboards cleaned and the bungalow was put in order. Having bid the lovely ladies of Moreton Island adieu, we departed for the ferry ride back to the coast and the car ride back home; home currently being Brisbane. Charles and I had settled into the idea that *home* was wherever we were; delightfully everyone welcomed us as family.

We were still very young during this time in our adventure, and most people we met seemed to care for us as they would their own children, safeguarding us on our fortuitous journey. While we didn't consciously understand that we were being cared for by the people of the world, we did realize that everyone treated us with extreme kindness; many seemed to go out of their way to make us feel at home. Even with other guys, who we usually referred to by name, rather than the ubiquitous *mate*; they always seemed to treat us like younger brothers, with the older guys watching over us. This understanding would grow much stronger as our trip progressed.

Returning to Brisbane and our floating home on *Paisano* brought some familiarity to our surroundings. We settled back in, returning to our four hour workdays caring for the ketch.

Wooden boats are a distinct species. In the view of Jonathan Wilson: "There is an irresistible aura about boats and yachts build of wood, an aura brimming over with the richness of creation. It flows from the strength and grace of trees themselves, through the hands of craftsmen who fashion them into proud new forms. It is the presence not only of substance, but of soul, created in collaboration between the earth, the sea, and the artisans who fit the wood with skill and care so that it will look lovely and last long." We were beginning to appreciate that as long as we traveled on this beautiful boat cruising the world's seven seas, we would be engaged with the never ending upkeep of a wooden sailboat. There were never any complaints.

✳✳✳✳✳

Unfortunately, employees of the American Consulate in Brisbane had other ideas for the two of us. When deported from the Fiji Islands, the consulate in Suva had issued Charles and I emergency passports with a restricted duration; they were limited to a length of ninety days. We were told the passports would need to be extended to their full five year term at the Consulate in Brisbane. Arriving at the consular offices, we stood in line, waiting to speak with the clerk. Approaching the counter, we offered the passports while requesting the term be extended for the full five years. We were asked how old we were. We both replied, "Eighteen." We were then taken aside by an employee of the consulate who asked, "Have you signed up for the draft?" Being stunned by the question and not knowing anything about the draft, we replied, "What draft?" Excitedly, the man behind the counter offered to send us to Southeast Asia tomorrow, if we'd like to volunteer. The inducement: some nice new boots, an M-16 rifle and an airplane ride to a place we couldn't identify on a map, Vietnam. We were mystified by his suggestion. We looked at each other while sharing a thought; then we looked at the man behind the counter like he was crazy. We had come to the office simply to have the term of our passports extended and he wanted to send us to war? Let's see, we confided to ourselves: "Being shot at by Vietcong versus maybe being eaten by cannibals in New Guinea; perhaps dying fighting for something we knew nothing about in a place we had never heard of versus living a life of unsurpassed excitement and adventure while sailing around the world. "Not a difficult choice," we concluded. We grabbed our passports and headed for the door.

✳✳✳✳✳

Paisano, built in 1924, was constructed of oak ribs with cedar planking glued and screwed to the ribs. She had teak decks that were common in those days and masts made from spruce with booms of similar hardwood. The deck planks and hull were sealed with thick cotton caulking and then pitch, a tar-like substance, was laid over the caulking to make a waterproof seal. Her main mast was seventy feet tall, the mizzen mast topped out at fifty feet. She had a beam of thirteen feet six inches, making her stable at sea and providing a nice salon down below for dining. A six footer could stand up without hitting his head on the ceiling, barely. She had a forepeak with two bunks and some sail storage space; two bunks were ensconced behind the settees in the main salon and an aft cabin with one large bunk for the owner. A three burner alcohol stove provided heat to cook the crew's meals; a small navigation station offered a table for parsing charts and reading sailing directions, the world's roadmap to: islands, coastlines, harbors and the planet's unlimited points of interest.

Electronics were scarce in those days. The boat was steered by a magnetic compass; global positioning satellites had not yet been put in place. She had a depth sounder for entering and leaving shallow harbors and a VHF radio for communicating with shipping on an emergency basis. The radio was almost never used while the depth sounder was used constantly.

Navigation was done with a handheld sextant. The readings from the sextant were paired with the exact time of a *mark* to determine boat latitude. A delicate chronometer, balanced on gimbals in its own finely crafted wooden box, was used to keep the correct time at Greenwich, England, while at sea. This time, known as Greenwich Mean Time or GMT was located at the prime meridian and has been used in navigation for centuries.

John had explained that *Paisano's* original purpose in life was to carry milled timber along the east coast of the U.S., which she did for a number of years. With the advent of larger, diesel powered ships, she became obsolete and was retired from the timber carrying trade. Soon thereafter, a sailing enthusiast found her sitting idle, decaying in a coastal harbor. She was purchased for a small sum and converted to a luxury yacht. She had the interior built-out: the salon, bunks, galley, forward and aft cabins all constructed of finely finished mahogany. A bright polish was applied to the woodwork giving her interior the look and feel of a richly paneled library. She then began to undertake the leisurely sea duty that she so richly deserved.

A number of years later John found and purchased the fifty six foot ketch; changing her name to *Paisano*. After refitting the boat in 1962, he began what was to become a six year odyssey that would carry him and others around the world in the voyage of a lifetime.

✳✳✳✳✳

Paisano was tied up to a floating dock at Norm Wright's boatyard. The dock was connected to shore by a gangway, whose angle would rise and fall with the tide, allowing easy access to the boat. Tethered on the outside of *Paisano* was a forty five foot yawl skippered by Didier Dubose, a Frenchman who was also leisurely circumnavigating the world's oceans with his beautiful wife, Bernadette and their Spanish crewman,

Jose.

Didier's boat, the *Vermillion*, was a unique yacht. It carried a bit more beam than the ketch, which caused it to waddle some in light winds, but also had the advantage of providing more space below deck. The increased area allowed Didier to install an upright piano amidships where his wife could display her musical talents. It's not often you see a piano on a small sailboat, but hearing Bernadette's melodic playing in the evening demonstrated the richness and tone that the piano added to their sailing experience.

Didier was himself an exceptional individual. He, like John, seemed rather young, being in his early forties, to be making a multiyear voyage of this type. Adding to his uniqueness, Didier had lost one arm, at the half way point below the elbow. He enjoyed telling stories of how he had been a member of the French Foreign Legion. Other times he noted losing his arm in an auto accident, explaining that he had been a professional race car driver. His stories never failed to entertain and were always punctuated with good humor and a glass of French wine. The owners of *Vermillion* had returned to France for the holidays leaving their crewman, Jose, onboard to care for their boat.

Through the many young guys Charles and I had met, we were invited to weekend parties where we were introduced to lovely young women. I had paired up with a sweet young lady of my own age; auburn hair, with a body to die for, named Barbara. She had graduated from high school and was working in town as a secretary. We spent many nights together, often with Barbara staying overnight on the boat. She enjoyed visiting on board; it was a diversion in her life that gave her a certain sparkle. She liked the way the yanks spoke and I enjoyed the uniqueness of her Aussie accent.

Charles had also paired up with a lovely young woman who lived in the suburbs on the west side of the river, not far from where *Paisano* was docked. Alice was in university, studying to be a teacher. She had an insatiable thirst to learn everything American. That made her and Charles a perfect pair as they could spend their evenings picking each other's brain while exploring each other's body. Charles and I spent

114

the holidays partying with the girls; we enjoyed the company of the lovely ladies and the many wonderful and open-hearted people we had met in a far off land.

∗∗∗∗∗

One mid-afternoon towards the end of January, while we were entertaining Barbara and Alice in the boat's main salon, Charles noticed the weather suddenly turning cool; the sun abruptly disappeared as though a hand had wrapped around it, stealing its warmth and light. The boat's interior rapidly darkened.

Charles hiked up the companionway to see why the sky had unexpectedly turned gloomy. Looking upriver, he viewed a large grouping of black clouds hovering over the city center; they extended their tentacle-like reach over the river to the residential area, on the west side of town. He had never seen such ominous clouds before. They had a coal black interior with gray edges; they tumbled, as though in a blender that had sent them spinning. The sky looked incredibly menacing, causing the hairs on the back of Charles neck to rise apprehensively. Soon the clouds began to head for the boats as though being drawn by a powerful magnet.

It was 3:00 in the afternoon; the wind rapidly began to intensify; we realized that trouble was about to befall us; I joined Charles on deck. Soon the wind was blowing sixty miles an hour, kicking up four foot waves in a river that usually had none. The small ferry that carried passengers across the river during morning and evening commutes was caught one hundred yards short of its landing; it was violently thrown about by the fury of the wind.

The ferry, powered by a tiny, one cylinder engine, lacked the ability to resist the overpowering storm; it was pushed helplessly towards the sailboats that were secured to the floating dock. The wind and waves drove the small ferry under the bows of *Paisano* and *Vermillion;* the current held her there to be thrashed by both the furious weather and the sailboats. The ferry was heaved skyward with each succeeding wave thrusting it up against the underside of the solidly stayed bowsprits of the madly bucking, pitching and rolling sailboats.

Fearing for their safety, panic began to make a menacing appearance amongst the thirty odd passengers who were unfortunate enough to be crossing the river that afternoon. There seemed to be no escape for them, they were horrified of being pounded to a pulp against the underside of the much larger sailboats; screaming erupted as the frail ferry continued to furiously fling itself against the wooden underside of the firmly secured sailboats.

Suddenly, the waves and rapidly running river current pulled the ferry to the outside of *Vermillion*; as she was sliding past, the driver threw a line to Jose, momentarily securing the ferry. Now the ferry had joined the sailboats, dancing on the crests of the storm generated, rushing waves. The three boats kept time, continuing their explosive dance as their sides converged in a pounding fandango surely destined to eliminate the weaker ferry.

Charles vaulted from *Paisano*, over two sets of lifelines, onto *Vermillion's* deck. There, he assisted Jose pulling the terrified passengers, in single order, from the deck of the slowly disintegrating ferry. Meanwhile, the subtropical temperature had fallen precipitously, a heavy rain lashed at our half naked bodies and two inch hail pummeled everyone.

The ferry continued to bash against the side of *Vermillion* adding to the fear of the riders still on board. Afraid that the ferry might sink, it looked more like it would break into pieces from the continual battering it was taking against the yawl's unyielding side. Once the frightened passengers were on deck, they crossed over *Paisano;* heading up the gangway to terra firma, happy to be safe from the storm's unrelenting fury and a horror filled afternoon on their usually placid river.

In the meantime, I had run ashore for help in securing both boats to the floating dock. Workers from the boatyard, huddled under cover of the boat sheds while watching the raging storm, raced out to help. Following my lead, they grabbed any lines they could find to secure the boats. Eighteen other boats, roped to moorings in the river, were blown down stream, dragging the anchors that held them in place. They were swept down-river by what was later reported to be ninety five mile an hour winds.

Charles and Jose were successful in off-loading all of the passengers, and the ferryman safely from the foundering ferry. As they crossed safely over to shore, the pressure from the pounding of the damaged ferry and *Vermillion* against the ketch caused all the lines securing her to *Paisano* to part. The two boats were pushed downwind by the massive strength of the storm's cyclonic winds. Turning broadside, the storm pushed the rafted boats alongside the ketch, raking her deck with an anchor that was firmly fixed to *Vermillion's* port bow. On *Paisano,* we focused our energies on repelling the yawl in a valiant attempt to keep her from damaging the ketch; we fell backward to her onslaught as immense pressures bombarded her hull while the ferocious storm continued its assault. As the yawl headed downstream, her anchor tore off a portion of the starboard cap rail on our boat; ripped off a bronze lifeline stanchion, hit stainless shrouds stabilizing the mizzen mast and lastly, caught on the metal and wood cradle supporting the mizzen boom, tearing the cradle from the deck.

The two boats continued their unguided journey down stream, finding respite against a far shore where the river made a ninety degree turn to the south. With the appearance of a marine cemetery, many boats lay on their sides; embarrassed, their topsides lay in the shore mud, driven to the water's edge by the overpowering strength of the storm. *Vermillion* and the ferry, still tethered, joined others resting peacefully in the shallow water of the near-shore.

The storm had lasted a short thirty minutes and then passed on, its fury spent on our small part of the world. Neither Charles nor I had ever before encountered a major storm. It was an eye opener to come face to face with nature during a nasty tantrum, a meeting we had hoped to avoid. It engendered in us the realization of just how fragile a soul can be and how easily the light of life could be extinguished.

In moments, the sun returned, the air warmed, waves ceased to exist and tranquility returned to the urban Brisbane River. We were soaked to the skin, had welts where we had been pelted with hail, and were exhausted from the adrenaline powered toil of our unexpected labors.

Seeing that we had work to do, the pale and scared girls, who had remained safely down below during the storm's wrath, excused themselves. The girls appeared frail and shaken from the experience; they said, "Call when you guys have a minute," while scurrying to more secure surroundings.

As calm returned to the storm-shocked Charles, he turned to me, confusion in his dark eyes. Hesitating, he spoke, "What the hell was that?" There was no response, only silence answered his wavering query. At a loss for words, my eyes met his, reflecting my own ignorance, but I said nothing.

Along with the boatyard employees, Charles and Jose helped tow boats and their moorings back to their designated resting place. We cleaned up *Paisano* as best we could and went below for a beer. Still shaken, we tried to relax and de-stress from the shock and fear of what had just happened. It was difficult to digest, seeing and hearing the screaming ferry passengers, the freed boats that became unguided missiles and the storms wide spread destruction. Roofs had flown off sheds, wooden walls were missing planks. We discussed what we had seen and how we'd reacted. We did our best to ease the bottled up tension. The beer helped.

Having survived what was termed a major tropical cyclone, we were surprised two days later when a film crew from the local television news channel appeared. They introduced themselves and asked if they could see the storm damage on the boat. Charles invited them aboard where they explained to us the story that was circulating around town. Citizens were discussing the heroic acts of the young boys on the sailboats; suggesting we had probably saved a number of lives as the ferry and passengers were being pummeled under the bow of the yachts. I pointed out to the film crew that it was Charles and Jose that saved the people on the ferry and it was them that deserved the accolades. I was busy enlisting others, trying to secure the two boats with additional mooring lines.

It appeared that my modesty was unacceptable to the news team; they interviewed both and filmed the damage on the boats. They filmed me winching Charles up the main mast to inspect for damage. We made the six o'clock news and were currently seen as local heroes. Now we had become everyone's friend and much to our dismay, everyone called us *mate* as we were greeted in town.

John soon returned from Tahiti and was shocked to see the destruction on his beautiful white sailboat. However, when he heard the story of the destructive storm, he expressed his pride at our brave actions in assisting the ferry's passengers.

After assessing the storm damage, John contacted his insurance company; *Paisano* needed to be inspected and repaired. An agent from the company came to view the boat damage, writing notes in a black binder he carried. Numerous points of damage were noted. The cap rail was replaced, the mizzen boom cradle was repaired as the taff rail was rebuilt; torn stainless steel shrouds were replaced. Two of the lifeline stanchions had been ripped from the deck; John decided to replace the old bronze stanchions with new stainless steel around the entire boat. Surprisingly, the insurance company declined to pay for the repairs stating, "John's insurance policy did not cover acts of God." That surprised us. While the storm was the initiating factor, it wasn't God that caused the damage to the ketch; it was the other boats.

During the repair work, Norm suggested to John that he rig our six foot fiberglass dinghy with an aluminum mast, mainsail and jib. He pointed out that we could keep up our deteriorating sailing skills by practicing in the river with the dinghy. We had not sailed for almost two months and it sounded like a good idea.

Once the dinghy was rigged, John, Charles or I could be seen sailing along shore until one day, when John had purchased some firecrackers. As Charles was sailing past the boat, John leaned towards the dinghy, lobbing a hand full of small firecrackers at him. Unfortunately for Charles, John made an accurate throw, putting a cracker right into the dinghy; as Charles made a hasty exit from the small boat he bent the mast and tore the new sail. Further inspection found that the fiberglass rail where the mast shroud attached had also torn making the dinghy all but useless for sailing.

*****

On the following Monday, a retired American sailed upriver and tied up at the boatyard. Hearing another Yank had arrived, John went to greet him with the two of us in tow. After greetings were exchanged, Phil explained that after being employed for thirty years as an engineer, he had recently retired. Not wanting to retire into the life of the lame and the lazy, he had been induced to continue working as a consultant for the company. The company had made a deal to employ Phil as he sailed around the world in his forty foot sloop visiting the company's satellite offices. The company would pay him for time spent in-house, thereby helping to finance his round-the-world cruise.

While not in a hurry, the idea of consulting gave Phil destinations for a world tour that kept him in touch with engineering, his love. He was a really nice guy who stayed a few weeks at the boatyard while fresh bottom paint was applied to his sloop, the *Destiny*. Phil toured Brisbane, provisioned his boat for the next leg of his journey and then sailed off to call on a company office hundreds of miles down the coast in Sydney.

While we really liked Phil: he had a pleasant demeanor, he spoke softly and intelligently. We couldn't understand why anyone would want to endure sailing alone for extended periods of time. It wasn't terribly difficult to rig a boat to sail single-handed, but spending weeks alone at sea didn't make sense to us. During a storm or after an unexpected injury or illness, handling the boat could become problematic. Apparently, it takes a special type of person for that sort of adventure, one whose understanding completely eluded our inquiring minds.

*****

During our stay in Brisbane, we were introduced to many friends of the boatyard workers and many families from around the area. Wanting to learn more about America, one young gent we met, Gene, invited us to his house for dinner and a chat. Afterward, our curious host would ply us with over-proof liquor and do his best, in the Aussie style, to drink us under the table. At the tender age of eighteen this wasn't a terribly difficult task. In the evening's late hours, after drinking Charles and I into oblivion, he would return us to the boat where we unceremoniously slithered into our bunks to sleep off the night's challenge.

In February, the marriage of Norm's son to his fiancée Mary, took place. After their church wedding, the new couple and guests returned to their parent's home adjacent to the boatyard. A large outdoor grass space behind the house served as the reception area. A tent was set up to provide shade for the party-goers; a band played dance music. We paid our respects to the newlyweds and enjoyed some good Aussie brew with the guests. It was nice to see the family line continued and with Norm's son following in his father's boat building footsteps, he was a proud father.

On weekends, the two of us often took off surfing with guys we had met. We traveled down the coast, riding with guys that owned their own cars. Cars were very different Down Under, many being more compact than those found in the states. They had names like Opal, Holden, Vauxhall and Rover. Whenever we heard the name Rover, we looked at each other and laughed, thinking it a dog's name.

We visited places like Surfers Paradise on what was known as the *Gold Coast*; the heart of the Queensland surfing beaches. Surfers Paradise had a beautiful, expansive, yellow sand beach, perhaps two miles long; it had plenty of room for the weekend crowds. There were no hotels at that time and the roads were not yet paved in gold. However, the surf was great; we met other guys in the water and on shore where quick friends were made. We told stories of our adventures in the South Pacific; the local guys filled us in with stories of the best places to surf on the mainland's east coast, with additional information about Tasmania and New Zealand.

Surfers Paradise was also very popular with the ladies. The local birds flocked to the beach on weekends drawn by a rivalry between regional lifeguard teams. They watched as lifeguards from various communities raced their surf boats in group competitions. A team of four lifeguards, wearing colored outfits with matching caps, rowed their brightly colored dories out through the crashing waves, around a distant buoy and back into shore again. With the size of the swell increasing, and much to their embarrassment, many boats didn't make it past the booming surf. We were curious about the colored caps that the oarsmen wore. Someone explained that the different colored caps allowed the judges to identify the different boat teams, as most boats looked identical from shore.

The lifeguards also wore Speedos at a time when most male beachgoers wore bathing suits that were more like boxer shorts. Charles and I were a bit embarrassed by the small size and sheerness of the Speedos, not feeling comfortable exposing our external plumbing, like the locals.

Having exhausted the weekend and ourselves, we returned to *Paisano* Sunday night. Continuing to pass the days working on the boat, we made her ready for the next leg of our passage. In the evenings we read and discussed all the great people we were meeting and the adventures we shared with the people of Brisbane.

Both of us were becoming attached to the girls we were dating. We had spent weekends and some weekdays together for almost two months; we were becoming quite comfortable as a pair. The women were lovely, the community was great, but the world was waiting.

While Brisbane lacked the native beauty of the South Pacific Isles, the common language, open and friendly attitude of the citizens and common culture insured a quick bond with the Aussies.

The guys we had met spun tales of the holiday islands off the East Coast that were visited regularly by large numbers of vacationing birds and blokes. It was there that they participated in what was euphemistically known as: *peak procreation vacations*. We had already been introduced to the beautiful women of Australia and their flattering bikinis, now we were being directed to where they liked to recreate.

When John returned from Tahiti in late February, he arrived solo, explaining that Jeanie would stay with her parents a while longer. She would fly in to meet us farther along on the trip.

John discussed sailing north, inside the Great Barrier Reef.

He explained to Charles and I how the reef protected the coastal region from the stormy conditions that existed during the winter Down Under. The reef was known for massive amounts of sea life and unrivaled diving with crystal clear water that provided one hundred foot visibility. John suggested day-sailing from island to island within the reef, stopping and visiting for a few days at each location. He surmised that sailing within the protection of the reef would also make our passage both safer and more relaxing. He highlighted some of the notable communities of the East Coast, including Cooktown in the far north of Queensland.

Of major interest to John was Endeavour Reef. While Captain Cook was searching for land, he reportedly threw heavy iron cannons from his ship in order to float clear of the reef and continue in a westward direction. John suggested we hunt for the enormously valuable cannons that, after two hundred years, might still be on the ocean floor.

✻✻✻✻✻

Could John have been dreaming? It was no secret that Cook dumped his cannons; surely someone would have salvaged them before now. Nor did it occur to John that they had no scuba gear, nor any training in underwater surveying that might facilitate their finding Cook's iron cannons on the ocean's sandy bottom. But they would face that hurdle when they got there.

✻✻✻✻✻

Paisano was tied up at the boatyard in the Brisbane River for three months. Being alone on the boat, Charles and I had met many people, had paired up with two beautiful local girls and had experienced some great surfing. As always, there was a warm spot in our hearts for the incredible time we had had, the generous and caring people we had met and the sweet women we had loved in our short visit to this endearing community.

Cruising through Paradise

VIII
Exploring the Great Barrier Reef

The boat was stocked with provisions, awnings were folded and stowed; *Paisano* was readied for departure. In March of 1965, she slowly made her way down river to blue water, leaving behind our riverside home of three months.

Bribie Island, the ketch's first stop after leaving Brisbane, was a short sail to the north. Epitomizing the term *Holiday Island*, this small speck of land off the east coast of Australia consisted of a recently built resort for vacationing Aussies. For people from the city it was a great place to get away, leave behind the cares of the working world and enjoy the temporary fantasyland that vacations encourage.

Since John was recently married and was without his lovely wife, he excused himself from the dating scene that we might encounter on the island. Rather, John had an epiphany. Our erudite leader had an understanding of the universal dating ritual and the raging hormones that coursed within the integument of his eighteen year old crew. With thoughts of how some single women might just be tempted by the wealth displayed by a beautiful yacht sitting at anchor in front of their resort, he made a suggestion.

Being the good spirited guy he was, John recommended that when we landed on a new island, I should say that the boat belonged to me. John went on to intuitively suggest, "When we go on to other islands, the crew change places, with Charles saying the boat belonged to him." The current *owner* would point out that the slightly older, portly John was merely one of the crew. Not surprisingly, John was found to be correct in his assumption of the dating rite as practiced by the locals Down Under. And for us, well, we received daily invitations to allow our hormones to express themselves.

More islands generated more ownership changes. When word got out who captained the beautiful white yacht that lay at anchor in the tranquil bay in front of the resort, a crowd soon encircled the current *owner*.

John gave us the go ahead on running up tabs in the bar. Drinks were very inexpensive at that time, a beer costing fifty cents; we could drink all night and never spend much of his money...and so we did.

The resorts all had bars, many with live bands that played on the weekends. When the two of us went ashore, we quickly hooked up with vacationing single women. In the evening, drinks flowed, music played, and we often ended the evening skinny dipping in the island's warm peaceful waters. Waking in the dawn's early hours, we usually found ourselves the guest of some lovely on holiday.

In this manner, we were learning the ways of the world. With the constant partying, it was difficult to remember all the beauties that we spent time with. There were blondes, brunettes, red heads; tall, short; all athletic and beautiful, we would have made mom proud! Indeed, it was a time to observe that boys were becoming men.

✳✳✳✳✳

Heading north from Bribie, Paisano rounded Fraser Island. We were searching for the navigational leads that marked the entrance to the passage through the Sandy Straits. Leads, like lighthouses, mark the end of a journey or the safety of a landfall; they mark the danger of a hidden reef or an outcropping of rocks. The sun was setting, making picking out landmarks significantly more difficult; its rays reflected off the surface of the glassy sea making our entire view one of a brilliant red-yellow-orange canvas. We searched the western horizon for the markers until noticing waves were beginning to break around the boat. Realizing we were getting into shallow water, and thinking that we had missed the entrance to the deep water channel that led into Hervey Bay, John decided to come about, retracing the last fifteen minutes of travel.

As he put the helm hard over, a pin connecting the rudder cables to the wheel fell out, making the steering wheel useless. John yelled excitedly to Charles and me to remove the cover plate from the aft deck where the rudder post was located. Charles ran below to grab the emergency tiller. Doing just what needed to be done: the cap was hastily removed, the emergency tiller was placed onto the rudder post, and John quickly regained control of Paisano. Having lost the mechanical advantage of the steering mechanism, it now required two of us to turn the heavy wooden rudder, changing the twenty-four-ton boat's course. Our rapid response prevented what could have been a significant disaster; we avoided grounding the boat on Wide Bay Bar.

Regaining our composure, we brought the boat about, finding that we had, indeed, overshot the leads. We picked them up on the second try, after the sun had set and the area around them began to take on the shades of grey that follow dusk. The focused light of a Fresnel lens spiked the darkness, guiding us, while shore lights began to twinkle in the twilight. Reassuringly, they led us to the deep water channel that led into the bay. We brought *Paisano* to rest at the old, wooden, Urangan Pier. Spending the night in the safety of a protected bay, we left the next day for Fraser Island; easier to find in the daylight.

Bribie Island led to Frasier Island to Herron Island and onto Keppel Island. At each island, the boat gained a new *owner* and lost the old. Stopping at beach resorts, most hosting only forty to eighty guests, *Paisano* anchored just offshore to make a pleasant and impressive vista for those vacationing at the resort. What a delight, and yes, the Aussie ladies did live up to their reputation of being some of the friendliest and most beautiful women on earth.

Paisano then sailed north to Wilson Island. A small island with white beaches, lowland scrub beyond the berm and coniferous pines spotting the higher elevations; we hiked inland on what we believed to be another deserted island. During our exploratory trek inland, the threesome ran into the island's owner, an eccentric young man who was raising a large herd of sheep for their wool. We first spotted him running, clad only in shorts, with a WW II army rifle held high in one hand. Unarmed, we were somewhat shocked to see someone running towards us sporting a weapon. With no method of defending ourselves; the initial shock of what appeared to be an impending assault was reflected in the expressions of fear on our faces. The runner saw our concern; he began to smile while waving a greeting with his free hand. Allowing our initial thought of taking cover to slip quickly from our minds, our heartbeats decreased, and our respirations slowed and we smiled as we returned the strangers greeting.

Introductions were made and we chatted for a short time. Aside from the owner, Allan, a few thousand sheep and a few hundred goats, the island was uninhabited. Allan explained his rifle was for hunting goats, inviting us to join him in his hunt of the unwelcome quadrupeds. He requested we kill as many goats as we possibly could, stating they were a nuisance, eating much of the natural plant food that he preferred to reserve for his sheep.

The island's owner explained that goats had originally been left on the island by passing mariners one hundred years ago. Knowing that the island's natural vegetation would provide sufficient nourishment to the feral animals, time would produce an expanding herd. On future journeys, when passing mariners were in need of food, they could stop at the island for fresh meat and goat's milk.

✻✻✻✻✻

Allan warned the neophyte hunters that they must be careful not to wound any animals. A wound could become infected, afflicting the entire island's animal population. Infected sheep could become a financial disaster for the island's owner. He did say to enjoy the hunt and invited *Paisano's* crew to linger on his island as long as they wished.

✻✻✻✻✻

The next day we broke out the arsenal maintained on *Paisano*. John had three rifles: a 30-30 lever-action Winchester, the type of rifle used by cowboys in the old west, had been put onboard the boat in New York. Someone in Brisbane had given him a .303 Aussie army rifle, and John himself had recently purchased a .22 caliber light rifle and a

.22 caliber pistol. The weapons were loaded with ammunition, more was stuffed in a satchel for reloading and we headed off on our first hunting safari.

Landing on shore, we went into stalking mode, searching for the oblivious goats that were calmly dining on the island's limited low-land scrub. After hiking a short distance, we encountered a group of the unwelcome animals, completely disinterested in the business of the human interlopers. They were preoccupied with taking their daily nourishment in a quiet, shaded meadow. Spotting a grouping of dead eucalyptus trees laying on their side, we took up position at the meadow's edge. Steadying our rifles on top of the fallen tree trunks, we took careful aim. Shots rang out, some animals fell, others ran; we dropped a small number of the pesky goats before the rest scampered for the safety of a nearby stand of trees. Both happy and surprised that we had hit something, we then marched off looking for another group of the intrusive diners.

This went on for most of the day; we returned to the boat tired and weary from our hours of scurrying over the islands hot, dusty and rarely used trails. Happy with our successful hunt, John expressed surprise that we could hit a goat from fifty yards. We admitted our own amazement at our excellent marksmanship; happy that we could be of assistance to Allan. We finished with dinner, cleaned up and did some light reading before turning in for the night.

What an incredible place; a small island off the coast of Australia, tropical in nature, beautiful by any standard; it was used as a sheep ranch without fences, as the island itself limited the movement of the undomesticated animals. Here was another slice of the seemingly unlimited paradises that dignified Australia's east coast.

Again we wondered how we were so lucky to have been graced with an adventure so beyond our wildest imaginations; perhaps fairy tales do come true?

We would pinch each other from time to time to insure that we were truly awake, that we were not experiencing a shared hallucination. Occasionally, we thought perhaps we had already died and were now on a passage through heaven.

Jeanie flew in to the mainland from Tahiti and had a float plane deliver her to the island that we were currently and ever so gently ravaging. Happy to be reunited with her spouse, the group dallied a few more days off shore before heading back to the mainland.

Charles, the most recent *owner*, had returned stewardship of *Paisano* to John as we headed west, toward the continent's east coast. Mackay was the first coastal lull for the crew; we were rapidly growing tired of drinking, carousing till all hours and partying in general. Arrival saw the ketch tie up at the main dock in town. As we were stowing the sails and getting the boat ship-shape, a reporter showed up from the local newspaper.

Seems our reputation had preceded us. With a photographer in tow, pictures were taken of the boat with a focus on John and Jeanie for the front page of tomorrow's newspaper. Titled, "Lovers make Round the World Passage," the boat's arrival and the story behind it was the most interesting thing to happen in Mackay in some time. And that pretty much describes Mackay in 1965, a nice place to visit, but...well, you know the rest.

Two days later, after picking up fresh provisions, we sailed north to Townsville, another north coast town that was still in its infancy; too small still to be called a city. *Paisano* received a warm welcome from the inhabitants, John and Jeanie had more pictures taken and an article in the Townsville Gazette. However, there was not anything notable in the area and we soon shipped out to our next port of call.

The next day found *Paisano* heading for a group of islands that sat a short distance off shore, at around twenty degrees south latitude. Known as the Whitsunday Islands, they sat as breathtaking specs of land surrounded by clear water that only reflected the mood of each day's sky. Covered with dense rain forest and surrounded with shallow barrier reefs, they were a perfect place for exploring. Quiet, warm, surrounded by a diver's paradise and with little settlement having reached northern Queensland, they were not much visited in the sixties.

Lying in crystal clear turquoise water, we found the islands to be both primitive and charming. Small, recently built resorts existed on two of the numerous islands.

Long Island presented itself with a beachfront resort that *Paisano* anchored directly in front of in eighteen feet of water. The water was so clear that seen from above, the boat appeared to be itself a cloud, floating in mid-air.

It was nice to be off shore again, visit a slower paced environment and revel in the lack of development on the island. Leaving the noise and activity that inhabits growing communities behind and slipping into the vacation attitudes that people wear while on holiday was always intoxicating, soothing, and ever so peaceful. The thought pattern here was to rest, explore the island some, and have a few beers and perhaps a vacation fling.

The *birds* seemed to love sunning in their skimpy bikinis, snorkeling in the tropical fish filled waters and frolicking throughout the evening hours. You couldn't have chosen a more perfect locale for skinny dipping; at times it was difficult to find an isolated piece of beach that wasn't already occupied.

After a few days of cavorting, the ketch sailed on to Hook Island, one of the more northerly of the Whitsundays. Hook Island was surrounded with a stunningly beautiful, sun-bleached, white sand beach. The last and largest of the holiday islands that we visited, this island paradise was covered with inland tropical forest and uncultivated tropical fruit trees that made hiking both fun and refreshing.

To our dismay, there was no surf on these islands. With safety concerns for *Paisano* being paramount, she was always anchored on the lee side of the island or in a sheltered bay. Lacking transportation of any kind, the windward shore was beyond reach. While surfing was a priority for Charles and me, protecting the boat from the swells and wind of the open ocean was a more pressing need. Occupied with meeting new people on each island, exploring during the day and partying during the nocturnal hours made up for the temporary lack of surfing. However, our interest in waves never faded in these most interesting of tropical locations.

Cairns was a novel town farther north on the coast of

Australia; the town marked a jumping off point to the Great Barrier Reef. A small town with a relatively large shipping facility, it was used to load sugar cane and timber for the export market; cruising yachts stopped in port mainly to refresh provisions.

The harbor was a fair distance from the open ocean and the ketch sailed some time to reach the town site. When *Paisano* did arrive, she found a small nesting of four sailboats grouped loosely together. We dropped anchor seventy five yards from the pebble-lined shore.

We found that we had arrived in a unique little coastal community. The town's citizens welcomed the foursome with another article in the newspaper, people greeted us warmly in the pubs, and we made lots of friends in the bustling community.

A small commercial fishing fleet lay at anchor in the bay, seaward of the port facilities. The fisherman caught swordfish, mackerel, sea bass, mullet, shrimp, tuna and barracuda in local waters supplying the community with fresh fish. Small fishing boats carried tourists, on holiday, out to the barrier reef where both the sport fishing and the diving were reported to be exceptional.

The community itself was a small outpost on Queensland's north coast. Perhaps fifteen thousand people lived in Cairns in the mid-sixties. It was a town that was growing rapidly and there was a palpable feeling of excitement among the pioneering citizens that had chosen to make their home here.

While walking in town one day, we met up with a law officer from the community. He reminded us of the sheriff on *Gunsmoke*, except he wore no gun. He must have been six feet four inches tall and weighed two hundred twenty pounds. Had he not been a law officer, he looked like he could have played professional football. He was polite, but stoic, with a look that denied the need for a sidearm. Greeting us with the colloquial, "Hey, mate" we were glad he was on our side.

In a small port like Cairns, the crew on the sailboats could easily visit with crew from the others. We shared sea stories, gave information about areas to avoid and often spoke of our home countries. The ketch brought the count to five boats in

Cairns harbor; gossiping over a beer was always a refreshing manner of passing the evening while getting to know those from other countries. There was a boat from Germany, America, France and two from Australia. They usually stayed a few days, and then headed on to their next destination.

One late afternoon, John returned to the boat with a couple of British submarine captains in tow. We wondered where he had found them, England being a bit far off. John introduced them to us; he explained they had met in town and the captains had suggested he join them upon returning to their submarines. So...John accompanied the captains to see their subs that were rafted together at the main dock in the harbor. After a tour of the submarines, the three of them shared some of the Brit's finer Scotch and then John, having reached a moderate level of inebriation, decided he wanted to show off *Paisano* to his new seagoing friends.

The three hefty males, portly gents, all sporting sagging bellies that promised an impending birth, almost sunk John's six foot fiberglass dinghy. They did, however, manage to make it out to the ketch where she lay quietly at anchor. The men followed John up the boarding ladder, took a quick turn around the deck and then headed down below to the boats salon where John opened a new bottle of Johnny Walker Scotch. John invited the two of us to join them in storytelling, drinking and more story telling. They allowed their minds to drift into the clouds that shroud sea stories from reality, mixing the two to create a tale of fiction and non-fiction that may please all in attendance. They continued their day-long drinking binge without any apparent metabolic limits on their ability to imbibe.

The hours passed with the telling of war stories and the emptying of a couple more bottles of Scotch. The captains, their speech slurred by the swishing of lugubrious liquid between tongue and jowl, suggested that John sail *Paisano,* "upp rever and ty up to orr bloody submines att the citi main werf." When John asked why they were docked at the city wharf, the skippers replied, "'Cause ere ain't any bloody navel sillities in tis own, tassall." Apparently, the subs had made an unscheduled stop in Cairns for needed repairs.

In John's drunken stupor he had related to the captains that he was constantly challenged by his boat's auxiliary generator, which was used to charge the boat's batteries. The majority of the time the generator preferred its leisure rather than fulfilling its intended purpose. The Brits offered to have their mechanics come aboard and repair the testy device.

The captains suggested tying up the white ketch to their submarines. They noted the "White, whit, bot might cash wit orr black sus, but really, hoo cares?" They jokingly went on to suggest they would enlist *Paisano's* entire crew into the British navy, giving them leave to continue the party on board the ketch, using her as their private pub.

They explained, "Oe dwink ah rum was dis, dis, distributted eh the sus's cew each, every, morning', but any ort of dwinkin' onbored after wus strictie forbidden, kno awlowed." Not to mention, it might be considered bad form for the captains to sit around drinking and partying all day while the crewmen of the submarines were standing their regular duty.

By this time the sun had set. John, speaking through a thick fog, but being clever enough to know when not to go sailing, promised to meet the British skippers on the beach the next day, after sobering up. He promised them, "Tomorrow we will sail *Paisano* upstream, adding her to the fleet of submarines."

The next day dawned much too early as the guys on the ketch were awakened by shouts from the beach. Our new friends, having regained their senses amid a semblance of sobriety and being military men that rise at dawn each day, yelled and waved to get the attention of the sleeping crew. Charles, being the smallest of us, rowed the dinghy ashore to pick up the two rotund English captains. Upon their return, John started the motor to power the boat up stream. However, the Brits would have none of it. They noted that *Paisano* was a sailboat, and, "Damn, if we shouldn't be sailing up stream, not motoring." John, not to be put down by the bravado of his new drinking mates, responded, "Hell yes, hoist the sails mates, we're going sailing!"

For Charles and me, this seemed a throwback to the days onboard the *Isabel Rose.* We looked at each other, rolled our eyes and laughed. Not knowing what was about to take place, we shared a common thought, "God help us!"

The submariners helped raise the main, mizzen and jibs. Charles and I weighed anchor. We headed up river until spotting the two submarines tied up next to each other at the wharf. As the ketch made a pass by the subs, the captains yelled instructions to their crew "Make ready to receive mooring lines." A look of confusion adorned the faces of those on deck duty. Not quite understanding what was about to happen, a crewman ran to the forward deck to receive the mooring line, as instructed. *Paisano* sailed a loop; coming around near the subs. Charles and friends dropped the sails in order to slow the boat, allowing her to drift unhurriedly abreast of the stationary subs.

As she came alongside the outboard submarine, I threw the bow mooring line over to the crewman on the sub's deck. I watched as the crewman, poised to receive the bow line, fell from the submarine into the water. He had leaned too far forward while stretching his hand out to catch my, almost accurately, thrown line. Everyone on Paisano laughed their heads off as the crewman scurried for safety from the oncoming yacht and tried to hide his embarrassment from his superiors. That gave the Yanks a point up for seamanship on their British brothers.

The group had successfully sailed the boat up to the submarines, docked safely and one of *their* crew went for a swim. Charles and I let out a sigh of relief that nothing more serious took place. This called for some serious laughter and, of course, more Scotch.

During the next few days, the captains practically made their home on *Paisano* while Johnny Walker Red flowed. Purchased *In bond,* a bottle of J. W. sold for three dollars in the mid sixties; not much of a draw on John's more than abundant bank account.

As the submarines were nearing the end of their shore-stay in Cairns, I began to notice a queasy feeling in my stomach. Soon, the smell of food was making me ill. I began to experience episodic diarrhea and started to dry heave from the odor of food cooking in the galley. At the age of eighteen and almost never having been ill, this was a bit of a surprise. The skipper suggested seeing a doctor. Feeling anything but human, I agreed; thinking that a very good idea.

John gave me money to pay for the doctor visit and I scheduled an appointment for as soon as possible. I went ashore on the appointed day and spoke with the local physician, explaining my daily routine and answering any of the doc's questions. He palpated my abdomen finding it very tender to the touch. The doctor's intuition led him to question the use of alcohol onboard. When I replied that we usually drank some, but recently had drunk a great deal of scotch with the submariners, the doctor reached a diagnosis of stomach ulcer and prescribed an alcohol free diet. I was shocked by the diagnosis; at the age of eighteen, I thought myself much too young to suffer from such an illness.

A few days later, following the directions of the doctor, I began to feel somewhat human again; meals soon followed. How nice I thought, I could actually maintain the food in my stomach. The odor of meals being prepared in the galley didn't make me ill. This whole episode of infirmity gave me pause. In all the trials and speed bumps of the past nine months, and for most of my life, I had been favored with excellent health. I pondered the ease with which we accept our good health and how helpless we become in its absence.

During the day, mechanics from the subs were ordered to come on board and repair the ketch's one cylinder generator that sat sequestered in a corner of the engine compartment. They spent days working on it; took it apart, cleaned it, put it together, made it run for a few hours and watched it stop. The engineers, being somewhat perplexed at their inability to make the simple but quarrelsome generator function properly, dismantled it again and carried the pieces on board the sub for a more in-depth evaluation. They soon returned the aging generator; it was shiny and clean on the outside, it sported fresh red paint; god knows what they had done on the interior. When started with the boat's batteries, it ran well. But after ten days, when the submariners had headed to sea, the generator again returned to its dysfunctional self. It was then accepted by all that it had been cursed by a Tahitian witch and would never again run correctly, if at all.

In discussions with the sub captains, prior to their leaving Cairns, John was reminded how dangerous it was to have a gasoline engine on board. The skippers alluded to how, "No Englishman in his right mind would sail a boat that was not powered by a diesel engine." Petrol, as they called it, was simply too dangerous. John was convinced to change out the gasoline engine for a diesel, "No more discussion, thank you."

Making inquiries at the boat yard resulted in finding a diesel engine that sat in an unused Fordson tractor, owned by a local farmer. The farmer had a red, "For Sale" sign on the tractor but when John made him a generous offer for only the engine, he happily accepted.

Taking out the boat's engine required Charles and I to remove a deck hatch that appeared to have never been removed. It was held in place by six thick bolts, was caulked and pitched so that it was not obvious to the casual observer that any opening existed in the deck.

The strength of a hydraulic jack was required to break the hatch loose; placed between the engine bed timbers and the deck above. The hatch made a loud popping sound as it was released from the secure grip of the deck. Once free, four men could lift the hatch from its resting place and put it aside on the deck. With the hatch removed the engine could be hoisted through the large opening by a small crane and lowered onto a pallet on shore.

The fuel tanks had to be drained of any remaining petrol and then flushed to remove any residue. The diesel engine was then dropped onto the engine bed where it was bolted in place. The boat's transmission and reduction gear were attached to the rear of the engine. New fuel lines were put in place and attached to the diesel's fuel injection pump, the fuel tanks had diesel fuel added and the engine was ready to test. With some light modifications, the engine sputtered to life bringing a smile to everyone's face. With the boat secured to the dock with her usual four lines, the transmission was engaged and the propeller rotated. All seemed well. Good Job! Well Done! Back slaps all around.

The next part of this project was replacing the deck hatch,

caulking and pitching it so that it, once again, became invisible. Since this was the first time Charles and I had done this type of work, it went slowly. It was messy dealing with the black tar that adhered to everything it touched. Soon, the two of us were half covered in tar and beginning to look like native aborigines. As our bodies and hands became pasted with tar, it was difficult to touch anything without watching the black mass spread with a viral intensity. When the job was completed, the hatch again became almost invisible.

Having lingered in Cairns for more than two months, John decided to leave as soon as the engine exchange had been completed. The crew said goodbye to all our friends, inviting many to the dock for a final farewell salute as *Paisano* headed out to sea.

At ten the next morning, with a host of friends watching from the dock, the boat's mooring lines were withdrawn and the transmission lever was thrust into forward gear. Everyone expected the boat to move slowly forward, away from the dock. To our surprise, instead of pulling ahead, she began to inch backwards. The boat had not stirred from where the engine exchange had taken place; no sea trials were undertaken, no further evaluation was done. Apparently, nobody had noticed that the diesel engine rotated in the opposite direction from the gas engine; the boat's propeller pushed the boat astern while the transmission was in forward gear. As you can imagine, the moment was fraught with embarrassment. The three of us exchanged curious glances as an expression of perplexity framed our faces.

At that moment, John's mind was percolating with thought. He reflected on how it looked to our friends gathered on the dock. We had received many Bon Voyages, celebratory dinners and generous gifts from the small group of friends who had come to see us off. But at the time of our scheduled departure, with the boat moving backwards, John had the look of a boy caught with his pants down. Our friends, seeing the boat moving backward, didn't at first realize what had happened. Someone yelled, "Put it in forward, John." John responded, "It is in forward." Those that had come to bid us adieu could not stifle the humor of the moment. Seeing the big white yacht moving backward, the gathering on shore burst out laughing as the color rose in John's unusually pale face.

*****

Our departure delayed, *Paisano* remained tethered to the city dock while John researched a remedy for our self inflicted malady. At first, Charles questioned if we could simply, "Put the transmission in reverse gear to propel the boat forward?" John replied that the bearings would quickly wear out, as the transmission was designed to function primarily in the forward gear. Discussion with land based marine engineers resulted in obtaining the knowledge that both right handed and left handed propellers existed and would be the panacea for the boat's current dilemma.

A left handed propeller that would fit onto the boat's prop shaft needed to be shipped from Brisbane and would require another week to arrive. Then the new prop would need to be fitted to the boats shaft, four feet underwater. However, no boatyards existed in Cairns. This impasse presented us with the opportunity to purchase scuba gear for both current and future use. With underwater breathing gear, the prop could be changed with the boat at its current, dock-side location.

After ordering the new prop, John found a shop in Cairns that stocked scuba diving gear. He purchased a new scuba tank, regulator and fins. While not having the luxury of taking a dive course, the college educated John gave us his best instruction, "Put the mouth piece in place and breathe." It didn't sound terribly difficult, and as expected, it wasn't. It may have helped that the water was crystal clear while the temperature hovered around eighty three degrees Fahrenheit.

Having delivered the scuba gear to the boat, an exploratory dive was made to view how the prop was held in place on the boat's drive shaft. A three inch nut held the prop in place and was backed itself by another large nut that functioned as a locking mechanism.

After a short period of waiting, the new prop arrived from Brisbane. Charles volunteered to make the shallow water dive; substituting the new prop for the old. He removed each nut in turn and found a prop that was securely held in place on the shaft by years of pushing the boat forward. With his adolescent strength, he couldn't budge the jammed prop. A wheel pulling device was borrowed and attached to the prop and the end of the shaft; the prop slid gently backwards toward the end of the shaft where it could be removed while the new left handed prop was installed.

Charles tied a rope to one of the blades of the old prop to prevent it from falling as it slid off the end of the drive shaft. This worked perfectly and was employed equally when installing the new propeller onto the shaft. The primary and locking nut were replaced. The job completed, with a bit of trepidation, John started the engine and put the transmission in forward gear. The boat began to move slowly forward and away from the dock as everyone on board let out a sigh of relief. *Paisano*, after three months in Cairns, was now ready to head north on the next leg of her adventure in paradise.

The beautiful white ketch was about to head out on a multi-day voyage that would take her out of sight of land. That was the cue for Jeanie to jump ship, purchase an airline ticket and go visit her family in Tahiti. She would rejoin the boat when we were comfortably ensconced in a large, peaceful and safe harbor. She flew out with good-byes to everyone, "See you soon." Apparently, she had not inherited her Tahitian ancestor's seagoing genes.

Departing Cairns allowed the three of us to spend some time away from bustling coastal towns. We headed off shore towards Endeavour Reef. The reef, named after Captain Cook's ship around 1770, blocked his progress from the east, as he sailed towards the unexplored north coast of the mainland. After impacting the reef and causing serious damage to his thirty meter ship, Cook allegedly dumped many of his iron cannons over the side. The lighter ship then rode higher in the water, providing sufficient space to clear the solid underwater obstacle while allowing Cook to continue his exploratory quest. He sailed to the shore, beaching the ship for repairs at the mouth of a small river that he conscientiously named after his ship. He founded a settlement on the north shore of the river's entrance, and not being bashful, named it for himself, Cooktown.

We arrived at the reef during low tide, the reef's uppermost surface being only one inch below sea level. Donning sandals, we were able to carefully walk on the sharp, jagged, surface of the coral. Inquisitive moray eels could be seen episodically peaking out of holes in the reef, sating their curiosity of the newcomers. Turtles swam in these waters; humpback whales, having birthed their calves in the warm waters of the tropics, swam south, cruising within their migratory corridors to the much cooler, nutrient rich waters around Antarctica. There, the baleen whales feasted on krill and schooling fish, including herring and mackerel, that fattened themselves on shrimp who also gorged themselves on the tiny krill that flourished in those waters.

Captain Cook had preceded us by almost two hundred years; surely someone would have found his cannons by now, if indeed they existed. Seeing the folly of a cannon rescue, we enjoyed the afternoon in a relaxed manner, slowly exploring the off shore reef. With *Paisano* safely anchored on the lee edge of the coral mass, we spent the night in blessed solitude; far from any landfall, bustling towns and more importantly, from any of the ubiquitous pubs that sate the thirst of weary travelers.

The next morning, after finishing breakfast and having totally dismissed the futility of searching for Cook's rumored cannons, discussion turned to our next port of call. It was back to the mainland to see what Captain Cook had named after himself. A short sail from Endeavour Reef, the crew of *Paisano* found Cooktown to be small, dusty and practically deserted.

In the early years of the 19th Century, a gold rush populated the area with entrepreneurial prospectors from Australia's southern provinces. Sixty years later, the majority of the gold having been removed from the ground, the miners deserted Cook's town en-masse, returning the dusty, unpopulated community to the providence of the crocodiles that sunned on the shores of the adjacent Endeavour River. The streets were unpaved, few people lived there and it looked like a place that most people had forgotten. After spending an afternoon exploring its few areas of interest, including peering through the dirt shrouded windows of a wood-walled museum that was securely locked; we decided that we should join the others in their concerted effort of forgetting Cooktown.

Being located on Queensland's Cape York Peninsula, Cooktown did serve as an excellent jumping off point to sail almost directly north to the vastly under-explored and little known island of New Guinea.

Tacking

IX
In Search of the Elusive Papuan Butterfly

The trip north gave us a few days to contemplate our impending landing in New Guinea, the major island of Melanesia in the Western Pacific. The name had an exotic ring; when we thought about the country, a picture of tigers, alligators and black natives with spears appeared in our minds. But no; wasn't that Africa? Prior to meeting John, we had never heard of New Guinea; somehow it had passed right by our high school geography class. New Guinea? New Guinea? Only a vast and unending blank peered back at us from our queried minds.

What we were sure of: everything would be new and different and surely primal in nature. Whatever we found, it would be completely foreign to the two of us, who had grown up in the confines of a concrete encrusted city on the opposite side of the planet. We eagerly anticipated a land unique unto itself; a country that would expose us to thrilling adventures that, like the majority of this entirely unforeseen adventure, was light years beyond our adolescent imaginations.

As our questions dug deeper into John's store of knowledge, we began to view our arrival with a great deal of excitement and some trepidation. In mid-sixties Papua, the eastern half of the island nation of New Guinea was still very primitive. We had heard whisperings that cannibals still existed in the outback, feasting on *long pig*. There were tribes, *bush people* they were called, that had never seen white men and little was known about the Sepik River area, an unmapped region of inland Papua. We wondered if any bush people lived on the coast or if we would even run into any local tribes. We hoped that we would meet with some unusual people with bizarre and alien customs; customs we had never before seen or read. We had great expectations; we were not to be disappointed.

*****

Paisano sailed on a broad reach for five days in glorious tropical weather. The winds were of moderate strength and steady; they carried the spirits of the many mariners who had died fighting for freedom in the Coral Sea. Slowly, we inched our way ever closer to the Equator, to Papua.

Arriving at Port Moresby in August of 1965, we dropped anchor in a large bay in front of the local yacht club. Not to be outdone by the inhabitants of other South Pacific paradises, Port Moresby had recently built its own yacht club for the expatriate Australians that lived and worked in country.

While somewhat rustic by yacht club standards, the building did have rudimentary showers on the first floor that gave bathers a short respite from the horrors of the incessant tropical humidity. In August, shortly after exiting the shower and toweling dry, a fine mist settled on the skin as bodies tried to cool themselves. Laying a short nine degrees south of the Equator, we did our best to protect ourselves from the furnace like temperatures that accosted us in this primitive land.

But the friendliness of the Aussies made up for the inhospitable climate that we encountered on one of the planet's largest islands. More important than the bath was the incredibly well stocked bar that resided on the second floor of the establishment. Taking advantage of the refreshments, in an attempt to maintain a reasonable body temperature, we downed copious amounts of well cooled domestic brew, making for some spirited discussions and meetings with unique characters.

Inhabited with the nightly crush of club members seeking to wash away the day's grit and well attended by the crew, the club was a great way to meet the influential of Port Moresby and enjoy the company of fellow sailors. And great sailors the locals were. Taking to their boats on weekends and sailing in a large bay on the outside of the harbor, the Aussies demonstrated their expert sailing skills as they battled each other, for beer and bragging rights in weekend regattas.

Settling into a routine of boat maintenance during

weekdays, the two of us did our best to keep *Paisano* looking good. Not only was maintenance important to the well being of a wooden boat, but it was also necessary to display a *good face* while visiting a foreign country.

Wooden boats have to deal with an unseen, but well known, pest in tropical waters. There, they suffer from a marine worm that burrows into the underside of their hulls. Known commonly as the Shipworm of the *Terendinidae* family, mariners have had to deal with them for as long as there have been wooden boats plying the seven seas. The worms invade healthy wood by chewing channels through the wood's solid fibrous structure. When the worms are discovered, the wood they have weakened needs to be excised from the hull and replaced by fresh whole wood. This problem highlights the importance of having bottom paint covering the submerged portion of a boat's bottom. The anti-fouling paint, an invention of the 20th century, emits a chemical toxic to worms and other plant life that might otherwise adhere to a boat's hull, completely covering its underside.

Natives, not being able to procure the expensive bottom paint, have devised brilliant methods of outsmarting the worms. They either put their boats on support structures above the water, or beach them to prevent an infestation. In so doing, they maintain the integrity of their wooden boat's hull and at little to no cost.

$$*****$$

One evening in the yacht club bar, Charles and I ran into two delightful women that seemed to be a part of the crowd, yet held back from the sometimes raucous events of the evening. Young girls; they had come north from the mainland in search of something different. They longed to avoid the blandness of city life in the land Down Under; Papua was anything but bland.

We picked up on their cool but diffident personas, introduced ourselves and joined the girls at their table. We shared stories of our trip and bought drinks on a couple of nights, getting to know the delightful pair. After having gained the girl's trust, I asked one of them, Joan, if she would like to go for a walk along the shore. It was incredibly romantic. Can you imagine: walking along the shore under a full moon in New Guinea? It was like being on another planet. We strolled along the water's edge, had a spirited conversation, while enjoying the sights and becoming better acquainted. I asked Joan if she would like to join me for a movie one evening; she accepted.

Back at the yacht club on another evening, one of the regulars, a fellow named Bill from Sydney, approached me and began a conversation; he soon inquired into my interest in Joan. She was a beautiful girl whose company I enjoyed. Bill's question gave me a scare at first, my thinking Bill was perhaps Joan's father. But his following questions put me at ease. Bill had noticed her and pointed out that she seemed a bit reserved, not the type of girl someone could easily hook up with. I agreed stating, "I think Joan is a beautiful girl." He bet me five pounds that I couldn't spend the night with her. At first I considered Bill's proposal an insult; I wouldn't simply try to pair up with Joan to win a bet. I really liked her, but I didn't mind the added incentive to my weekly income of nothing.

On the following evening, I met Joan at the yacht club; after having a couple of beers, we went off to a movie together. After the movie, something terribly grainy and boring, we returned to the club and had another beer. I suggested we head for her place. Joan acquiesced and together we walked the short distance to her quarters where we spent the night together.

Joan and I had a great time in each others' company; I liked her reserved ways, she enjoyed my companionship. And of course being from two disparate backgrounds, we had a great deal to talk about. She was a lovely girl, quiet, but strong willed, knowing what she wanted from life. She had traveled from a settled modern country to spend a year in a hot, humid, primitive part of the world. She shared her adventure with few countrymen and lots of natives that really didn't understand what the Aussies were doing in New Guinea, but really didn't care, either. It was an opportunity for Joan to see another part of the world, let her spirit soar and peek beneath life's surface, peering into the unknown.

It was an enlightening experience; one that she would remember all her life and adding me to her memories was a bright spot in her trip. She requested my silence about our evening together; sending me on my way in the morning, she informed me we would meet at the club after dinner that night.

A couple of nights later, with Joan being occupied with her girlfriends, I again, met up with Bill. Trying to be silent about my pairing with Joan when Bill asked what had happened, I extended my hand for the five pounds I was owed. Bill dutifully pulled out his wallet and handed me a bill with a congratulations and a hand shake. We followed up with a nice cold beer.

✵✵✵✵✵

During a drinking bout at the yacht club, a result of the one-upmanship that commonly takes place when alpha males have too much to drink, John accepted a sailing challenge. As the rams butted heads, each boat owner argued that his boat was faster than the others; a competition was suggested to prove whose boat was truly the swiftest. Ron Devereux's forty seven foot *Matoma*, the current sailing stud in town, challenged John to a sea-borne duel. John declared that *Paisano* would wipe *Matoma* and the local fleet and the losers would be buying drinks that night.

Paisano was now entered in the upcoming weekend regatta, but without the knowledge of Charles or me. We had found, after inspecting the topsides of the boat that she needed to be spot sanded to bare wood, primed and then repainted as some of her topside paint had bubbled in the intense sunshine on the trip north. Without John's knowledge, we had begun the repair process during the week, not realizing that the primer would not dry in the extreme tropical humidity of Papua's August.

Without the primer drying and being sanded for the next coat, nothing further could be added. That led to *Paisano* showing up on race day Sunday, with what looked like patchwork on her topsides, in essence putting on a *poor face*. Unfortunately, there was no way of covering the unfinished woodwork, it had remained wet and simply looked bad.

Not only did the boat look bad, but she was poorly sailed. While the two of us learned quickly and were extremely adaptive, we had no prior racing experience. We had only set the spinnaker on the ketch twice prior to race day and did not know how to handle the sail well. With its five thousand square feet of sailcloth, the spinnaker was difficult to handle in the best of conditions.

On the downwind leg of the race, in the midst of a jibe, the massive blue and white paneled sail suffered numerous small rips, catching on the unprotected tips of a cotter pin during the maneuver. Someone had been errant in not covering the pin the last time it was attended to. Sailors know that anything with an uncovered sharp edge on a boat is almost guaranteed to cut or tear clothing, skin, or sails, and at the worst of times.

From there, the race continued to deteriorate, with *Paisano* coming in a distant second behind what should have been slower boats; a good example of the importance of tactics and proper sail handling in boat racing. In our defense, it needs to be pointed out that we were completely unschooled in this type of boat and equipment handling, a genre of sailing completely opposed to cruising. A sail of that massive size takes much practice to handle properly and should never have been set that day. But then again, John wanted to win.

The poor race showing made John incredibly angry. He lost face to the local sailors, tore what was a hugely expensive and beautiful five thousand square foot blue and white patterned spinnaker and looked bad doing it. Even though it wasn't our fault, the resulting debacle meant Charles and I were in for a bad time. Paradise was about to take a one hundred eighty degree turn south.

✳✳✳✳✳

The following week the skipper decided the boys needed to, "Get a job." We thought John was suffering from a cerebral aneurysm; apparently, we had not gauged his rage accurately. We were in Port Moresby, New Guinea, not exactly the center of a hot job market, although each day was blazingly hot. But

148

John wanted us to get a job? His anger still percolating from the past Sunday's regatta-loss motivated him to reach out to those on shore. Basking in the glory of the palace of revenge, John had formulated a plan to make us suffer. He found work that would occupy Charles and me, while keeping us out of sight until he could work the edge off his displeasure. Unfortunately, we were about to find out what really hot was, descending deeper into another circle of hell.

Through a connection made at the yacht club, Charles and I were invited to visit a job site in the Papuan bush country. We had to rise from our bunks at six in the morning, a time we had forgotten existed. In the morning, we would row ashore, taking showers at the yacht club before the temperature reached eighty degrees. A fellow worker picked us up on his way into work; transporting us some miles into the countryside where we met up with others working for an Australian construction company. The company was building a housing development in the bush and would happily accommodate John's request to, "Put the boys to work."

We began each day by meeting at the company's compound where a dining hall and business offices were located. A driver would deliver us to different work sites, dropping us off for the morning. At lunchtime, another driver came for the two of us, transporting us in to the dining room where we could eat with the other workers and boss boys from different crews. We found it interesting that we were the only Caucasians that worked in the bush. At noon, we would wash the dust off, eat and drink as much as possible, then it was back to the blazing hot bush where there was no shade, only an excess of humidity coupled with a surplus of ravenous insects. The mosquitoes buzzed, they reconnoitered and they attacked with smart bomb precision extracting sufficient blood to maintain a vampire. Having moved away from the coast to the inland job site, we lost the cooling ocean breeze that blew in the afternoons. The already unbearable heat increased a notch.

In essence, we were given jobs as visiting boss boys. A boss boy headed native work crews. An Aussie would give instructions to Charles and I, we would relay it to the boss boy and the instructions were then given to the laborers who used hand tools to manually build the required structures.

In the beginning, working with the island's natives was an incredibly interesting task for us. The bush people were inconceivably funny when viewed through the eyes of two foreign teenagers. On the job-site, where they were tasked with constructing the sidewalks for a housing subdivision, the workers were seen wiping motor oil on their skin. At first Charles thought the oil was a type of lotion to protect them from the pitiless rays of the sun. When he asked why the oil was being applied, he was told it was an attempt to provide a barrier that would repel the ravenous mosquitoes. Thirty-weight seemed to work quite well. While we found this intriguing, neither Charles nor I were wholly enticed to follow the example of the natives.

During their daily labors, the natives chewed a local substance called betel nut. The nut was about one inch in diameter with the consistency of hardened peanut butter. After chewing it into a softer mass, a bite of lime was added to the mix apparently creating a chemical reaction that activated a lightly intoxicating chemical in the mixture. The mass turned bright red, causing the mouth, teeth, gums and lips of the chewers to display the same bright red tint while a mild grin adorned their faces. The Aussies called them *chewers* while viewing them with disdain.

While the red mouths of the workers did not evoke envy in either of us, I was curious about the effect of the mixture. I inquired of the boss boy if I could sample the betel nut, but the boss boy was adamant with his, "NO!" Somewhat surprised by being told no by the Papuan, conjecture led me to believe that the bright red substance could have a negative effect on my well being; I, astutely, let it go.

Another amusing feature of the natives was their facial ornamentation. Some of them had slit the lower edge of their ears and put bone and other light weights on the lobe causing the skin to stretch over time. Some of them had ear lobes that hung four inches below their ears; they could be lifted up and hung on the top of their ear. They looked really odd. When we thought about it, we realized that the natives probably became

150

bored with little to occupy their time in the bush; aided by chewing betel nut, this was a non injurious way of passing time and it did give each one of them a distinct *look*.

Others had pieces of bone that were cut into thin slivers like tooth picks. They planted one end of the bone in their cheeks with the slivers standing straight up giving their faces the appearance of a radiant sunburst. Still others had cut the cartilage in the center of their noses and placed bones there. We weren't quite sure if we were in some sort of African movie or were having a dream when we went to work in the morning. But the natives were the same each day and Charles and I could only marvel at the diversions these primitive people enjoyed in their spare time. We never did ask where the bones had come from.

Sometimes it was a challenge to stifle a laugh at the natives' expense, but we did our best to hide our amusement at the Papuans' appearance. If Darwin could have observed these primitive bush people, he would have smiled inwardly, seeing how evolution seemed to have passed right by this island.

Charles looked at the native men and wondered, "If this is what the guys looked like, man, what could their girlfriends look like?" Not wanting to ask, or possessing the daring to verbalize his curiosity, he let this question go unanswered. We never did see any of the native women.

Communicating with the workers was also a chore. The natives spoke a unique language. Pidgin English was a blending of words derived from German, Dutch, English and the tribal tongue. This language was an amalgam created from the languages of various groups that had ruled over the island at various times in its history.

As with most primitive groups, and some advanced societies, there was a pecking order. The boss boys really stuck out, being the biggest and most physically intimidating. These attributes gave them ready access to their foreign employers, allowing each to be chosen as a group leader. Charles and I spoke directly with them. The boss boy would then pass on instructions to his men. Never would we speak directly with the workers, as they were frightened by their leader. They received orders from him and communicated information solely to him. A finely honed chain of command existed in the bush. Any breach of this protocol could be injurious to the offender.

When Charles became intrigued with a worker chewing betel nut one afternoon, he walked over to inquire about the substance. Hearing Charles' question, his boss boy rapidly walked over and in a tacit manner informed Charles that if he wanted to know anything, he should ask the boss boy, not his subordinate. The average worker was about five feet two inches tall, the boss boys usually four to five inches taller.

This punishment, in the guise of employment, turned out to be a great lesson for the two of us. We spent all day in the bush, an eight hour shift in a dusty, sweltering, humid, mosquito ridden countryside with no real duties except to watch the workers work. After a few days of watching the natives doing their jobs, the novelty wore off as boredom rapidly set in.

In a challenge to our own intellectual myopia and having a great deal of time to ponder our surroundings, we began to question why this development was being built. Who would live in this place and why? It seemed a God-forsaken piece of earth that no one in their right mind would want to inhabit; a major variation from the many paradises we had visited in recent months. It was as though we had left the planet earth and been deposited, through no effort of our own, on another planet that resembled what westerners might easily conceive of as hell. Something told us that the indigenous people of this island might have felt the same way. Unfortunately, the natives lacked the knowledge and ability to extract themselves from this hostile environment; they lived today on their under-explored island as they had lived for centuries, with little contribution or interference from the outside world.

After the day's work, many of the guys would gather around an outdoor icebox that was stored in a shed at the company headquarters. There, we would drink beer to cool ourselves, rid our minds and bodies of the heat demons and wash our throats clean of the day's dust. It was also a perfect time for the two Yanks to answer questions about our trip posed by the other workers.

After two weeks of mind numbing work, we had finished our sentence of toiling in the seventh circle of hell. Completing the final day of labor, the company foreman came to speak with the two of us; it was time for a paycheck. The foreman tallied the bottles of beer we had consumed during our two weeks on the job. He added the lunches we had eaten, generously supplied by the company each day during a short break from the boredom of our mindless inactivity. Subtracting the cost of our freely advanced refreshments from our gross earnings resulted in a paycheck of seven Australian pounds and change.

Stunned, both Charles and I had a difficult time accepting that two weeks of work, minus beer drank and food consumed, resulted in a gain of fifteen dollars. We later thought, perhaps this is how management keeps the natives poor. Feed them, let them drink away their pay and give them a few baubles at the end of each two weeks. Not our idea of gainful employment.

In retrospect, we had to admit that the two of us really didn't do any real work. We were simply *there,* which helped us in accepting the fact that we were paid for essentially doing nothing. Reflecting on our "jobs" led us to the realization that being away from John so that he could work off his race-induced anger was the real reason for our sudden employment and not an avenue for financial gain. After two weeks of employment, our financial position had not really advanced, but at the same time, it had not deteriorated. And more importantly, John's anger was assuaged by knowing we were not especially enjoying our labors beyond the berm.

We returned to our regular four hour work day on *Paisano,* thrilled to be done with the punitive drill of semi-conscious inactivity that filled our days in the Papuan bush country.

While working off our sentences in the outback, we had met a young man, in his mid twenties, who was living on the outskirts of Port Moresby with his family. He invited Charles and me to come to his home, meet his family, and share a Sunday dinner. After finishing our chores on the boat, Charles and I rowed ashore on the appointed evening where we rendezvoused with Jeff at the yacht club. He drove us through the heart of town and out the opposite side into the country, where his modest home was located. Jeff was on a three year work contract with the construction company that had employed the two of us.

Jeff was married with two small kids; his family was living in a quaint company cottage set up on the outskirts of town. His wife was intrigued to meet the two boys that were sailing around the world, she was not much older than the two of us, and asked Jeff to invite us to dine with the family that night.

Arriving at Jeff's house, we were greeted by Julie and their two children, Steven and Susan. As we entered, Julie mentioned that there was some exciting news on the television. Charles and I had not seen a T.V. for over a year and, thriving on our disconnect from modern civilization, were not especially interested to see what the excitement was about. Ushered into the living room by our hosts, we could not escape viewing the seventeen inch black and white screen; a plume of smoke could be seen rising towards the heavens from a city somewhere. The view was being shot from a helicopter flying overhead; the announcer was providing a narrative to the world about the burning of Watts.

"Watts? Watts?" what is Watts? Neither Charles nor I could remember the name. Los Angeles, our home city, was so far from our minds; we had forgotten Los Angeles and its suburban troubles. A melting pot of the world's peoples, race relations was always strained. The Civil Rights Act had been passed by congress the year before. The law could be changed overnight; it took much longer to change people's minds, their attitudes and their practices. The poor blacks were treated unequally, unfairly and unjustly. Pricked with the unholy thorn of inbred prejudice and scorn, something had set off the people of that neighborhood in the southeast sector of Los Angeles; the citizens were looting and burning the community; anarchy reigned; the battle cry went out: burn, baby, burn!

*****

What did Patrick Henry say in 1775? "Give me liberty or

give me death," a battle cry for an emerging republic. I don't suppose he meant that only for himself? It was almost two centuries later; the blacks were due their seat at the table.

*****

Not knowing why part of our home city was burning, we were as shocked as our hosts and somewhat embarrassed at the actions of our fellow citizens. The four of us had a short discussion on the troubles of that distant city, however, not being terribly interested in what was taking place on the other side of the planet, the television was soon turned off and discussion turned to local activities.

Charles and I had a delightful evening. We told stories of our utopian adventures and how we had arrived in Port Moresby. We shared that we didn't know where we would be heading next. John's goal was to reach Papua and collect butterflies; we never did really discuss where the boat was heading next. Having complete trust in our learned leader, we allowed his intuitive compass to guide us.

Dinner was great, Jeff and Julie were excellent hosts; it was nice to sit in a home and relax with polite discussion and a glass of wine. The family had come to Port Moresby to work construction in the bush for a few years. True, it was somewhat uncomfortable and they were far from their families, but the money was good. Their banked savings would afford them a nice home when they returned to Melbourne, at the completion of their work contract. As the evening wore on, we said our goodbye's to the family; Jeff returned us to the yacht club. From there, we pushed the waiting dinghy into the calm waters of the bay; setting the oars in their locks; Charles rowed us out to *Paisano* where she lay lazily at anchor enjoying a light evening breeze.

Not having enjoyed any time surfing in New Guinea, we began to search out information on beaches where waves could be ridden. The Aussies' reaction to our inquiry was a vacant stare. All they did was work on the island. Recreation took place when they returned to the mainland for holiday. It appeared, again, that no one had ever come to New Guinea on a surfing safari.

Seeing our disappointment at not being able to use our long idled surfboards, John made a suggestion. He asked if we could ride the boards behind *Paisano* while she was under sail. I didn't think so. I replied, "The boat doesn't move fast enough." But Charles piped in, "Why not try?" After all, we were trying to stay on John's good side; he wanted us to have some fun; it was worth the effort.

Charles and I raised her anchor, hoisting the sails while John maneuvered the boat into the large bay. There, we would have plenty of room to tack or jibe the boat when necessary.

Tying a loop in its end, Charles put a fifty foot line out behind the boat. He threw his board over the side and jumped in after it as *Paisano* sailed ahead. Crawling onto his board, Charles paddled to get some momentum going and then caught the line as it slid silently through the water. Allowing the boat to pull him at its faster speed, Charles stood up on the board, riding it like a Herculean water ski.

While not as exciting as riding a wave, it was better than not using our surfboards at all. Charles was picked up and I took a turn, surfing, gliding, and dreaming, re-entering paradise as we were towed behind *Paisano*, tethered to a stern-cleat. We enjoyed returning to the water, refreshing our souls. John was happy to see us enjoying ourselves. After our two week ordeal in the bush, it was a happy reunion with the ocean.

Soon afterward, John was joined by Jeanie as she flew into the airport outside town. Leaving us to safeguard the boat, the two of them departed the coast; trekking to the interior of New Guinea's bush country. There, the natives were having the bi-annual Enga Games that played out as the local tribal Olympics. Also known as the Highland Games, the natives dressed in their best outfits decorated with feathers from the most exotic and colorful birds on the vast island. The tribesman paraded with displays of indigenous birds: the Blue Eyed Cockatoos, the Orange Breasted Fig Parrot and the colorful Kingfisher. Of special interest, the prized Bird of Paradise feathers, known locally as the Bird of the Sun, with their bright colors and long plumes crowned the fringes of highly valued, hand carved masks. The natives showed off their wood work, especially their distinctively painted masks that were sought after by regional collectors.

While most competitions were foot races, bow and arrow marksmanship or spear throws, occasional conflicts grew out of disputed competitions. Conflict, always conflict. It seems there is no place on earth to escape the constant bickering between tribes, states, countries. These differences of opinion were occasionally settled with rock throwing between the conflicted parties with results of bloody bruises and sometimes broken bones.

John and Jeanie returned from their inland trek, thrilled that they were present for the rarely seen native games. Now that we were again in the good graces of John, it was time for us to go hunting. The Carnegie Museum in Pittsburgh had sent John on a mission. He was to collect as many different butterfly species as he could find. Unbeknownst to them, there were over eight hundred distinct butterfly species in Papua. Learning this, we feared we could spend the rest of our lives in New Guinea. Not an attractive thought!

The butterfly nets that had been stowed on board two years previously were unpacked from their storage place. Small white boxes with soft cotton padding appeared and were readied for filling. Led by a native guide, John, Jeanie, myself and Charles were driven out to the bush where we headed off on footpaths into the mountains, searching for the rarely glimpsed Papuan butterflies.

Not to be party poopers, Charles and I made a pithy attempt at humor; trying to keep a light air about *the hunt*. Hunting goats with guns was fun, it was manly, and it was cool; but hunting butterflies with nets? The picture of the four of us running around in shorts taking murderous swipes at fleeing butterflies didn't fit our newly acquired image as macho men of the sea. As maturing eighteen year olds, we felt as though we would be locked up in white jackets if any of our friends saw us hunting with those silly nets.

But the butterfly hunt was successful. Copious flights of butterflies, or Lepidoptera, were intercepted in mid flight. They were skillfully captured, netted; they suffered a death by compression; a semi-compassionate end to their short lives. Their poor little bodies were crushed between thumb and forefinger, as John had instructed. It seemed almost criminal to kill the beautiful little creatures; they added color, beauty and diversity to the area where they lived. However, the Carnegie was waiting; the bloodless slaughter went on.

We returned to the boat each night to rest; refreshing ourselves after a hot day in the bush. A few days into the hunt, and having collected some of the most beautiful butterflies we'd ever seen, John said the attack could be halted. He had enough butterflies to fill the small white boxes; the museum would be pleased, we could put an end to the hunt. We returned to the boat and prepared our motionless bounty for transport.

The butterflies were placed one in each cotton padded box and sealed with a small piece of tape. The fauna of Papua, while not being terribly elusive, was artfully colored and extraordinarily interesting. Butterflies we had captured and boxed had names like: the Map Butterfly, *Araschnia levana*, for its striated wings created by distinctive wing-venation; the Owl, *Caligo illioneus*, had two large eye spots on its monochromatic wings; and the Queen Victoria Birdwing, Ornithoptera victoriae, with its colorful elongated bird wing-like contours. Named after the monarch, the Q.V. Birdwing is known as the largest butterfly in existence. While not being especially interested in butterflies at the outset, both Charles and I became respectful observers of the ingeniously designed and uniquely adaptive critters. Seeing them flitter freely in the country put us in awe of nature and her unlimited creativity. It was another "Wow" day.

*****

It did, however, completely escape our notice that both of us could be seen as potential butterflies. Currently in our immature larval stage, we were going through a metamorphosis that would take us from ignorant young boys to something grander. But for the time being, that was a work in progress.

✳✳✳✳✳

John packed the small white boxes in a larger brown box and sealed it for posting. He had now completed his mission, the one for which he had traveled over three years, navigated around the North American continent, through the Caribbean Sea, the Pacific Ocean and sailed many, many thousands of miles. With a raised brow, Charles and I sensed, without admitting it, that perhaps another motive laid at the foundation of this most exotic and lengthy trip.

Getting the ketch ready for her next leg of the voyage, provisions were purchased at local stores. John had given instructions to the two of us to bring the boat into the pier where the supplies for the trip were being delivered.

Friends from the yacht club, including Joan, had come to see us and the boat off on the next leg of our endless quest. After starting the motor and raising the anchor, I steered *Paisano* toward the small pier where we would load supplies and exchange our Bon Voyages.

Putting the throttle up to full, the boat cut through the water at a sprightly six knots, heading on a tangent for the side of the pier. Charles turned and looked at me with an inquisitive look on his face, he knew something was up. Those on shore noticed the boat's high speed and thought something was wrong. If she continued at this rate, the rapidly moving ketch would pass the pier and run ashore, smashing the boat to pieces.

But I knew what I was doing. Mentally calculating when I would have to begin slowing the boat, I waited until the last moment and then throttled back the engine, jammed the transmission in reverse, and put the engine to full throttle again. This maneuver had the effect of flawlessly stopping the boat directly next to the pier with no harm done, except to the hearts pounding in the chests of those observing the impending crash. If John had seen the folly of my scheme, he probably would have throttled me.

But John had taken Jeanie to the airport where she hopped a return flight to Tahiti. She would visit with her parents until the boat reached its next safe port. John then rejoined the

159

boat for our departure and the next leg of our seaborne trek. Actually, with John's commission for the Carnegie Museum having been fulfilled, he was now on a slow but steady return trip home.

Having enjoyed the wonders of New Guinea and survived the seventh circle of hell, we bid a lukewarm farewell to this less than tropical paradise. While not a paradise on the scale of the South Pacific isles previously visited, it was a land of unequalled mystery, incredible fauna, colorful flora and mild mannered native peoples. Papua did have a place in our hearts for its uniqueness. Besides, who do you know that's ever been to New Guinea?

Staysil set

X
Go West Young Men

Leaving Port Moresby on a robust southeasterly wind, *Paisano* headed west-southwest through the northern reaches of the Coral Sea.

The Coral Sea was known as a famous battlefield during World War II, where massive sea battles were fought between Japanese and American naval forces. The Japanese were preparing to take the island of New Guinea and were only a short hop from invading Australia across the narrow Torres Strait. May of 1942 saw the crippling of two Japanese aircraft carriers that greatly weakened the Japanese fleet, putting the brakes on their southern migration; oil, more land, occupation, the greed, trauma and pain of war.

After the infamous attack on Pearl Harbor, the imperialist Japanese were also island hoping across the Pacific in an easterly direction. Their goal: the U.S. mainland. They had taken the islands of Guadalcanal and Bougainville in the Solomon's, were heading for the Hebrides and the Philippines as they continued their advance towards Midway Island. A difficult and deadly time in the Southwest Pacific that occurred more than two decades earlier; it was dramatically contrasted to the peaceful and leisurely passage of *Paisano* under sail.

✳✳✳✳✳

The Torres Strait was named for the Spanish explorer Luis Vaez de Torres; he first sailed through the region in the early 17th century. Crossing westward through the Straits, the ketch headed for Thursday Island, located in the Prince of Wales Channel. Thursday Island received its name from Captain Bligh who sailed west through the region on his way to Timor months after the infamous loss of his ship *Bounty* to Fletcher Christian in 1789. He stopped at T.I. for a short respite from his historic, open boat journey on a Thursday.

T.I., as it was known to locals, became the pearling capital of the world in the second half of the 19th century. It was a magnet for divers from Australia, Japan, many of the Pacific islands and the pearling luggers that transported them. In the mid 1880's over two hundred schooners could be counted resting at anchor in the bay. Thursday Island became the recipient of the local *Pearl rush* that greatly inflated the population and created an industry where previously none existed. The industry, crippled by its own over exploitation, limped along until the early years of the 20th century.

Inhabited by the Torres Strait's islanders, in the mid sixties, Thursday Island was a sleepy place. It was nestled in the midst of a number of small islands making up the Torres Strait Shire. T.I. measures less than two miles long and one third mile in width; surrounded by bleached white sands while most of the island was covered with palms, ferns and bougainvillea; the island rose to a height of twenty five feet above sea level. This tiny isle was inhabited by locals with nothing to do except share stories with visiting yachtsmen, fish and drink.

Having met some of the local islanders; Charles, I and John sat and drank a beer in the T.I. pub one day. We listened as locals explained how they keep themselves occupied on this small jewel of an island. They articulated a custom that was truly unique to Thursday Island; it was their inimitable manner of celebrating the passing of family and friends.

The islanders didn't believe in the mourning process that the three of us were familiar with from the western world. After laying someone to rest, the deceased's friends and family from the surrounding islands, would gather at the T.I. pub to celebrate the life of their late relative or friend. It would be a happy time; a commemoration of the life of the recently departed. Each individual who knew the deceased would stand up and tell a story about the good times they had had together and what a joy it had been to know them. Then, they would drink a cheer to the spirit of those that pasted, those that had departed on their ethereal journey to rejoin the mother spirit.

A month later, another celebration was held for the late friend, again noting the high points of their life and how they were an asset to the Shire's community. On the one year anniversary of their passing, a third celebration was held continuing the festival of life. In essence, this seemed like a great way to continue drinking and partying throughout the year and a nice way to remember loved ones; less tears, more cheer.

Fortunately, there was not much work to be done. The days that were passed in inebriated celebration were not a drag on the local economy. Actually, there was no local economy. Thursday Island now served as a meeting spot for yachts cruising the world as they left the Pacific Ocean behind and headed west into the Indian Ocean, an ocean with characteristics uniquely its own.

While there, we met a couple who had sailed out of New York and were heading east. They were circumnavigating the planet in a leisurely fashion, in a twenty four foot sloop. Charles and I were amazed to hear that Josh and Carolyn were actually sailing around the world in a boat whose interior had the dimensions of a medium sized closet. They had the pioneering spirit necessary to make a trip in close quarters; or perhaps they were just confused, after all, they were sailing contrary to the prevailing wind direction. Not allowing convention to interrupt them in their search for adventure, they were a courageous couple.

Sharing a beer, we traded information about our trips, sailing stories were spun, and a book exchange between the boats took place. We wished the intrepid sailors well and parted ways with a verbal, "Good sailing" salute.

You really have to be in love to spend years together on a boat that required one person to sit down while the other turned around in the main cabin. Either they would bond as one or kill each other during their close-quarters journey. Fortunately, they were sailing through the tropics which required very little in the way of clothing, as storage space aboard their tiny boat was scarce.

Leaving Thursday Island found the ketch continuing on a westward course in combination with a little too much southerly that resulted in us getting lost in the Gulf of Carpentaria, off the northeast quadrant of Australia. After sailing for a day on the wrong course, John noticed the water around the boat appeared to be a light brown. He questioned the color: we knew it was inconsistent with the open ocean. Charles turned on the depth finder showing that we were sailing in twenty feet of water, not nearly as deep as it should have been.

Grabbing his hand held sextant, John thought it best to take a sun sight that would pinpoint our location. The sextant, a currently out of date navigational instrument, was used in the eighteenth, nineteenth and twentieth centuries to measure the angle between a celestial body and the horizon. In this case, John took a sun sight that measured the angle, in degrees and minutes, between the lower edge of the sun and the ocean where it met the horizon. John explained that doing some calculations with this number resulted in what was termed an "altitude or azimuth." When the sun sight was taken, the exact time was noted on the chronometer and then referenced in the Nautical Almanac, which provides the sun's exact location above the earth, at a specific time, on any day of the year. Those figures are used to locate the latitude of the boat in a book called the Sight Reduction Tables for Marine Navigation. With the results, John then charted our exact latitude.

He paired the latitude with information derived from dead reckoning: a combination of the speed and direction of the seas current, the boat's sailing speed and course sailed over time. Parsing our plotted location on a chart of the area indicated we had wandered too far to the south, entering the gulf.

John ordered Charles to bring the boat about and follow a heading north by west. Soon, *Paisano* was sailing gently through blue water on a course that led the ketch through the Arafura Sea. Sail for another day, hang a left at Croker Island and enter the Gulf of Van Diemen. Continue on a short distance; to the right was the capital of the Northern Territory: Darwin.

Truly a place of high energy and exploration, Darwin was located on the far northwest coast of Australia, far from what was considered civilization. The Northern Territory spanned thousands of square kilometers with very few inhabitants. An arid, undeveloped region, there was little to sustain settlers that tried moving inland from the coast.

Using Darwin as a base, locals labored in the coastal region, building, and planting. Fishermen worked off shore and a small town grew up to service the needs of the pioneering inhabitants.   Inland, miners searched for gold, opals, and oil. While some gold and countless opals were discovered, oil was a needed energy source that didn't exist in the dry bush country of Northwestern Australia.

And of course there were pubs. Pubs were everywhere and, as usual, the visiting Americans were very popular with the Darwinites.   Dancing and drinking throughout the night usually allowed Charles and I to hook up with a local lady and invite her back to the boat for a tour. I met Sally; Charles met Jeanie; together we explored the community and shared tales of adventure that each had experienced in our travels.

No one was actually from Darwin; everyone had come for one reason or another. The girls, young and high spirited were not quite ready to settle down and form a family in the southern cities. They supported themselves working in a general store, while maintaining an open eye for adventure. Wishing to find out more about the planet they inhabited; Darwin was a good starting point for Aussies wishing to go on a walk about.

Darwin became an international town due to its proximity to Asia. It was known as a jumping off point for overland travelers heading north to Singapore, Indonesia and Thailand. More energetic trekkers could make their way farther north and west, eventually reaching central Europe. Inversely, Europeans who were interested in exploring the land Down Under could reverse the path disembarking Asia from Singapore and entering Australia through Darwin.

✳✳✳✳✳

Most small communities we visited had a custom of the citizens strolling along the docks on a Sunday afternoon, checking out the visiting boats in port. The big white ketch received a lot of "ohs!" and "ahs!" as she was a spectacular looking sailboat. Unfortunately, most onlookers were unable to see her under full sail, when she was in her real glory. She cut a very impressive figure on the ocean; but one that was reserved for those lucky enough to see her at sea.

One afternoon, while Charles and I were working on the boat, a young lad appeared on the dock, checking out the ketch. Charles noticed him on the dock, but ignored him, returning to his chores. After scrutinizing the boat for a period of time, the onlooker introduced himself as Gus; he began asking questions about the trip and the boat in general. Hearing Gus's interest in the boat and being the friendly chaps Charles and I were, we invited Gus aboard and gave him a tour of the boat. She was truly a beautiful sailboat, well kept by the two of us; no expense was spared in maintaining her. Sitting down below in her salon was like lounging in a small wood paneled library, a place where a snifter of Brandy and an old, leather-bound copy of Verne's 20,000 Leagues Under the Sea, would not be out of place.

Gus was duly impressed and continued to question us about our trip: "Where are you heading and how long will it take to get there." Having heard these questions on multiple occasions we were not suspicious of any ulterior motives.

However, not long thereafter, the three of us received an invitation to dine at the home of the territories Crown Officer. We had no idea who the Crown Officer was, however, in our wide-ranging travels, we had met many new friends; receiving invitations to visit their homes was not uncommon. Word often spread quickly when we arrived at a small coastal port; we made headlines in many newspapers, our arrival being noteworthy in numerous sleepy coastal communities. Citizens being both hospitable and curious about the boat; they were keen to hear about our adventures in paradise. We told stories about our travels while learning from our hosts about the community we were currently visiting.

Learning that the Crown Law Officer was the head legal representative of the Australian government in that expansive region, we questioned if we had run afoul of the law. Arriving at his home on the appointed evening, the crew of *Paisano* was greeted at the front door by our recent visitor, the inquisitive Gus. Suddenly, things became somewhat more transparent.

Seems Gus wanted to go for a boat ride; who could blame him? Gus, at twenty two, had recently graduated university and had not yet settled into making a life for himself. He was young and adventurous, longed to get away from home and an open ocean crossing on a beautiful sailing yacht sounded just the ticket. The ketch had two vacant bunks in the forepeak and Gus suggested he could help by standing watches as *Paisano* traversed the Indian Ocean.

Chatting with his father over dinner, John related that yes; we could take his son with us to our next port of call. Learning that we were planning to stop for a short interval at Christmas Island and then would sail on to Ceylon, Gus asked if he could continue with us all the way to that distant nation, a four thousand mile voyage.

Gus presented a good argument, "There was no return transport from Christmas Island." No airport existed on the island, rarely did yachts stop there. When Gus's father supported the idea, pressing John to accept the additional crewmen, he surrendered to their request. Upon further questioning, John replied, "No, the trip was probably not dangerous." And, "Yes, this would be the adventure of a lifetime for your son." John agreed to take him on as additional crew; dad agreed to pay for his food and transportation home.

Darwin was well known to seamen for its unusually large tides. The daily tidal fall was found to be eighteen feet. For eighteen feet of water to leave the shoreline and then return in less than twenty four hours was a mighty task. In order for that massive amount of water to make its round trip, it was necessary for the current to move at a very rapid pace. To take advantage of the speedy outgoing tide, boats always departed port while the tide was ebbing. Those boats entering port set their incoming passage to coincide with the flood tide, making their transit time that much shorter while consuming a great deal less fuel.

Disappointingly, there was no place for Charles and I to surf around Darwin. We found ourselves ensconced inside a large gulf that was protected from ocean swells by the surrounding land mass. We were getting tired of visiting places that had no surf, but hey, the pubs and the young women were nice to hang out with. Again, it was difficult to complain. And we were getting an education on the ways of the world: its diverse cultures, its varying viewpoints and its contrarian opinions.

*****

Once again, John's Jeanie had flown into port to join the boat while we dallied in Darwin. Not much of a place in contrast to Tahiti, Jeanie put in a vote to continue on our westward journey.

John had convinced Jeanie to remain onboard, sailing with the boat on the next leg of her trip. The Indian Ocean is known for its calm weather and placid seas; John told Jeanie she probably wouldn't get seasick and it would be a pleasant passage. Charles and I reaffirmed John's statements, hoping that Jeanie would join us.

Gus came on board the boat on the day we were set to leave Darwin. Having said his good-byes to his father, he brought his traveling gear onboard.

Gus was ushered to his quarters in the boat's forepeak. He was surprised to see a broad deck support, which ran from the underside of the deck through the middle of the tiny cabin attaching itself to the keel below the floor of the forepeak. The wooden support was set between the two bunks, dividing the small cabin into two equal sections. Seeing the post creating a narrow opening to his bed, he inquired, "How the heck do you get into the bunk?"

Charles gave him a demonstration; feet first, then slide the rest of your body onto the thin mattress. This was done while holding onto the deck support to prevent falling on the floor. Don't even think of sitting up, as the bottom of the deck hovered twenty inches above your head. If you were claustrophobic, you might have a difficult time in this space. Below the bunk was open storage space for extra sails; two four inch portholes were located on each side of the forepeak, allowing light in and providing a view of the outside world while resting or reading in bed. At anchor, the portholes could be opened to allow fresh air to enter.

Timing our departure with the ebbing tide allowed us to make good time passing from the harbor. The ketch transited through Beagle Gulf, named after the ship that carried Charles Darwin in the nineteenth century; we steered west toward the Indian Ocean. With the trade winds at our back, Paisano made fair time on a westerly course into an ocean that we had not yet set eyes on. Due to the unique weather conditions, we had no idea how long it might take us to reach our first port of call almost fifteen hundred miles distant. Calculating our average daily sailing distance of one hundred fifty miles, our studious leader came to the conclusion that we should reach Christmas Island in about twelve to fifteen days, our longest voyage to date.

Sailing downwind was not *Paisano's* best point of sail; she labored at a paltry three to four knots for a few days. With the light wind coming from astern while a moderate swell crossed her bow at a ninety degree angle, the ketch rolled from side to side as each wave passed beneath her. The unnatural motion of the boat caused Jeanie to become ill, she then retired to her cabin for most of the journey.

Leaving the mass of the mainland behind, the boat fell into what is well known to sailors in the Indian Ocean, the dreaded *Doldrums*. A sailboat without wind is like an automobile without gas. She sat, mostly becalmed, laboring along while we searched the ocean surface for wind created ripples that signaled an impending renewal of the currently absent trade winds.

During our downtime created by the weather's fickle breezes, we would practice taking sights with John's sextant. He taught us how to sight through the eyepiece; we shifted the adjustable arm that would focus on the sun through a number of reflective mirrors. Having found the sun in the eyepiece, we would adjust the arm until the bottom edge of the sun just touched the water's surface at the horizon. At the exact moment of their meeting, we would note the time and start researching its meaning in the navigational texts. While taking a sight didn't sound like a difficult task, doing it on a moving, rolling, or pitching boat resulted in a figure that could be less than accurate. In that instance, numerous sights could be taken and the average of several used to accurately calculate the boat's position.

The wind picked up, we sailed for a couple of days and then the wind ran off, as though it had business elsewhere. Reading became the mainstay of our days, as there was little to do when the boat didn't need a helmsman to guide it.

The ocean's surface a mirror, it reflected the rays of the brilliant orb overhead. Having lost the cooling breath of the trades, we searched out darkened areas on the boat to shade ourselves from the tropical heat. There was so little wind that the boat would literally whirl slowly, making lethargic loops; being pushed about, here and there, by the currents that traverse that mammoth body of water.

A fishing line was thrown over the stern in hopes of catching fresh food for dinner. The boat didn't have a functioning refrigerator, an icebox sufficed to cool our fresh food. As we left port, a twenty pound block of ice was sequestered in the icebox; it would last a few days, perhaps a week, cooling our supply of fresh vegetables and meat. When the ice melted and the fresh food was consumed, we were compelled to turn to canned food to nourish ourselves. Canned food in the sixties especially that found in distant locales was only marginally superior to hunger; catching fish became a priority.

A fresh wind appeared and *Paisano's* sails filled with the mild breeze. She began sailing, at first slowly, but at least on a straight course. Then with stiffening winds, she accelerated up to her cruising speed of six knots. With some days spent in windless drifting, the crossing from point A to point B required a total of twenty one days, somewhat longer than expected.

Arriving at Christmas Island, we found an Australian island that was located two hundred miles to the south of the Indonesian coast; much closer to Jakarta than to the Aussie mainland. First settled by the British in the nineteenth century, Australia took over management of the island in 1958, only seven years prior to our landing. Long a nesting place for seabirds, the island was covered with guano, a polite word for bird droppings.

The Australians colonized the island while setting up a factory for mining, drying and loading the processed guano onto large tanker ships for transport to the mainland. There it was bagged and distributed to gardening stores throughout the nation and the world.

With modern factory machines controlling the process, few employees were required to man the fertilizer plant. Large trucks delivered the mined Guano to the processing facility. From the plant, conveyer belts laden with the dried powder snaked towards shore, transporting the desiccated guano to the ships that were anchored next to one hundred foot high cliffs. The scene was right out of Ian Fleming's <u>Dr. No</u>. At the shore line, large cranes intercepted the conveyer belts and curved out over the water where they dropped the white guano through a long chute into the holds of the freighters moored below; the ships were suspended under a massive dust cloud as the endless ribbon of guano cascaded into their vacuous bowels.

The ketch had anchored in Flying Fish Cove, a large calm bay with crystal clear water. The cove had a small sand beach where we could leave the dinghy after rowing ashore.

We had reentered paradise. New Guinea, with its multiple circles of hell, was becoming a distant memory. On shore, we met the colonizing Aussies who, apparently all drinking from the same cup of boredom, spent most of their off-work hours drinking, playing snooker while drinking and having drunk sufficiently, bonking each others' wives. The community of eighty inhabitants made for an interesting behavior study of what human beings will do when constrained on a small island, in the middle of nowhere, with not much to do.

One of the local young girls, the daughter of a factory worker, apparently also bored with island life, rowed out to the ketch in a small dinghy one afternoon. Not having heard her approach, we were startled to hear someone say, "Hi, what are you guys doing?" Looking over the side of the boat we spotted Jane, who introduced herself and began conversing with the guys working on deck. She was invited aboard and explained how island life was for a poor young girl of her age, which she swore was sixteen.

Apparently, the lack of island diversions coupled with the actions of her adult mentors on the island, had infected her with the need to mate with passing sailors. Her real reason for the visit to *Paisano* was to check out the crew, while mentally questioning if any would be a suitable conquest. On her first visit she toured the boat while learning about our travels. During her tour, she had time to make an appraisal of the three young guys who were tidying up. Having made a decision on her prey, Jane excused herself, rowing her dinghy back to shore with a smile and an, "I'll see ya guys."

The four of us spent time ashore; we met the locals and visited the island's club. Drinking cold beer to stay cool, we played snooker while learning about the island from off-duty workers.

One of the foremen from the plant invited us to tour the guano factory; it was really interesting--remember we were only eighteen--but didn't compare to stalking butterflies in New Guinea.

Touring the island was virtually impossible as there were no paved roads and few vehicles. Those vehicles that did exist were occupied with guano excavation. Surfing was out of the question; where we could get to the coast, it was lined with hundred foot cliffs. On many of the cliffs and near the cove where we had anchored, the shore was lined with coconut palms, adding to the beauty of this mid-ocean gem.

✶✶✶✶✶

An interesting inhabitant of Christmas Island was the coconut crab, *Birgus latro*, so named for the food that it feasts on. The crab's body was three to four inches wide and nine inches long when fully grown. The crab stood four to six inches tall when ambulating on land. The crabs are known to climb a tall palm and cut the hanging fruit, allowing it to fall to the ground. It will remove the husk with its powerful claws, carry the interior nut thirty feet back up a tree and then drop it to crack open the shell. It has a giant claw that the crab uses to tear the coconut in half. It also possessed a smaller claw used to stabilize its food. The crab is considered the largest land-living arthropod in the world. Lacking gills, the crab is land based and, like the monitors on Moreton Island, has a prehistoric appearance.

The island was practically covered with coconut palms providing sustenance to a large crab population. The crabs are omnivores, feasting on other island fruit and occasionally rodents. It was a fearsome looking creature; one we had never seen before. We were just in awe of the oversized claw on the crab and were stunned to find that if you approached a walking crab it would slowly back away, not wishing to interact with humans. However, we were also warned to stay clear of the claws if we encountered a crab that was dining.

✳✳✳✳✳

On another afternoon, while walking around the few streets of the settlement, we happened upon an unmarked road that appeared to encounter little use. Following it a short distance, the road opened onto a small clearing populated with animals made of stone.

There we met an Asian gent with whom we could only communicate with hand signals. Not sure of the language he was speaking, it was completely indecipherable to us. After a tour of his garden, fully narrated in his unintelligible language, our host invited John and me to sit on a horse he had made with stones from the surrounding hillsides. Charles took a picture of us on horseback while I held a wooden rifle supplied by our host; it had been shaped from an old, dried piece of driftwood.

This modern day hermit had gathered the small, two inch diameter granite stones from different parts of the island and carried them to his garden. Mixing dried Guano with water, he formed his animals from a paste that bound the stones firmly together. With the abundance of time on his hands, he had created an eagle, goat, bull, some crabs and others. He fashioned them around a garden filled with a variety of stone plants. Oblivious to the world that surrounded him, our hermit host appeared happily at home in his mid-ocean hideout.

When returning to the settlement, John inquired about the

Asian man we'd met. He was told that the gent was a recluse who preferred to live on his own; his days spent searching the island for interesting new ideas for his inanimate zoo. The Aussies thought he was senseless; had no idea how he had arrived on the island or how long he had lived there.

Noting that the crew had returned to the boat, Jane decided to row out to *Paisano*, which lay like a beautiful pearl in the center of a tranquil, shell shaped bay, in the middle of the Indian Ocean. Jane wanted to speak with her future conquest; it was time to put her plan of seduction into play. She had chosen me, indubitably for my good looks and muscular physique. I began conversing with her while she sat next to the boat, remaining in her dinghy during this mid-afternoon visit.

Beginning to perspire under the blazing sun, Jane jumped in the water to cool herself. Surfacing, she leaned back against her small boat holding it with her hands spread behind her and above her head on the boat's cap rail. Her hair wet, it encircled her head, highlighting her brown eyes, while shedding cooling drops of saltwater that fell softly onto her shoulders. She let her legs dangle below her; she had the angelic look of a young mermaid.

Looking down, I noticed that Jane had removed the bottom of her bathing suit. My eyes widened, "Wow, nice view," the thought swirled around my mind as dormant hormones began to emerge from their sleeping place, urged on by Jane's cherubic features. Noting my interest, Jane suggested I come ashore in the evening and stop by her house for a rendezvous. Jane pointed out that her father would be working on the night shift at the plant; we would have the house to ourselves.

Settling on the time of eight o'clock and giving me directions to find her house, Jane put on her bathing suit and pulled herself into the dinghy. Paddling for shore, she turned her head and gave me a smile, saying, "See you tonight." I watched as she paddled away with a twinkle in my eye and a smile on my lips; my quiescent hormones percolating with thoughts of our evening tryst.

That evening, the crew had dinner on board the ketch. After

cleaning up, we headed for shore to visit those at the club and have a few beers. After a couple of drinks, I excused myself; heading for Jane's house.

Arriving after dark, I found the house in the midst of a small development, a block from the main street. I knocked on the door; Jane answered in her nightgown. She grabbed me by the hand, leading me into her bedroom near the rear of the house. Jane had created a cozy nest for our secret rendezvous where she could fulfill her most current erotic fantasy.

The room was filled with the scent of her perfume. Pheromones careened from wall to wall, floor to ceiling; they attacked my eyes, my ears, my nose; they injected themselves into every pore of my skin. My breathing increased, my heart rate sprinted, my desire rose. Jane had lovely sparkling eyes, a bright smile and long, soft auburn hair. She was difficult to resist, so I decided not to. She hungrily jumped on me, kissing, probing, and caressing me all over. My hands found her warm body; the soft mounds of her breasts yielded under my inquiring hands; I felt the hot flesh of her burning desire, we rapidly became one. I eagerly drank from the fountain of sensual delights offered by this gorgeous sixteen year old girl/woman.

After a few minutes of lively lovemaking, we heard a noise at the front door; the handle swiveled, the latch released, allowing the door to swing open; footsteps could be heard as someone entered the house. I was shoved forcefully out of bed; unceremoniously landing with a thud on the floor. A soft voice whispered an admonition to run for the back door; Jane's father had come home early.

I jumped into my shorts, throwing on my shirt as I headed for the back door. Finding the unlocked door without difficulty in the dark, I ran the fastest hundred yard dash of my life.

Spotting some lights on the exterior of a building a quarter mile from the house, I headed for what looked like an unoccupied warehouse, hoping to leave Jane's father far behind. When I finally did reach the building, I could see some men standing around under a night-light, outside a side entrance to the building.

I stopped running, took a couple of deep breaths and tried my best to breathe and act naturally; walking in a nonchalant manner until I reached the building. Three men stood together speaking in a light conversational tone while one sat on a motorcycle. I said, "Good evening" to those I met there, not recognizing anyone until my eyes scanned right, towards the bike.

Sitting on the motorcycle, with a beaming smile on his face, was Jane's father. A short man, with a stocky, muscular build, he said, "Hi" and inquired what I was doing out there at night. "Oh, just out for a stroll," I replied, trying as best I could to hide the fact that I had been running, not to mention bonking his sixteen year old daughter. Not surprisingly, even at my fastest, I was no match for his motorcycle.

Much to my relief, Jane's dad, in his heavy Australian accent, suggested, "You should carry a torch while walking after dark." Ready to make his exit, he ended with a, "Good night" and rode off into the darkness, a loud laugh escaping his throat as he departed the group.

Apparently, Jane's father had a great deal more insight into the games his offspring played than she realized. Relieved, I headed back to the club to cool myself with a frosty brew; thanking God for not having me killed that night.

XI

Legend has it that Sighting an Albatross is Good Luck

Paisano left Christmas Island before the aberrant social behavior that had infected its inhabitants metastasized to the crew. Sailing to the south of Indonesia, we left a wide girth between the ketch and the infamous Malacca Strait. The Strait is a narrow, perhaps twenty miles wide, waterway that separates the island countries of Malaysia and Indonesia. Having attained infamy throughout history for its roving and sometimes pernicious pirates, the Strait is a place smart yachtsman avoid.

Finding Christmas Island on a chart, Charles noticed it was located ten degrees south of the Equator. Our next port of call, Colombo, lay seven degrees north of the Equator and some two thousand miles distant. Having sailed fifteen hundred miles to get to Christmas Island, we expected an extended time at sea on the next leg of our fortuitous foray into the unknown.

Heading farther west, and closer to the Equator, we were again embraced by the breathless doldrums of the Indian Ocean. Parsing the sailing directions illuminated a little known fact of the winds in that area. In the West Indian Ocean the trades blow east towards India in summer months and then reverse direction during the winter, when they blow west towards Africa. We had not yet entered the western segment of the Indian Ocean; we continued reading, finding further information of great interest.

The area around the Equator lies between two wind masses that, in concert, create the trade winds. The trades blow gently from both the northeast and southeast at about eleven to thirteen knots, converging at the Equator. As they meet, large amounts of precipitation are dropped, allowing the drier, hot air to rise where it creates dramatic, high altitude thunder and lightning storms. Having attained sufficient altitude, the cooling air circles back to the north and south, descending again between thirty and forty degrees of latitude; there, another cycle of endless trade winds are created. As the air rises, it leaves a vacuous area a few degrees above and below the equatorial line, uncommonly known as the *Intertropic Convergence Zone*. Unfortunately, as *Paisano* attempted to cross from the south to the northern hemisphere, she again became the temporary prisoner of the placidly calm *zone*. Sitting for days on a sailboat that could not move on the windless sea and only being able to read for so many hours, boredom became a numbing agent that could not be avoided.

Starting the boat's engine in an effort to motor out of the becalmed sea was fruitless. The engine was started, the transmission was put in gear and a clanking sound was heard inside the transmission casing. The clanking sound was the transmission giving notice it was seizing and then the engine stalled. Trying again was met with the same unsuccessful conclusion.

After attempting to start the motor several times, it was surmised that a bolt securing the transmission and the reduction gear cases had broken. With the transmission engaged, the bolt was swept in between the spinning gears. The gears jammed, the engine stalled. Our multiple attempts were all for naught. We had installed a diesel engine that ran perfectly well, but whose gears could not be engaged to put the boat in motion. The good news was that with the engine running, we were able to charge the boat's batteries supplying much needed electricity. However, without the power to motor her way out of the surrounding high pressure area, the ketch sat in place while being pushed this way and that by the whim of the ocean's meandering currents.

Once again being concerned about running short of fresh food on this lengthy leg of the trip, someone would troll a fishing line over the boat's stern with the hope of bringing in a fresh meal. Due to the boat's lack of motion in the calm seas, prowling sharks usually reached our catch before someone could reel it in. Not being especially interested in fishing anyway, it was the noise made when a shark hit the fishing line that made us aware we had caught something.

On one occasion, we were lucky enough to pull in a fish head, but were not terribly fond of fish head soup. The sleek, rapidly swimming sharks had a great meal at our expense. In an attempt to turn the tables, John loaded the 30-30 Winchester rifle; we then used the fish head to bait other sharks into coming to the surface.

Gus tied the fish head onto a rope line and let it float just below the water's surface to see how far the pelagic marauders would come for their meal. If a shark came close to the bait, Charles would shoot at the scavenger with hopes of serving him for dinner. Unfortunately, when he leaned over the boat's aft rail to get a better aim at the approaching hunter, the observant predator's sharp eyes would see his movement and the salivating shark would veer off, avoiding a death by gunshot.

As the hungry hunters approached the fish head, they would turn sideways, giving us a front row view of their gaping mouths; an incredible sight; we were close enough to count the shark's numerous rows of teeth. But as the sharks closed on their prey, we were disappointed to find that the rifle's bullets did not penetrate far below the water's surface. The sharks showed that they were wiser than we had anticipated. Swimming six or more feet below the bait, the sharks cautiously stalked the fish head before attacking it. At that depth, they were safe from the shallow penetrating force of the Winchester's bullets. As they say, "smart fish don't bite." Outsmarted by the sleek predators, we bemoaned the fact that there would be no shark fin soup served on *Paisano* that night.

Finally, we were lucky enough to get to the fishing line before the sharks, pulling in a four foot barracuda during one of our unremarkable afternoons. Unfortunately, the long sleek fish had little meat on it. Its razor sharp teeth were integrated into the fish's skull and its sleek body consisted mainly of sturdy bone. But Jeanie demonstrated that raw fish was a delicacy that we could enjoy with the fresh juice of a lemon and a dash of soy sauce. She cut small pieces from the fish's body and passed it around with a slice of the fresh fruit. We dipped it in soy; finding the flavor to be excellent. Jeanie taught us to call it Posen Cru, adding that she used the marinated raw fish in a delicious vegetable salad with fresh shredded coconut and hard boiled eggs; a Tahitian delicacy.

✻✻✻✻✻

During the windless afternoons, after tiring of reading, we often sat on deck and played cards to pass the time. Shorts were the customary outfit for the males and Jeanie, who had become a fun addition to the group on this crossing, wore bikinis during the hot afternoons on the boat.

With *Paisano* slowly, laboriously, spinning in circles like a wounded fish on the glass covered sea, Jeanie would partake of the afternoon card games on deck with the guys. Sitting cross legged in her bikini before the eyes of a group of adolescent towers of testosterone; there was no surprise when she won most of the hands.

We did our best not to drool at the sight of her lovely nineteen year old beautifully formed, gently curving, and lightly tanned, Tahitian body. Her skin was golden; she had delightful almond shaped orbits lit bright by the white of her dark eyes and a smile that could melt the toughest man. Her hair was jet black; framing her face, it created the picture of a heavenly cherub. Da Vinci couldn't have done better. She was the only female around for hundreds of miles and thank you God, she was a masterpiece.

Having Jeanie on board was an enjoyable change from the usual male dominated crew. She conversed with the guys, told stories of her homeland in the Society Islands and, on occasion, made fun of our youthful ignorance. She did as she liked and gave instructions, through John, on how she wanted things done. Young and innocent, she was smart and resourceful when she wanted something.

Unfortunately, she was sick most of the time we were under way. She spent much of the trip in her bunk while we were sailing. As most islanders are, and although she was a good swimmer, she had an exaggerated fear of the sea when out of sight of land.

The typical boat used in the islands is the outrigger canoe. Even to a modern day islander, if you remove the outrigger, you remove the boat's stability, making it more likely to roll over. Jeanie had a deadly fear of the boat overturning. Most people sailing hundreds or thousands of miles from land have an intuitive understanding about not being able to make it to land by swimming, so her fear was understandable. On numerous occasions we would explain to Jeanie that *Paisano* had thousands of pounds of lead in her keel. That weight would counteract the heel of the boat while sailing, but without that visual outrigger, her innate fear of rolling over persisted.

✳✳✳✳✳

One afternoon, while we were playing cards on deck, John spotted a large seabird flying overhead. The bird circled around the boat and made a landing on the top rail of *Paisano's* stainless steel bowsprit. John jumped up in surprise yelling in his excitement that it was an albatross. The albatross, *Phoebastria albatrus*, had a white body with long dark wings. It had a wingspan wider than John's arms and often grows to a length in excess of ten feet.

The bird's extended wingspan gives the albatross the ability to fly thousands of miles without stopping, rising with strong updrafts and gliding on warm air currents that carry it seemingly forever. Males are better known for their adventurous flights that can take them nonstop around the world.

Barring a premature death, the albatross can live sixty to eighty years. The birds grow up to one meter tall and have shown themselves to be monogamous by nature. They prefer to spend the majority of their lives at sea, except when they return to shore to mate.

The albatross has been immortalized in Coleridge's, "Rime of the Ancient Mariner," where a foolhardy sailor killed a bird that landed on his ship. Believing that the bird was a visitation from God that brought the ship good luck, his shipmates tied the sailor to the mast and hung the dead bird around his neck so that he might suffer the same fate as the albatross. That action was meant to appease the Gods and prevent the bird's demise from bringing God's wrath onto the ship. Another ancient, and lesser known myth, suggests that the albatross is the reincarnation of drowned sailors.

Our visiting bird flew off from the lounging ketch's bowsprit and made a few circles in the air before coming to rest on the boat a second time. John attempted to crawl forward with a camera in hand and snap a photo of the magnificent seabird. When he moved too close for the bird's comfort, it took off again, circled the boat a couple more times and made a final landing on the bowsprit, giving its regards before heading off into the blue. What a sight and surely a stroke of good luck on what had been, up to that time, a less than exciting transit through the serene and windless waters of the Indian Ocean.

With the high pressure area surrounding the becalmed boat persisting, another afternoon found us tying a line to a deck cleat, putting three hand-hold loops in it and launching it over the side; it was time to play in the water. We made a slow survey of the surrounding area to ensure that no sharks were stalking the boat. Charles stood guard with the Winchester in case any unwelcome guests wandered into the area while Gus was amusing himself in the water. He put on a dive mask and went over the side grabbing hold of a loop in the line. After a short minute in the water, he limply climbed up the wooden boarding ladder onto the deck, complaining that he felt like his arm was going to be pulled from its socket. The boat was only moving at a paltry two knots; we thought the slow speed would not be a cause for concern. However, it was too much of a strain for Gus. Even moving at that foot dragging speed, Gus's short swim resulted in red bruises on his cheeks from the dive mask. Another day was another lesson for us enterprising adolescent travelers.

Eventually, the wind did grace the Indian Ocean with a light breeze and we began to make way through the brilliantly clear waters of that vast body of water. We sailed west, passing south of the Indonesian Archipelago, and then headed in a northwesterly direction sailing for Colombo, the capitol of the island of Ceylon, currently known as Sri Lanka.

✳✳✳✳✳

There's a spiritual aspect to sailing that isn't often recognized by those that haven't. Standing our usual three hour watch on *Paisano* gave us the opportunity to see every aspect of the weather; of day and of night, every phase of the moon and sun, pouring rain, starless and star-filled nights.

As we sat talking one afternoon, I remarked how I had seen the moon, glowing with the incandescence of a bright bulb, set into the distant horizon at the edge of the illuminated sea. It was an exceptional sighting, one that I had never been privileged to see before. These new and unique experiences allowed me to realize that there was so much more to life than I had yet learned during my short stay on earth. How did Shakespeare put it in the sixteenth century? "There is more to heaven and earth than exists in our philosophies."

I felt as though the planet had exposed itself to me in an intimate fashion; one that I would never forget. Nature's way of reaching into the depths of my soul and planting a new idea, "You're new here son, keep your eyes and ears open, your real education is just beginning." And so it was...

The crew shared how they had seen every type of sunset: in clear skies, clouded and overcast so that the sun was only a dull, warm circle amongst pale grey clouds.

We had witnessed the sunrise in equally diverse conditions. We had observed it in seas so calm it appeared as a sheet of glass reflecting the new born light of the nascent day; rough water strewn with foamy white caps diffused the waking days light; pouring rain in the midst of a mid-sea squall almost obscured the brightening morn; brilliant, luminescent, sunshine that made a blatantly loud announcement, to those that were oblivious to their surroundings, that yes, "The Day has Dawned!"

Charles spoke of how eerie the starless night could be. With no moonlight to give some vision of the sea around him, he felt as though he was in a darkened room with wind blowing his hair about while he stared at the helm's crimson-lit compass. He remarked how on a dark, cloudy night, "I had difficulty seeing the outline of the boat's sails."

Gus added that being in the middle of the ocean after dark was a bit scary for him; a thousand miles from land made him realize how important the wooden deck under his feet was to his survival. Both *Paisano* and the ocean gained a great deal of respect from Gus on his maiden blue water voyage; one that he would never forget.

Gus also gained a profound respect for the wind. At times it was completely absent, leaving the ketch to be pushed about by the might of the ocean's currents. At other times, the wind would thrash the boat with waves that crashed on her bow, blowing spray on everyone, while the boat lunged ahead with patient yet strong surges, plowing through the endless surface of the sea.

At night, we became accustomed to seeing flashes of light as fish, porpoise and whales swam through clouds of dino-flagellates that cause the water to light up with transient phosphorescence that kept us aware that we were not alone out there.

These solitary times on watch were a time of soul searching, of contemplation and of observation for the adolescent crew. Charles and I had only rudimentary educations; our minds had become like sponges on this vastly captivating trip. What we found so incredibly fascinating was that almost everything we did, everywhere we went was a completely new and foreign experience. Up to this time in our lives, we had seen few noteworthy events. Now, it was as though we were having the experiences of a lifetime all jam-packed into two years; it was inspiring, overpowering, and humbling. The accumulation of incidents was molding us into the men we would soon become. Again, we moved to pinch ourselves.

The wind picking up led those on board to notice something new. As the boat plowed ahead through the mildly undulating sea, Charles noticed a movement in the periphery of his vision. Not knowing what it was, he watched the water for a few moments; there was no repeat of his vision. After completing his watch, Charles took a turn around the deck before going below; he found a small fish four inches in length. It was a member of the flying fish family-*Exocoetidae*-that flew onto the boat at night, not realizing that its flight would be interrupted by the boat's deck. Having failed to fly far enough or high enough to clear the boat, the fish fell motionless onboard. It had taken its last breaths as *Paisano* dashed ahead. Charles lifted the dead fish and sent its lifeless body back to its deep sea origins.

✳✳✳✳✳

The crew began to sight many ships passing at night and kept a sharp lookout for moving lights. Lying off the southeast coast of India, the tear-drop shaped island of Ceylon was in the path of one of the world's major shipping lanes. Ships departing India headed south past the southern tip of Ceylon and then steered either east towards Malaysia and Australia or west towards the Red Sea, Suez Canal and the Mediterranean Sea. From India and Ceylon: tea, rubies, sapphires, teak, bananas, coconut oil, silk and highly sought after cooking spices were transported to all corners of the globe. In return, wheat, rice, petroleum and western technology were imported to the region.

As *Paisano* approached the west coast of Ceylon, we once again fell victim to the high pressure grasp of the doldrums. She lay sixty miles southwest of Colombo, and again due to her dysfunctional gearbox, could do nothing to make way. After rolling around on the southerly swells for two days, John decided to make a radio call to Colombo. He was fortunate enough to hook up with our old friend from Australia, Dedier Dubose, who happened to have his radio tuned to the emergency frequency. Dedier had been relaxing in Colombo for about three weeks; fortuitously, he was on board to hear John's call for help. Dedier volunteered to come out on *Vermillion*, hook up with *Paisano* at sea and tow her into port, where we could tie up at the same dock.

For the crew, it was a bit of an embarrassment. *Paisano* was a beautiful and proud boat. To not be able to sail into port was one thing, but being towed into port by another, smaller, French sailboat, was disheartening. But when we thought

185

about it, getting off the windless sea and into port where we could stretch our legs on land would be a nice change; especially after more than three weeks at sea.

Vermillion arrived at our position the next day at ten in the morning. Charles had arranged towing lines to heave over to the rescuing boat. Once the two were tethered, she could tow *Paisano* slowly into Colombo. Ten hours later, the boats were berthed without incident, side by side, in the bay. There, we were surrounded by the 19th and 20th century British colonial architecture of government buildings in the burgeoning capitol city of Ceylon.

It was nice to finally reach land, have a cool, fresh water shower and some fresh food. We had been at sea twenty three days, partially due to the windless condition of the sea. It was a relief to get off the boat and walk on a surface that didn't move.

We visited with Dedier, his wife Bernadette, and their crewman Jose. We shared a glass of wine and told stories of adventures that had taken place since last we met. It had been a year since the two boats had crossed paths in the Brisbane River; it took some time to catch up.

✳✳✳✳✳

Ceylon was like no land we had visited before. Known in ancient times as *Serendip*, it was truly a country of discovery. The people had dark complexions with straight ebony colored hair as dark as the hardwood tree. Sparkling white eyes and shining teeth illuminated their smiling faces. They were an extremely handsome people.

The country was populated mostly with humble working class citizens who survived on a meager income. Luckily, the ocean was rich with sea life and the land lush with natural resources. The majority worked hard and ate well, but little progress was seen from generation to generation.

Sinhalese education was practically non-existent. Carpenters' sons became carpenters, taught by their fathers. Housemaids bore a new generation of housemaids, and farmers begot future farmers. There was not really any economic progress made during the 20th century for those that could not afford to go abroad for a "higher" education. The country and its people were mired in the stagnation of their poverty; they were unceasingly frustrated by the paucity of their knowledge that resulted from the lack of any structured education.

We later found that most of the land was owned by few families; they controlled the gem trade that made them fabulously wealthy as well as the tea, mango, coco, cinnamon and banana plantations that covered the small island. For the sons and daughters of plantation owners, life was good.

The island was peopled by two religious sects that were constantly at each other's throats. The minority Tamils harassed the majority Sinhalese, making life in Ceylon hazardous at times. They had started a minor civil war in the fifties, and it continued to the mid-sixties, the time of our arrival. Fortunately, it was both sporadic and found mainly in the countryside, outside of the capitol city.

✶✶✶✶✶

We had been in town for a short time when word reached a transplanted European, who lived in the outskirts of Colombo with his family; boys with surfboards had landed in town. He was intrigued by the fact that we were circumnavigating the world by sail, but was more interested in the surfboards.

Mark was an entrepreneur that currently occupied himself with making movies for the native market. Movie making was a challenge in Ceylon due to the uneducated population, the religious restrictions of the Hindu majority and the low economic scale where the majority of Sinhalese existed. Being a movie star was certainly an exalted position here, but great riches did not flow to those that graced the silver screen; better to be born to a rich family.

Mark was a gregarious expatriate Englishman who enjoyed meeting new people and doing different things. Surfing on weekends was a great form of diversion for him. He explained that when he was occupied with very different types of activities, it helped to keep his mind fresh, stimulating new ideas. When he heard we had brought our surfboards, he invited the entire crew to dinner and questioned us about our plans in his adopted country.

Charles explained that we were on a world cruise aboard *Paisano* and did not know what plans John had for our stay in Ceylon. John added that he had completed his butterfly mission in New Guinea; he now wanted to play things by ear, allowing the world's winds to blow him and *Paisano* where they would. He remarked, "I hope to visit places off the beaten path;" an idea he had already embraced.

Mark requested that Charles and I accompany him on surfing safaris when he was freed from his daily endeavors, during the weekend. He suggested we share the surfboards, trading off with each other during the day of surfing. He offered to commandeer two cars, and with his driver, ferry everyone to beaches where he knew waves were breaking. Mark pointed out that he had lived in Ceylon for more than two decades; he knew the coastline like the back of his hand.

John and Jeanie were also invited on these weekend surfing expeditions, but they found touring the island's many historical and religious sites more to their liking. Being newlyweds, they also enjoyed doing things without an entourage.

Driving the coastal roads of Ceylon was a test in itself. Their pusillanimous vehicles were small and under-powered. The four cylinder engines barely had enough torque to move the laboring autos with four adults on board. However, when they did get going they became a guided missile that was a threat to all in close proximity.

The roads were narrow; they had no curbs, no sidewalks. In the country, villagers commonly walked down the middle of the road when no cars were present. Automobiles being few in the countryside, half our time in transit was spent sounding the horn and slowing for pedestrians using the highway as a foot path. Getting somewhere was both time-consuming and precarious but was a great deal more pleasant than walking or using public transport.

Speaking of public transport, there was a bus company that ferried passengers around the capital in old, red, double decked British buses that were usually overloaded with commuters. It was amusing to see so many passengers standing on the rear entry platform, the excess weight causing the platform to sag to within a few inches of the road. On occasion, the platform would yield to the disproportionate load and the uneven road, spitting sparks as its underside scraped the pavement's surface.

Obviously, the citizens of this island nation had a great deal of faith in their Hindu gods; those buses would not have been safe without Krishna's spirit sustaining them.

✵✵✵✵✵

Having completed a blue water voyage through a major portion of the northern Indian Ocean, Gus made arrangements to return to his home in Australia's Northern Territory. Gus had just completed the voyage of his dreams, but was looking forward to getting home and beginning the life he had spent four years studying for in university.

Having grown attached to his young shipmates, it was a sad departure for him to be leaving *Paisano*. We all shared a farewell dinner, drank a toast to his future good fortune and bade him farewell.

The next morning, Gus packed his belongings, called a taxi, and headed for the airport. He headed home to Australia with a smile on his face and memories of the days he spent on Christmas Island and in Colombo. He reflected on the voyage across four thousand miles of never ending ocean and the days spent with four people from different parts of the world; people with different ideas and different outlooks. He was welcomed into the group as a brother and felt as though he was leaving family behind. He was awed at how, simply by asking, he became an integral part of what became a profound and thorough friendship during a short but eventful oceanic voyage that was previously only a fleeting thought in his fantasy filled imagination.

Somewhere on the coast of Ceylon.

XII

How Do You like Your Curry?

The weekend surfing safaris found us traveling all over Ceylon's west coast; nothing else mattered to two of us, we were in heaven again. After months of cruising the world's oceans, we finally had arrived in a place where we could once again paddle into the water and reignite the dream. Those ear to ear grins, first spotted in Hawaii over sixteen months ago, were again in residence. The two of us were like fish, we lived to be in the water and felt as though something was missing when we were not. With the water temperature on the coast of Ceylon hovering around eighty four degrees, it wasn't difficult to spend hours each day surfing; so we did.

An incredibly stunning spot that Mark wanted to show us was a bay that rimmed a small native village on the southwest coast. The village consisted of a sparse grouping of a hundred or so wooden huts crowned with thatched roofs; they sat just inland of the tree-line creating a stunning silhouette when viewed from the sea. Lit by single bulb luminescence, cooking was done on an open hearth with the fire fueled by gathered firewood from the surrounding jungle.

The community of Galle was located an hour and a half to the south of the capitol. It was situated on a crescent shaped bay lined with sixty foot coconut palms. The tall, arched palms, heavy with maturing fruit, grew in the midst of dark green grass that stretched down to the sparkling white sand that lined the gently curving bay. The boats of village fishermen were left to rest on the beach until needed for the next day's fishing. Three foot swells rolled into the bay, heaving the crystal clear blue water towards the sun and sky as they passed. And of course, there was absolutely no competition for waves as there were no other surfboards in Ceylon. A true portrayal of a *surfer's paradise*, we had every wave to ourselves.

On the north side of the bay, on a knoll overlooking the

ocean, rested a single story white-washed building; the Galle Hotel. Employing an energetic wait-staff of tall, lean natives attired in spotless white linen uniforms with white pugrees on their heads; they strolled around the hotel shoeless, speaking only the local dialect. When I attempted to speak to one of the waiters, I was met with a look of confusion; I then realized that no one at the hotel spoke English. At this time in history, only wealthy Sinhalese vacationed at the Galle Hotel. There were no visiting emissaries from afar and there was no need to speak English. The menus were all printed in the native tongue.

The view from atop the knoll was breathtaking. A panorama of white sand beaches reaching out to endless ocean sprinkled with small wooden fishing boats; manned by two or three fisherman with nets slung heavily over the gunwales, the view continued until it abruptly landed on the far shore lined with tall, lanky, coco palms; heavy with fruit; they waltzed lazily in the mild afternoon breeze.

The rooms at the hotel were small but sufficient, with mosquito netting hanging over the centrally placed beds. An electric fan circled slowly overhead in an attempt to keep the ravenous mosquitoes, moths and related insects at bay. The rooms had hand painted wash basins set on a small round wooden table with a pitcher of water and a hand towel; there was no running water. The shared bathrooms were found in the hallway. Floors were all a flat red tile, whose cool, smooth surface made it a pleasure to walk upon barefoot. In all, the place had the look and feel of a well-kept relic from British colonial times. It was like walking through a movie made of the British Empire before its collapse.

The dining room had rows of long wooden tables set on hardwood floors hewn from the native Rain Tree. They had been worn smooth from decades of scrubbing, leaving them with a polished glass-like patina. The long tables were used for communal dining and the food was incredible. We did not know the language; we could not read the menu nor could we ask for interpretations from the waiters who spoke no English.

Mark asked us what we liked and then ordered our food. Taking delight in the fact that he could speak the local dialect and we could not understand a word of what was being discussed; Mark decided to have some fun with the two of us. We heard the waiters stifling laughs as they put heads together deciding what to serve. Understanding that something was up, we shared a knowing look and wondered what Mark had in store for his English speaking guests.

When Mark ordered the meals, he apparently ordered our portions with an extra splash of curry; the curry made our eyes water like we were at a funeral. As tears cascaded down our cheeks, everyone roared with laughter. Even though we imbibed copious amounts of water, it did nothing to quench the burning sensation that currently resided in our throats. "Ahhhh," we mumbled, "How do you control this internal fire?" I felt that my body was about to burst into flame. The waiters bent over roaring with laughter.

Attempting to hide the fun he was having at our expense, Mark asked in an inquisitive tone, "How do you like your curry?" The two of us responded that it was great, very tasty, as we wiped the tears that poured freely down our cheeks. Enjoying the joke as much as the others, we joined in the laughter, as we tried our best to diminish the flame that burned in our throats while controlling our draining sinuses. The wait-staff offered tissues, while they giggled in their girlish manner.

✳✳✳✳✳

The next morning, Charles and I made our way down a small hill to the water's edge, on the bay side of the hotel. The shore around the knoll was lined with rocks six to twelve inches in diameter, covered with algae. At high tide the rocks were unseen, hiding just below the water's surface. With the tide having ebbed, the slippery rocks now had to be navigated in order to enter the bay. Standing on a rock in ankle deep water, I waited for a swell to pass to put my board in the water, jump on and paddle out to where the waves were breaking.

Before I could make my move, a small wave passed, knocking me off balance. I tried to counter the wave's push backward but overcompensated, causing me to slip forward. Both feet slid off the rock I was standing on, my right foot landing on an unseen critter that had attached itself to a submerged rock. I felt something hit my foot, but decided to ignore it; I was more focused on the waves I had been watching as they rolled into the bay. It was going to be a great day of surfing.

After a few hours, with both Charles and myself riding numerous waves, I began to feel a burning sensation in my right forefoot and soon could only stand on my heel. This made surfing somewhat precarious and increasingly painful. Having surfed a couple of hours of the afternoon, I decided to leave the water after riding a wave into shore.

On the beach, waiting to greet me with yells of joy and waving arms, were the skinny, young kids from the village that was located just beyond the waving palms; their long, dark hair hung forward, almost blocking their vision. They had been watching as we surfed throughout the late morning and early afternoon hours. It was the first time they had ever seen surfers riding waves. The fact that it was happening directly in front of their hut-like homes made it all the more special.

In my youth I was a tough kid, I didn't give in much to complaining, but by this time, the pain in my foot had increased to the point where I could barely walk. The red color in my right foot grew in intensity as did the burning I had noticed earlier.

The village kids volunteered to carry my surfboard back to the hotel, fighting each other to get a hand on the rail, as I hopped on one foot behind them. An elder from the village, seeing I was having difficulty walking, quickly walked over and grabbed my arm; putting it around his shoulder, he helped me hop up the hill to the hotel.

As we reached the top of the knoll, I turned and looked into my helper's eyes. I saw warmth within him, a smile deep within the soul of that humble fisherman. I was moved by the man's warmth; surprised by his help. I gave thanks for his assistance; the fisherman nodded in reply and silently walked off, returning to his village. Random acts of kindness are no anomaly in paradise.

Inspecting my foot revealed little; even if it had, there were no medical facilities in the area. The skin had closed around the wound and nothing was visible from the surface. The others asked me if I could deal with the pain for the night; suggesting we go to Colombo, where I could see a doctor, in the morning. No one wanted to leave this idyllic location earlier than necessary, a thought I readily agreed with.   In acquiescing to stay the night, I had no idea that the pain would continue to increase while being joined by a throbbing sensation, preventing me from enjoying any slumber that night.

Evening brought on another delightful meal artfully spiced with local ingredients and, again, an overabundance of curry. The tears flowed from both of us, our noses ran and the intense fire was again lit in our throats.   While we were still only eighteen years old, the hotel was liberal in providing copious amounts of cold beer to help douse the fires that raged within us.

The main dishes of curried chicken and curried fish were served with aromatic rice and various vegetables, also spiced with excessive amounts of curry.   It seemed that as long as we were to remain at the Galle Hotel, the dining room would be the playground; Charles and I, the defenseless playthings of our hosts.

Having finished dinner and entered into a slightly altered state of inebriation, I said good night and, with a limping gate, headed off to my room. I tried to get some rest, but with the pain in my foot, I spent the entire night tossing and turning. For myself, the night couldn't have ended too soon. That night was one of the most miserable of my life. By morning my right foot had swollen significantly larger than its normal size and the pain was equally intense.

Breakfast was served at the hotel where the spice of the food stoked the flame in our throats to a level just below the burning registering in my foot.   Incredibly, I was now burning both inside and out.   Regrettably, the curry did nothing to quell the throbbing pain I felt.

Tears streaming down our faces, we happily bid adieu to our white robed hosts and began the long ride north to Colombo.   The drive was a visual cornucopia of plant types and colors, the bright green glow of the countryside creating a stark contrast to the white beaches, blue ocean and black pavement of the road. We passed through small villages that were bisected by the primitive highway; our course wove along the coast where the ocean's swells made a thundering thump as they crashed upon the unoccupied shore.

Then the road twisted inland towards forested areas overgrown with naturally growing teak, coco de mer palms, ebony, and java fig; their green canopies crowning the brown trunks that supported them from far below. Surrounding the base of the trunks were colorful shrubs sprinkled with frangipani, multitudinous species of wildly shaped orchids and lantana, adding a multihued foreground that painted an exotic landscape of naturally scented flora. From branches high above the ground, the voices of purple heron, rose-ringed parakeets, mynas, and the black hooded ibis broadcast their messages for all to hear. Waves of energy emanated from the verdant growth as it sprang into the air. The area was so vibrant, so alive; you could almost see the plants growing.

The villages had their own unique points of interest. Inhabitants could be seen walking barefoot towards their homes with caldrons of water balanced delicately on their heads, others carried groceries wrapped in a cloth about their shoulders; cyclists, riding leisurely through the village, carried piles of small cut branches to stoke a fire for cooking.

Many of the villagers wore light colored wraps that contrasted sharply with their dark skin. With their sparkling bright eyes and obsidian hair they were an incredibly handsome nation of people. Doing most everything by hand led to a physically demanding life, causing the Sinhalese people to age prematurely. Looking into their faces, you could see how the ravages of time had left its mark on their deeply etched skin.

✳✳✳✳✳

I slept at Mark's house that night; the next day his lovely wife Victoria, a former Miss Ceylon, ferried me to the doctor's office. After hearing the history of what had happened on the shoreline at Galle, a brief visual examination followed by a touch here, a prod there that almost caused me to fly off the

196

exam table; the doc surmised that my foot was impaled with sea urchin spines. He opined that he could not remove the deeply sequestered spines without making an even bigger mess of my foot, an outcome we both wished to avoid.

The doctor ordered me to bathe my right foot in hydrogen peroxide three times a day for twenty minutes during each application. He explained that the bubbling action of the peroxide in concert with the natural healing processes of my body would, given time, expel the spines from the underside of my foot.

His instructions were to let the spines protrude from my foot until I thought they could be extracted with tweezers, without breaking off the tips. In the meanwhile, I was given crutches to walk on and was not allowed weight-bearing on my right foot. The doctor prescribed a mild tranquilizer to help me sleep.

The doctor had said something that had struck a chord in me. He spoke of the "Natural healing processes of the body," a thought that seemed completely appropriate, yet sounded so foreign to me. In Western medicine, I was taught it was the medicine that caused healing to take place. If the medicine couldn't heal an injury, then a surgeon would often intervene through surgical excision. But to consider the body having the ability to heal itself was something that had never occurred to me. It began me thinking…

In a few days the spines began to emerge from the reddened and swollen sole of my foot. I grabbed them with the tweezers as instructed, removing about eight three-quarter inch long spines during the next week. As I extracted the first spine from the underside of my foot, my eyes opened wide as I saw its length. At first I was surprised by how deeply they had penetrated my foot, but then thought about the pain I had been suffering and it made sense that the foreign material would be of significant size. With the spines removed, my foot rapidly returned to its normal color, the pain resolved and I could again bear weight. Now, it was back to the beach; I had not been in the water for ten days.

＊＊＊＊＊

For centuries, India had been a major destination for sailors in search of new lands and exotic spices. Ceylon was on the major shipping route to and from India and many ships had foundered off the coast during monsoon season storms. The sea floor off the Sinhalese coast was littered with cargo from centuries old sunken ships: some precious, some not.

In addition to his numerous talents, Mark was a scuba diver who took advantage of the crystal clear water that surrounded his adopted island home. He had some very interesting mementos from his dives that he wished to share with me.

In his bedroom, Mark had what looked like a very old sea chest made of a light colored hardwood, bleached from decades underwater; it was held together with heavy metal support straps that were rusted from their years under the sea. The chest measured thirty inches deep by three and one half feet long; it stood thirty inches tall. When Mark opened the chest, the rusty hinges creaked as though they wished to spin their untold yarn of sinking in a ferocious storm and having lain undisturbed for centuries beneath the sea. The interior appeared to be full of clumps of a porous, grey concrete.

Mark told me to hold out my hands; lifting one of the heavy grey clumps, he dumped the oblong mass into my palms. He explained that originally these were canvas bags brimming full with silver coins. During their uncounted years beneath the sea, the canvas had rotted away while madreporic coral had formed around the coins creating the rough clumps of rock that I now held. It was easy to see the coins, their smooth silver edges contrasting sharply with the irregular edges of the abrasive coral. When asked where Mark had found the treasure chest he replied, "Somewhere off the coast." No further clues to the origins of his silver treasure chest were offered.

Mark did show me a picture of himself underwater with sharks circling around him. He explained that on a dive north of Colombo, he encountered a school of eight foot sharks that surrounded him and gave him the scare of his life. He recounted actually living his worst nightmare: deep in the water, running low on air and surrounded by the predacious animals. He had to do everything in his power not to panic. Somehow, he managed to escape his predicament and exited the water, body intact. Observing that there was someone nearby to take a picture, I didn't think his position was terribly precarious. Actually, the sharks that surrounded him looked like Nurse Sharks from the family *Ginglymostomatidae* who are known as bottom feeders. They are not known as human predators, but the picture certainly caught your eye. Then, I reflected on the fact that Mark had his movie lab available to him; it wasn't much of a stretch to see him super-imposing a picture of the sharks over a picture of himself diving in safe water.

✻✻✻✻✻

Both Charles and I noticed that wherever we went, we always had one of what we thought was Mark's friends along. Noticing that Mark never drove the car when we went surfing, it finally dawned on us that Raj was one of his servants, not a buddy along for the trip. Mark was one of Ceylon's elite; he didn't even drive his own car. When I was driven to the doctor's office, it was Raj who chauffeured us, while Victoria rode beside him as a passenger.

Victoria also never drove a vehicle. We later learned that she was never taught how to drive and had no wishes to learn. She was the child of a privileged family; she had married into another privileged family; driving a car was a menial task that could be left to others.

Her duties in life were first as a beauty contestant, and she was gorgeous, with a face that made average men weep. Later, she became an ambassador to the Sinhalese people as Miss Ceylon, and then as a challenger in the Miss Universe competition. Having failed to gain that prestigious crown, Victoria was married off to Mark, who had come to Ceylon to forage in the jungles, dive on the coasts and make movies in his adopted country.

Mark and Victoria had a small son, five years old, who was

the mango of their eye. Taken care of by a full time nanny, he was smothered with love by everyone in the household. Victoria was currently occupied by raising her son with the nanny as surrogate, and overseeing the daily operation of her household.

The house itself was maintained by numerous individuals: a nanny took care of Mark Jr.; there was a cook, a gardener, a driver, and another woman who assisted the nanny when not occupied with housekeeping. Mark went to work each morning and Victoria spent most of her day preening. While she had the freedom to do as she wished, she was always driven by Raj and accompanied by an escort.

*****

Back on *Paisano*, Jeanie had continued to harass John about his liberal ways with the crew. On other boats, she pointed to Dedier and how he interacted with his crewman Jose; the owner didn't do any of the work and treated their crew as subordinates. But John enjoyed getting his hands dirty; he wanted to share tasks with the guys; we were a team. From a casual observer's view you might think the three of us were brothers, especially since we were nearly the same age. But truth be told, we were wealthy owner and not very wealthy, unpaid crew.

Unfortunately, Jeanie wanted to put on airs, play the pretentious *Tahitian Princess* that she wasn't and have others around act subservient. These feelings finally came to a head in Ceylon. Actually, they couldn't have risen earlier, as Jeanie was rarely on the boat, preferring to spend the majority of her time in the more familiar surroundings of her parent's home in Papeete.

Speaking between ourselves, the two of us wondered how John could continue on this trip; surely we were having a great time, but he was recently married and we questioned why he didn't have his newlywed wife with him. Not wanting to pry and John not volunteering any information on the subject, our curiosity went unanswered. But we knew, if we were in John's shoes, our wife would be with us.

200

On numerous occasions, we had heard John and Jeanie arguing on the boat. We couldn't imagine what problem might arise that was worthy of arguing about in paradise. In our adolescent ignorance, it seemed to us that nothing was so important it demanded sufficient energy to warrant such conflict. But there it was. John the millionaire wanted to be one of the guys, get his hands dirty and play with his toys. Jeanie, the millionaire's wife, wanted to be treated like the snob she was becoming. Perhaps they weren't the best matched couple?

With the ongoing bickering, we were really disappointed in how things were turning out. We thought the whole idea made John sick to his stomach. Here we were, sailing around the world on his beautiful yacht and all she did was complain. His imperious new wife was ruining John's idyllic vision of his adventure in paradise.

Due to the continuing marital strife and the hostility that was circulating within the boat, the two of us decided to move off *Paisano*, giving John and Jeanie some space to work out their problems. Remember, we were living in a space that wasn't much larger than a closet, privacy was non-existent. Nothing definite was decided except to allow things to settle and see what time would bring.

In the meantime, Charles and I moved into a small apartment that our new friend Mark owned. It was located around the corner from his house on the outskirts of the city. A small one bedroom apartment, sparsely furnished, it was much more spacious than the main salon we had shared on *Paisano*.

We informed Mark of the intense conflict raging between John and Jeanie; we expressed the sadness we felt as the squabbling was beginning to pry apart the strong bond that had formed between John, I and Charles. At this time, we had sailed together for fourteen months and could almost tell what each other was thinking.

We knew each other's habits, our likes and dislikes. John trusted us implicitly and would do anything for us. The feeling was reciprocated in our minds. We hated to see John and Jeanie bickering, it made us feel bad and we knew this was no way to act in Paradise.

Understanding the currently conflicted nature of the boat's inhabitants, Mark invited the two of us to have our meals at his house. This invite was not really a strain on Mark's household. He had a cook who prepared the family's meals and there was always room for two more at the dinner table.

Food for the two might have added a dollar a day to the household budget; again, not really a problem. Eating at Mark's was a new experience in the culinary arts. Of course, the meals were prepared to the local taste, again the tears flowed. We consumed heaps of curried meat, fish and cooked vegetables with rice.

After the first meal, Charles pointed out his running nose and tearing eyes, asking "if we could have our dishes prepared with a dash less curry?" Nodding in agreement, Victoria made a mental note to request the cook season the food for the boys, lightly.

Meals were served in a round stainless steel dish with a one inch vertical rim. The custom in this country was to use your hands to scoop up some curried veggies or meat, add some rice, perhaps use a piece of chapatti, a flat bread, to wrap the mass and try to get it in your mouth without dropping it on your lap.

At first, this was quite a challenge, the use of utensils being mandatory in the Western world. As you know, eating food with your hands is frowned upon at home. Becoming agile with our fingers took some practice. In the meantime, we were a topic of discussion and derision for our clumsy manners at the dinner table.

*****

At the dinner table one evening, Mark explained that he had run into an American couple who were touring Ceylon on their way to India. They had brought some interesting drugs with them and had invited Mark to indulge. Mark had replied that he would be available to meet with them at his home on the weekend, when their visit would not interfere with his movie production schedule. Mark suggested that we be around to meet with our countrymen and perhaps explore some new ideas with them. Not yet having indulged in any drugs, nor truly understanding their meaning, the two of us were hesitantly curious. Upon Mark's invitation, we made plans to attend.

Coastal Ceylon

Refreshing ourselves in Benji's River

XIII

Paradise Becomes Psychedelic

On Friday evening, Mark arrived home with the young couple that was touring his adopted country. The gent was tall and slender; he was dressed in loose fitting white clothing, wore sandals and had long hair that fell to his shoulders. This was at a time when long hair was an anomaly, so we knew right off that this would be an interesting encounter.

In addition to his saintly garments, Mark's guest had an air of spirituality about him; he was traveling through the region visiting ashrams, temples and other religious sites with his female companion. Having brought some LSD with him from the states, Paul wanted to *turn on* Mark and friends.

At that time, Charles and I had no idea what LSD was; we thought *turning on* was getting a really good ride on a wave. But Mark's guest Paul went on to tutor us, explaining that LSD was a psychedelic drug synthesized in a laboratory. He continued stating, "It produces mental hallucinations and other unique psychological effects." When he asked us if we wanted to join in, our curiosity overcame our caution; we responded positively, "Sure man, I guess?" While we were very young and ignorant about many things, we were roving the world with an open mind; hoping to explore its wonders, its secrets, its beauty and its oddities; we deemed this to be another facet of our ongoing education.

Neither of us had ever taken any drugs before, we were what was referred to as *squeaky clean*. We weren't sure what we were supposed to do or what we should expect. The term psychedelic had not yet entered our lexicon; we didn't know what LSD was or a hallucination, but we were certainly open to new and exciting experiences. If this was something that Mark thought was O.K., then we would follow the lead of our British mentor.

It seemed that many places around the world utilized some sort of mind altering intoxicants. In Fiji, the natives drank kava

kava, in New Guinea they chewed betel nut, and now it was an introduction to LSD in Ceylon. None of these substances were illegal, simply frowned upon by the majority. Surely we had had our fill of Scotch and beer in many locales, but these were commonly accepted intoxicants in most parts of the world, only producing facial grimaces in those that dwelled in ultra conservative areas.

Paul mentioned that some people might experience an out of body experience after ingesting the LSD. Charles questioned why anyone would want to leave their body; he didn't quite understand what would be achieved by that type of "trip." Contemplating the idea, he thought perhaps it would allow him to transport home and say hi to the folks; or he might see strangely colored lights that he could dance with in the sky. Could we see through walls or through each other? Or could we look into each other and see what we were truly becoming as human beings? That could certainly be enlightening. But he still couldn't quite comprehend how anyone traveled without their body? At that time in Charles' life he understood that his body was the totality of his being.

We all sat down to dinner at Mark's house; we ate a well prepared meal, mildly spiced with curry and shared some red wine. Mark and Paul spoke about current world affairs, of which Charles and I mostly listened. An hour later Paul distributed the LSD and mescaline to those around the table and we ingested our first dose of mind altering drugs.

As it turned out, each had his own personal experience. Some seemed not to notice anything, others slight distortions of reality. I was given a dose of mescaline, a derivative of *magic mushrooms*, as there was not enough LSD to go around. Being the youngest, I was often the low man on the totem pole.

The mescaline seemed to heighten my senses, perhaps the substance allowed me to see clearer. Mark's house was behind an eight foot wall with sharp broken glass on top, which seemed to waver somewhat when I looked at it for a while. Previously, I had ignored the rim of broken glass crowning the wall, now I questioned its existence. Shame, I thought, living in Paradise behind a wall topped with shards of broken glass.

As I sat outside on the door step, I could hear the sounds of people rampaging in the streets. Ethnic strife had begun in Ceylon in the early fifties and this night was an example of the unrest that might take place in the country after dark. That answered the question of, "Why is there a glass rimmed wall surrounding the house?" As in many third world countries, the wealth was unevenly distributed; some of those that had not, would always attempt to take from those that had. It was not a problem that was unique to Ceylon.

Bored with the lack of visual stimuli outside, I wandered back inside the house. Allowing my gaze to slowly revolve around the room, I noticed a wooden credenza perched against a side wall. I walked over and picked up a book perched on the tabletop. It was titled <u>The Family of Man</u> and consisted solely of photographs of people's faces; there was no text, no descriptions. The people were from all over the earth, different nationalities, different races, yet each was beautiful in his or her own way.

I was struck mainly by their eyes, and the depth in their expressions. Deep, endless pools finding their bottom in the root of their souls. I wasn't sure if it was that book or the mescaline or both that impressed me so very much that night.

It did help to open my mind to the thought that we are all members of one large family on this planet that we need to recognize that and peacefully reconcile the problems that conflict mankind. I remembered from my history classes that in all the years of man's existence on this planet, he had been continually at war someplace around the globe. Currently, there was a small skirmish in a far off place called Viet Nam. Wouldn't it be interesting if *the family* could somehow come to embrace the thought that we are all related and should work out our problems in a peaceful, sensible and mature manner?

It must have been the mescaline, too silly a thought for reality. However, this seemed to be the cardinal moment in my own personal soul searching; a new consciousness was beginning to emerge from within me that was to be the origin of my quest for a more tranquil life in a peaceful world. One that everyone could live in, one in which the suffering of the masses would be diminished. This was a profound experience for me, it appeared that my own personal doors of perception were beginning to open, if ever so slightly.

Charles had a somewhat different experience, having ingested LSD with some bottled water found in the house. Mark had a pet mongoose which was kept around the house to protect the family against snakes; a part of the reality of living in the countryside of a snake infested island. Ceylon is home to the celebrated and venomous cobra; over eighty species of snake live in country. With the proliferation of the slithering vertebrates crawling around the countryside, the mongoose has become an important member of many households. The mongoose, from the family *Herpestidae*, is a small animal covered with dense fur, the size of a large squirrel. It has very sharp teeth and is both extremely fast and agile; they have the ability to grab a snake by the neck, killing it before the snake can strike.

Charles sat crossed legged on the floor. He played with the mongoose while attempting to form a mental connection of some sort. Unfortunately, the only thing Charles connected with was some fecal matter the mongoose left behind on his leg. Aside from that, he noticed no special visual effects or physical manifestations from his experience with LSD.

Mark, on the other hand, had opened a conduit to God; he had visions of saints floating overhead, looking down on him from heavenly heights; they had golden halos adorning their heads, like those seen in renaissance paintings. The saints were smiling, which greatly pleased him. He believed he was receiving a sign that his life was being lived correctly; that the gods were happy with his ways; a very nice response to the mind altering drug.

This was a glimpse into another aspect of life with which we were completely unfamiliar. Drugs, which became common place in later decades, were practically unknown in the mid-sixties, especially in places like Ceylon. At that time, America was still very much a God fearing country where drugs were not something that was known or accepted. But we were on an unparalleled voyage of adventure and discovery, trying to be open to all experiences that crossed our paths; we were curious, our curiosity was for the time being, sated.

For the two of us, weekend surf safaris continued to different parts of the island nation where we enjoyed the waves at various surf spots and where the swells were uncontested by other wave riders. During those treks along the coast, the beauty of this Garden of Eden never failed to create awe in us.

*****

One afternoon, we met one of our neighbors walking on the street near Mark's apartment. Seeing what was obviously strangers in his neighborhood, Rashid introduced himself and we exchanged pleasantries. We were an unexpected sight on a side street in the country; we had to be learned about by the curious citizens of this suburban community. Rashid asked if we would care to come to tea at his home one afternoon. Looking forward to making new friends in a foreign land we currently called home, we responded positively. Rashid stated he would come by our apartment in a few days; we agreed with his plan. Having completed conversing with our new friend, we said, "Goodbye," as we parted ways.

A few days later, Rashid, the twenty five year old son of a wealthy family with interests in the nation's gem trade, came by the apartment to escort us to the home of his parents, a few doors down the street. Rashid was a short man, had dark hair and skin; he wore a mustache which was the current style in Ceylon. He had bright white teeth and eyes that contrasted sharply with his dark skin and hair. The Sinhalese people were easy to look at, especially the women.

The homes in the area had flat walls that faced the street with an occasional small window to allow light and fresh air to enter. The exterior facade made a show of humility; no demonstration of wealth was visible to the outside world. Once indoors, we were invited to sit in a richly decorated living room. The floor was covered with thick wool and silk Persian carpets; the room had soft-pillowed plush chairs and a large couch. The windows were draped to keep peeping eyes from straying.

Rashid asked us if we would like some tea. After receiving

a positive response, he exited the living room. In a short time, he returned with a young woman, his sister, whom he introduced as Sarah. Sarah wore a traditional Sari of green cotton with a silk shawl layered over her shoulders. With jet black hair and ebony eyes, she looked both beautiful and exotic in her native dress. Sarah sat and conversed with the group, learning about our travels, our observations and thoughts about her country. The four of us passed a pleasant afternoon in conversation while drinking some incredibly fine tasting, locally grown, black tea. When Charles asked what type of tea he had served, Rashid told him its name, "Earl Grey." He went on to explain that the tea was an old blend of black tea and Bergamot, the extract of a small citrus fruit grown in Southeast Asia and the Continent. The mix was first introduced and bestowed on a British Prime Minister in the first half of the 19th century. The small island had remained a British colony up through the early years of the 20th century, when it had finally gained its independence. It is believed that the new tea was a gift from a visiting Sinhalese emissary. The Prime Minister was an English Earl named Charles Grey.

During our afternoon chat, Rashid explained that he worked at his parents' jewelry shop in the heart of the capital. He informed us of the existence of sapphires and rubies that were found in abundance in the river beds of his country; land owning families became very wealthy by mining those gem bearing rivers. He went on to give details of his family's factory in the countryside. There, they employed silversmiths and goldsmiths. The artisans would design and create settings for the precious stones. Stone cutters were employed to cut and finish the rough gems; when the finished stones were set, the ready for market products were sent to town where they were sold in the family store in the jewelry sector of central Colombo.

Looking around the room, Charles noticed there was no television to be seen. When asked, Rashid responded that television did not exist in Ceylon, but he knew what it was from reading about it. Charles reflected back on his years growing up in California, the programs he had watched with his family and how it seemed to be a focal point of family life in the states, especially on Sunday evenings.

He turned to Rashid saying, "You don't know what you're missing." Rashid responded that Charles was correct, he didn't know anything about television, and therefore he hadn't missed anything. It took Charles a few minutes to digest Rashid's sharp response.

As the afternoon wore on, finding his conversation with the visiting Americans agreeable, and beginning to formulate a mental plan, Rashid mentioned that he had a cousin who was a very wealthy landowner. His parcel of land was so large that over the years villages had been built on it. This was prior to his cousins inheriting the land. He asked us if we would like to travel into the country and do some sight-seeing? He wanted to share some of his country's natural wonders with his new friends. Sensing the potential for an interesting adventure, we were elated by Rashid's suggestion and replied positively.

Days later, traveling first by train and later by taxi, Rashid led us to his cousin Benji's home in the inland reaches of the countryside. There, we were met by a pair of eight foot ivory elephant tusks standing guard as they curved over either side of the entryway to his home. Inside, we viewed hand carved furniture that his servants had spent years laboriously carving from solid blocks of aromatic sandalwood. Benji's home in the country was modest, yet full of the furnishings that could be modeled from locally grown materials. To us, its natural beauty was inspiring.

Benji, a young man of twenty five, arrived and we were introduced. He led a tour of the house that we hadn't yet seen. Many rooms, scantily furnished with incredibly intricate carved pieces, some painted, some natural wood, completed his home. The walls were mainly bare; some pictures of Hindu saints: Shiva, Vishnu, and Krishna, were found adorning the walls in one room.

Our host requested food be prepared by his wait staff and we were invited to lunch. Having learned our lesson, we requested our curry be lightly spiced and hoped to see some fresh fruit on the table. Not to be disappointed, the meal was perfectly spiced; the table was full of locally grown fresh fruit including: banana, mango and papaya. A local specialty, bottled carbonated coconut milk, was served over ice. When the cap on a bottle of coco milk was removed, a horrific odor, similar to that of the sewer, escaped the bottle, making it an unlikely export. However, the taste was incredibly good, the drink's saving grace. Tea was served after lunch and then a walk around the garden was undertaken to assist in digesting the afternoon meal.

Benji and Rashid excused themselves for a moment. They spoke in private and it was decided to give their guests a tour of Benji's land holdings. Using one of Benji's cars, a short ride deposited the group at a river that ran through his land. The river was fed by rain water from the mountains to the cultivated areas of his property and eventually to the sea. On the riverbank, in a small thatched hut, lived a hermit who transported people across the river on a strongly constructed wooden raft.

Having lived in the grass hut for over a decade, the hermit had dedicated his adult life to serving the people of the villages found on the far side of the slowly flowing river. His raft allowed villagers easy access to the coastal region and the capital city. Although the hermit may have denied any need for money, a meager income was derived from poling the raft laden with villagers.

The nameless man had long flowing grey locks that reached below his shoulders. A matching curly grey beard grew from his narrow and tanned face; it hung half way down his chest. He wore a loin cloth around his waist that reached his knees and nothing more; his bare skin carried a dark leathery sheen from years in the sun; he spoke only his local dialect. Strangely, he appeared none too happy to see Caucasian faces at *his* river. Obsequiousness was not one of his faults.

Ignoring his lack of civility and upon our host's invitation, we all undressed and cooled ourselves in the refreshing waters of Benji's river. The heat of the tropics seemed to never leave us during our travels and too much time spent directly in the equatorial sun could be traumatic. After refreshing ourselves, we dried off; Benji humbly asked, "If you would like to see some of my elephants?"

Leaving the local Siddhartha to his raft and his personal Shangri-La, the group headed off toward Benji's compound where the animals were housed. There we found Benji's favorite elephant with one leg chained to a wooden stake. He explained that the stake, fixed deeply into the ground, was called an *alheka*.

Being curious about the strength of the alheka, Charles asked, "Would that slender piece of wood really hold the elephant if he wanted to make a break?" Benji replied, "No, it is symbolic and the elephant understands that he is supposed to remain there until a caretaker moves him." He added that the only reason the elephant would run off was if for some reason he became frightened.

The elephants of Ceylon have been present on the island for over 5000 years. They were first captured in 40 A.D. as described by Pliny. The massive animals were used during royal celebrations and were ridden by the island's kings. In later times, the elephants were exported to India for use as tools of war and to ancient Burma to be used in state ceremonies.

Benji's elephant had numerous uses in the country. It was a living, breathing bulldozer; it could topple trees and move heavy objects. It was also a mode of transportation through the densely overgrown jungles where they often encountered leopards, monkeys, crocodiles and numerous species of snakes. The elephants were prized possessions that were well taken care of and, due to their massive size and weight, treated respectfully.

It appeared that Benji had everything a person could ever want. He owned so much land that villages housing hundreds were built on it and rivers ran through it; he owned homes, cars, elephants and much more. Soon we were shocked to find that he was afflicted with a disease that he would rather not have possessed.

As the group was walking towards the elephant Benji brought us to see, he suddenly stopped moving. Noticing Benji halt his forward motion, I looked at him to see why he had stopped. At the same time Rashid grabbed Charles and

I, pulling us away by the arm. A servant who was standing nearby ran towards our host, forcing his mouth apart and placing a stick between his teeth; he held him to prevent his falling over and injuring himself.

Benji at first was rigid. He began shaking as though he were freezing cold; he would have fallen had it not been for his servants who physically supported him. When his tremors ceased, the help carried him to his home where he could rest. Apparently the seizure that had wracked his body also exhausted it. It would be days before he left his bed again.

Benji had epilepsy. Unfortunately, there was no medicine available that could help control the seizures that regularly tortured both his body and his mind.

That incident was a staggering shock to the two of us. This fine young man, who seemed to have everything, and shared much with his friends, also had a grave debilitating disease. This was a disease that was then little understood and was, with the primitive medicine that existed in that place, untreatable. We thought that Benji would have traded everything he owned if he could rid himself of the powerful seizures that put such severe limitations on his life. Poor Benji we thought; surely the poorest of rich men.

At our age, Benji's illness had a profound effect on us. We had never before seen an epileptic seizure; it was scary to observe, no doubt much worse for the recipient. But it didn't seem fair. How does God give a young man so much earthly riches and then infect his body with a dysfunctional brain that suffers neurological storms, completely incapacitating him? Was it that his excessive material wealth was being balanced with a dysfunctional physical body? Never before had life's duality been demonstrated so clearly, at least not to us. It was certainly humbling and a major point was added to our continually growing stores of knowledge: all the money in the world couldn't buy Benji's health.

Rashid led us to another of Benji's houses in the country, where we spent the rest of the day. There Rashid explained about Benji's family and how they had attained their massive land holdings. After the British granted independence to Ceylon in 1948, the land was returned to its rightful owners.

Being the descendant of a powerful and wealthy Maharaja and his sole heir, Benji had inherited all the holdings of his estate.

Benji's task in life was ruling over his landed holdings and caring for the welfare of the peoples that lived in his domain. That piece of information literally boggled our minds. But in the back of those minds, a thought continued to perplex us: how could someone be so graced and cursed at the same time?

In the evening, the three of us shared a meal at Benji's home where we discussed the affairs of the world. Hearing views of someone living all his life in Ceylon, we heard a non-American interpretation of what was going on in the world. We were often on islands or in places with no news apparatus; we paid little attention to world affairs. The information Rashid discussed was all news to us and we had to admit to not being especially conversant in international affairs.

Rashid seemed to be a genuinely fine person. He had invited the two us to view the interior of his country. He wanted to show off what a bountiful and magnificent land he called home. We were very impressed by our visit to the countryside. We were thankful for our meeting on the street that one afternoon, grateful to have met Rashid and appreciative of his and Benji's hospitality.

It was also an eye opener on how life progressed in a country like Ceylon. If you were born to a wealthy family you lived a comfortable life. If you were born in the country and lived on Benji's land there was little opportunity for personal growth; the children received only a rudimentary education. The poor simply survived and often times by serving the rich.

During our evening conversation with Rashid, we explained how we spent our days surfing on the coast, a vastly different lifestyle than Rashid was familiar with. Not understanding the point of our activities, he asked, "Why do you do this?" To him, our activities seemed an unproductive use of time. I described our work caring for the sailboat, which we were not currently occupied with. I went on to explain that surfing was a form of recreation widely practiced in other nations.

I didn't want to explain the details of our current absence from the boat, but suffice it to say, at the moment, we weren't gainfully employed. I explained that surfing was good exercise, lots of fun and we enjoyed time in the sun and sea. To our dismay, Rashid was not interested in joining us for an afternoon at the beach; Rashid was a responsible individual; he had work to do.

Having exhausted the evening hours in titillating and insightful conversation, as the clock struck eleven, we turned in for a night's rest. The next day, having consumed a breakfast of fresh fruit and tea, we made the return trip to Colombo and our current home away from home.

Working

XIV

They did write the Kama Sutra

Mark's many interests and his quest for learning and experimentation led him to share his business offices with another Englishman who had immigrated to the suburbs of Colombo. Arthur Clarke, a prolific science fiction author of over one hundred books, had the prescience of mind to write about space travel, computers and satellites before they existed. He used the islands' primitive and peaceful environment to sequester himself in a serene locale where he could study and write.

The tranquility of the native surroundings allowed his mind to wander, to seek, to contemplate. In this lush but soothing hideout, his unbridled intellect sprung to life, he was more creative, ideas flowed, and pages filled. The jungle provided a calm that protected his considerable genius from the conflict and trauma of the modern world. He had found a reclusive sanctuary in Ceylon, far from the maddening world, and it served him well. We found his statements to be well founded upon viewing the movie created from the science fiction best-seller 2001-A Space Odyssey that Arthur had written. But that was a few years later.

Mark was currently involved with making modern movies for the Sinhalese market. He filmed a James Bond type movie that was funnier than it was adventurous, at least to us. When the heavyset Sinhalese *James* came into a hotel room, he checked to see if it was bugged by taking an electric razor from his suitcase and walking it around the walls of his room. Most people in Ceylon had never seen an electric razor and would be easily fooled by substituting it for a real bug detecting device.

Remember this was well before cell phones; television had not yet arrived; people were not savvy about techno devices. And much more so in a backward third world country, where the price of admission to the movies was the equivalent of a penny. Another scene had the local *James* crawling through a thirty inch diameter tunnel that was fabricated from cardboard. It was funny stuff, but if you lived your life in the interior of Ceylon, it was probably pretty exciting.

There were few women in Mark's movie, even though it was a James Bond thriller. In Ceylon, he could not show a man kissing a woman on the screen, and sexual relations or even sexual innuendo were strictly forbidden. That made his movie pretty benign to western eyes.

Mark finished his movie and it did well at the box office. It played at hundreds of theaters all over the country, winning accolades from the local press. Happy with the result of his latest production, Mark made plans for his next movie.

✶✶✶✶✶

During our next weekend's surfing safari Mark mentioned he had met some really cool guys that would like to join us for a surfing adventure. It was becoming apparent that Mark was Ceylon's unofficial ambassador of good will; he met every one of interest that came to the island and seemed to get involved in everything that was happening.

We were introduced to Brad and Bill on the following Saturday at a new surf spot on the south coast. Surprisingly, they were both Americans whose work had taken them to Italy where they currently resided.

They were both young, good looking and strong. They had gotten involved in movie making and were currently employed as actors on the European motion picture circuit. They had done so well that they were considered stars in low budget movies made for the Continental market. Not to be made fun of, those *B* rated movies resulted in a nice living for the guys while they traveled the world in search of exotic filming locales.

Brad bragged that he made a nice income as a star in those low-budget movies. He crowed that his exalted position as an actor afforded him a nice villa in Italy where he had a Maserati parked in the driveway. The film company that currently employed them had come to Ceylon to film a James Bond type movie, a very hot film genre in the mid-sixties.

The film company was ensconced at the Mt. Lavinia Hotel, a classic colonial hotel located on the west coast some twenty miles south of the city. With polished wooden floors, a wood paneled dining room and an outdoor dining area shaded with colorful umbrellas, the hotel was a picturesque spot. It functioned as a perfect base for their film making activities.

Actually, the hotel was so striking that the film company decided to shoot many scenes there. They used the beach to film the stars swimming in on a mission. They shot the outdoor dining patio for meetings that the movie's characters conducted during the film. It was really interesting to onlookers and a small crowd usually gathered when they were shooting.

Both Bill and Brad were body builders with huge muscles. Charles thought he was knowledgeable of the term *muscle bound* that applied to both of them. They obviously spent hours each day at the gym. Charles thought that their excessive muscle mass decreased their flexibility making it difficult for them to move well. Allowing his thoughts to be verbalized, he was highly surprised when Brad, with all his bulk, declared, "I can easily do a standing back flip." Charles almost fell over when Brad provided proof of his statement, performing a back flip on the beach.

The producers and the director of the production had handpicked them specifically for this film, taking full advantage of their physiques. They were the good guys in the film and had numerous shots taken with their chests bare. They were also good stunt men; Bill jumped off the hotel's second story roof, falling onto a platform made from empty cardboard boxes padded with mattresses from the hotel. It looked like a very exciting and rewarding means of making a living.

We were open to sharing our surfboards and the actors were excited to join us on our surfing adventures. When Brad and Bill were not working on the set, they had nothing to do but study their lines and wait around. Surfing along the palm lined coast of Ceylon was a great way to pass the time and stay cool under the blazing tropical sun.

One day, while sitting on our boards waiting for some swells to roll in, Brad questioned me about my home town. I was surprised to find that we had both lived in the same community in Southern California. Both of us had resided in Monterey Park and attended the same high school. It was quite a shock to meet someone twelve thousand miles from home who had gone to the same school. We formed an instant bond, became good friends and spent much of Brad's and my free time together.

During one of our surfing afternoons, Brad turned to me and asked, "What are you going to do with your life?" Having thought about this previously and not come up with a satisfactory answer, I replied, "I don't know." During the month of November I had turned nineteen. I felt no closer to knowing where my life would take me or what I would be doing when I arrived. Brad now felt a kinship towards his new friend and wanted to help guide me in some direction. Being happy with his own career and the handsome income it provided, he suggested that I think about becoming an actor.

I was young, had the juvenile good looks of a leading man, was physically lean and muscular and could speak well. It was not an area of endeavor that I had previously considered, but I responded positively; that I would consider it. It was a good thing Brad did, planting that seed.

✳✳✳✳✳

A nice aspect of their movie making venture in Ceylon was that Brad and Bill had a generous expense account written into their employment contracts. And everything was very inexpensive in Ceylon. Everywhere we went either Brad or Bill, Mark or John paid the bills, food flowed and so did the drinks.

Once again, it was hard to remain sober. However, in a conservative country like Ceylon, where Buddhism and Hinduism flourished, no girls were ever part of the celebrations. When we inquired into why we never met any women while traveling in country, Mark pointed out that in Ceylon, women do not go outdoors except when chaperoned. Relationships were arranged by the family and any young women having an extra-marital affair, would be kicked out of her parent's home, if not murdered, for dishonoring the family.

The Kama Sutra, written in the 2nd century by the Indian scholar Vatsyayana, is the Hindu text on the art of love making; however, this was only to be indulged in after marriage. The island had a very strict moral code, and we realized we would not want to be responsible for such a horrible punishment being visited on any young lovely. So, it was a time for male bonding and with the time we spent together, the waves that were shared and the new experiences we enjoyed, it was a fun time of island exploration and personal growth.

*****

Soon, it became apparent exactly how our new friends became so physically well developed. On a Friday, after surfing on the south coast all afternoon, the group made an evening junket into the country. We stopped at a hotel, had dinner and drinks and then went to walk around. We enjoyed the freshly scented air and visited the gardens that we had been told were especially beautiful. Surrounded by tea plants imported from China's Yunnan Province, an aromatic scent permeated the air.

During our walk, we stumbled upon a black sedan that was parked on the grass in the midst of the gardens; Brad saw the out of place vehicle and verbally mocked the errant owner. Gathering his massive strength, he started shaking the car from side to side. Observing his behavior and thinking it kind of funny--remember we were only nineteen and had been drinking--we helped test the vehicle's stability.

With the other three of us joining Brad, seemingly before we could blink, the car had rolled over onto its side. Charles, suddenly seeing through the shrouded cloud surrounding his intoxicated senses, was shocked by the violent action of our small group. We must have drunk more than he thought. When he looked back on the events of that night, he was astonished at our juvenile behavior and its destructive outcome.

We rationalized that we were in the company of wealthy people; money really didn't mean much to them and we were part of the party. However, this display of bravado and unbridled passion had reached a fiercely destructive level; it gave us youngsters pause. It also gave us some early insight into the damaging consequences of anabolic steroids, a substance that was currently unknown to us.

✻✻✻✻✻

For these now nineteen years old voyagers it would be decades before they would understand the effects of those muscle building drugs and the episodes of uninhibited rage they produce. But they had just witnessed one of those episodes; it was both an eye opener and intimidating.

✻✻✻✻✻

Charles voiced concern for the owner, "Imagine the shock of the vehicle's owner when he returned to find his car lying on its side?" Thinking it best to leave the site of our automotive mischief, the group jumped into a taxi and headed back to a coastal hotel where we could relax and converse about our current state of affairs. Charles told the actors about the trip, the places we had so far visited and explained the current conflicted events that brought us to be living at Mark's apartment.

With discussion continuing on into the night, another round of drinks was ordered. An elderly waiter appeared with the drinks and placed them on the table in front of us. He turned and looked at me; I looked up into the waiter's face, being shocked by the man's serene appearance. I had never seen a face with more character in it. He was an older gent, perhaps sixty years old, bald on top with a fringe of white hair; his skin well-tanned from the tropical sun. His face was deeply creased by the harshness of the weather and the decades of his life.

To me, it was as though I was staring into the face of God. I was incredibly moved by the countenance that rested gently on the surface of the waiter's face. It demonstrated to me that

222

a person's character may perhaps come from the construct of their entire life, and that the type of employment undertaken during a lifetime, while an ingredient of that construct, was on its own, unimportant. Having done his duty, the waiter walked off, thanking his guests for a generous tip.

After finishing our last drink, the actors returned to their hotel, the surfers returned to our apartment outside Colombo. Again, I reflected on the waiter's face that I had seen that night, the violent behavior of our friends and continued to wonder at the sometimes petulant and at other times extravagant nature of our lives.

The experiences of our days were accruing in an ever growing volume of extraordinary episodes and meetings with remarkable men. After having traveled for eighteen months, these experiences were beginning to have a deeply influential effect on the two of us. They were adding to our knowledge in a manner that was hastening our maturation and broadening our education in a way that would have a profound effect in future years.

✳✳✳✳✳

With Brad and Bill on the island, we had someone to play with during the week. Mark was busy making movies from Monday thru Friday and, aside from surfing, there wasn't much for us to do. It was beginning to dawn on Charles and I that were it not for the wealthy people that surrounded us, who always readily volunteered to pay the bills, we wouldn't be doing anything. The two of us were bereft of money of our own; we were in a foreign country where we couldn't work without government approval. We both had a high school education that might carry us far in Ceylon; however, the average wage here was less than one hundred dollars a month. Not promising.

Following on those thoughts, our minds turned to ideas for sustaining ourselves. Not being sure what our future on *Paisano* might be, we thought about turning Ceylon on to the surf scene. We did know surfing and thought we could make a reasonable living shaping and selling surfboards to the local population, hence the founding of "Surfboards Ceylon."

Mark arranged for introductions that culminated in a meeting with government officials. We had enlisted the bureaucracy; we probed to learn if licensing was required for our nascent venture. The skittish officials replied that licensing was indeed necessary, adding that we would need to hire locals to do the physical labor.

Apparently, business owners in Ceylon were limited to administrative tasks, while the indigenous population did the manual labor. That was a surprise to us as we were planning on doing the fabrication of the surfboards ourselves. The officials also stated we would be required to use home grown products in the manufacture of the surfboards.

Inquiring if they had the foam blanks, from which surfboards were shaped, in country, the officials replied, "No." That would make it difficult to build surfboards, since the main ingredient was missing. Fiberglass, a relatively new material in the U.S., was also not available and would need to be imported.

Not allowing the constant obstacles that cropped up to dishearten us, we continued our evaluation of the possibilities. So excited were we with the idea for our new venture that we ran out and had business cards printed with the company name and logo. The name, "Surfboards Ceylon" sat in the center of the card with the outline of a surfboard, horizontal side view, beneath the name. They both were superimposed on the Sinhalese Lion, the symbol of the nascent nation. They really looked good, motivating us to eagerly push forward with our emerging endeavor.

Since most materials would need to be imported, discussion soon turned to how much it would cost to build a surfboard. Shipping costs would need to be factored into the cost of manufacture. Not to mention that government permission would be required for the imports, which the authorities were reluctant to grant.

Then someone had an epiphany. After reflecting on the homes we had driven past in the countryside; mostly primitive native homes built from unfinished domestic woods with palm frond roofs, little electricity and no indoor plumbing; the lack of automobiles on the roads and the general poverty of the citizens, speculation arose about the people's ability to afford a surfboard. We questioned what the per capita income was of these hard working people?

Upon further reflection, we also realized that we had never seen anyone doing anything but fishing on the coasts, and that was commercial fishing done on open wooden boats powered by an outboard motor. The country had not yet developed sufficiently to embrace something like surfing; at that time, it just wasn't done. Nor were any other recreational sports seen being played.

When it was ascertained that most families lived on an income of one dollar per day, we came to terms with the fact that building a business around coastal recreation was probably not realistic. Even if we could get a large number of citizens to buy our boards and become avid surfers like ourselves, they didn't have the ability to transport the surfboards to the beach. Surfboards in the mid-sixties were at least nine feet in length and weighed thirty pounds or more. Without cars no one could ever make it to the beach with sufficient energy to do any surfing. We had encountered, in our rush to build an industry around surfing, what Melville had noted a century earlier, "Headwinds are more prevalent than the winds from astern." The hammer had fallen on Surfboards Ceylon.

That denouement pretty much put an end to the entrepreneurial zeal of our new venture. We did, however, continue to ponder in what direction to turn in an effort at finding gainful employment.

⁂ ⁂ ⁂ ⁂ ⁂

Brad and I went surfing one day during a break in Brad's filming schedule. By this time we found it easier to store the surfboards at the hotel, decreasing the difficulty of transporting them each day. Brad hired a taxi that took us from the hotel to a close by surf spot. The wind was completely absent from the coast that day as beautiful four foot swells rolled towards shore. With the lack of wind the surface of the water was like glass; perfect surfing conditions.

While sitting on my board waiting for a set of swells to roll through, I became fascinated with the surface of the water; I could not divert my attention from its radiant glare. The water seemed exceedingly beautiful, the sun's rays reflecting on the surface, causing it to light up like a dazzling sheet of white fire. Unfortunately, the glassy surface of the water functioned exactly like a polished mirror, reflecting the brilliance of the sun's rays directly onto the retina in the back of my eyes.

The intensity of the sun's reflection caused my first, and thank God only, case of severe retinitis. Ceylon lays only seven degrees north of the Equator; the sun there is exceptionally bright. The reflection on the water was bright enough to burn the sensitive cells lining the interior of my eyes.

It felt like there was sand under my eyelids, scraping the surface of my corneas each time I moved my eyes or blinked. The irritation created a migraine headache that caromed from eye to eye to ear and back again. Returning home, I lay with a wet cloth over my closed eyes and forehead trying to dispel the pain.

During that afternoon, as I endeavored to rest and decrease the discomfort caused by the sun's rays; a military jet fighter began to fly over our apartment. The speeding aircraft buzzed the community at a very low altitude. Like a pelican flying only high enough over the water not to get wet, its elongated wing barely touching the top edge of a cresting wave; the plane's wing barely cleared the building's rooftops. The sound of the jet had the effect of magnifying my throbbing head pain by a factor of ten.

After the jet's fly-over of the apartment, it flew a circle and, surprisingly, buzzed the apartment again and again; like a wedge being hammered into my skull, each pass exacerbated the throbbing between my ears. Having added agonizingly to the thundering misery I felt, I prayed that the creep in the jet would crash before my head split into pieces. I couldn't fathom why a military jet was continually flying so low over a highly populated area; not that I really cared; I just wanted the sound of the deafening engine to stop. Much to my delight, the plane suddenly did stop flying overhead and the offensive thunder of the jet's engine ceased to repeat itself.

As the roar of the plane was hushed, I immediately felt some relief in my aching head; I embraced the surrounding quiet, clinging to the healing silence. I almost felt as though the pilot had been purposely harassing me in my excruciatingly painful condition. The next day, I heard a radio report that the pilot, while making a too sharp turn over the city, had lost control of his craft and crashed, killing himself and two people on the ground.

There was a great deal of familial anger when it was reported that the pilot had been killed in the accidental crash of one of his nation's few jet fighters. He was the son of a leading Sinhalese family and there would be hell to pay if anyone was found responsible for his crash. The idea that their delinquent son could have been responsible for his own death never entered the family's thoughts. Not to mention that his flight pattern, flying low over the residential areas of the city, was illegal; it was reported he was showing off for his fiancé with his ill-fated maneuvers. As for the two deaths on the ground, a payment of a few rupees was made to the surviving families and they were soon forgotten, swept under the rug like so much dust.

I didn't dare entertain the thought that the strength of my prayers might have had something to do with the sudden and disastrous outcome of that offensive flight. While being sorry for the loss of life, I was intensely happy when the screaming blast of the aerial trespasser had been extinguished.

During that afternoon and night the throbbing in my head persisted; I felt as though I lay on a bed of nails; being hit with a hammer would have been a relief. I continually placed a wet cloth over my eyes and forehead. Again, I tossed and turned all through the late hours, sleep not making an appearance that night. The next day, the pain in my head finally began to abate, the next night I was able to sleep and the following day, felt almost human again. I had no idea that the rays of the sun could be so potent. In my youthful innocence, I was astonished to find that simply staring at the water's surface could cause such agony.

Time was slowly passing as we continued to enjoy the endless days of surfing on Ceylon's scenic coast. We realized that this heavenly existence couldn't go on forever; we needed a plan for our future, it was a time for meaningful thought. Discussion was focused around *Paisano* and if we should, or could return to crew the boat. We were having a great time ashore; we hadn't recently contacted John and didn't know what plans might be formulating.

Deciding it was time to meet with John, do some probing to discover if we had a future on the ketch, we set up a time to meet with him. He asked us to return to the boat so that we could continue our journey as a group. Apparently, there was no animosity amongst the three of us.

John alluded to the government not allowing the crew to leave the boat without hands to sail it, in essence stranding John in Ceylon. Inversely, John could not deposit two young American boys in Ceylon without any means of support. A conundrum existed that would have to be resolved to everyone's satisfaction: John's, mine, Charles' and the government's.

Charles decided to return to *Paisano* and continue to crew the ketch on its westward journey. I, after considerable discussion with my new friend Brad, decided to head for Australia. I had had a great time in the land Down Under; I really liked the women I met there and had made ready friends with the guys we had surfed with.

Brad offered to give me money to pay for passage on a steamer to Singapore. Once there, I could find passage aboard a ship heading south to Darwin on the west coast of the Northern Territory. I liked that idea; I really liked Aussie attitudes and wanted to spend more time pursuing life in Australia. However, it seemed the divine hand of fate had other plans for me.

The filming of the Italian movie was soon completed and Brad was looking forward to returning to his Italian villa. He, Bill and the film crew had departed Ceylon and were on their way home to Italy. I booked passage on a ship sailing to Singapore, via Malaysia; passage was about to begin in the next few days. Due to the small amount of money that I possessed, with a heavy heart I sold my surfboard. I reasoned that the board would be too difficult to carry along with me; besides, someone in Ceylon would surely enjoy it.

Charles returned to his bunk on the boat. He and John could sail the boat alone if necessary; or perhaps they could find another crewman to replace me. As it was, they were not quite ready to leave this Indian Ocean jewel quite yet.

After enjoying an incredible three months surfing coastal Ceylon, making forays into the densely packed jungle interior and meeting many new friends, it was time to head on. With an optimistic view and no idea what the future might hold, at the ripe young age of nineteen, I stepped aboard my transport in early February of 1966, at three o'clock in the afternoon for a five p.m. departure. I never looked back.

Surfing at Galle

Port Moresby, Papua, New Guinea

XV

Go East Young Man?

The *Asian Princess* headed out to sea leaving behind the colonial skyline of Colombo and its striking inhabitants. Heading south, skirting the southern tip of Ceylon, she turned in an easterly direction towards Malaysia, cruising at a moderate speed of twelve knots.

A modern freighter, the 7,000 ton ship was clean and well maintained; she had a small dining room where the few passengers on board could take meals with the ship's officers. Her guest accommodations numbered twelve.

At dinner, the crew showed their amazement at having a nineteen year old on board, traveling alone. The officers were a bit priggish; in a feeble attempt at humor they alluded to the ignorance and immaturity of their young male passenger, calling me *kid* in a demeaning tone. It appeared that I, with my recently acquired assemblage of divergent experiences and youthful good looks, was a challenge for the ship's semi-accomplished officers. But yes, they did look both handsome and polished at the dinner table in their sharply pressed dress whites.

Traversing a distance of approximately fifteen hundred miles in slightly under a week of travel, the ship made its first port in Penang. She anchored in mid-harbor like many ships currently in port; her deck crew readied the ship's equipment to off-load cargo carried from India. Afterward, she would receive cargo that needed to be delivered to more distant ports.

Penang was a large port with an international fleet of cargo ships anchored offshore; mountains of goods were delivered to this southwest Asian port while others were shipped out. The port city was completely uninteresting, a veritable melting pot of everything that you would want to avoid in life. The water in the harbor was brown, the cranes unloading the ships created a cacophony of irritating sounds and the air smelled foul from diesel fuel exhaust. Not part of the world of island paradises that I had grown accustomed to.

However, looking forward to some uniquely Asian points of interest, I was excited to head to shore on a chartered skiff that carried travelers and off-duty crewmen into the passenger wharf. From there I headed into town, searching for new things to see and do. Walking around the city for hours, I found little to rouse my interest; I stopped to have lunch at a seaside restaurant. The food was poor and the city as uninteresting as the harbor was offensive; disappointed, I returned to the ship to relax, glad to be out of the distasteful city.

The Asian Princess had to wait for a shipment of cargo that had not yet reached Penang. Having free time and never having observed it before, I found the management of cargo to be interesting. Barges were employed to carry the cargo from shore out to where the ships lay at anchor, onboard cranes and winches were employed to lift the cargo from the deck of the barges and then lower it into the vacuous holds of the ship. Inside the holds, crewmen used a forklift to shuttle cargo to its resting place for the next leg of its travels. The cargo was secured in place with tie-downs, preventing it from shifting in rough weather, and the job was done. To off-load the cargo, the process was reversed. When the late consignment did arrive it was loaded; in two days the *Asian Princess* shipped out for her next port of call.

Kuala Lumpur, the capital of the Malay Archipelago, consisting of hundreds of small islands, was much larger and more interesting. The key land mass is the Malay Peninsula bordered on its eastern shore by the South China Sea, which also separated it from East Malaysia, located on the island of Borneo. The peninsula, known as West Malaysia, was inhabited by the majority of the country's population of one hundred million souls. It had gained its independence from the British only three years earlier; this Southeast Asian paradise was blessed with some of the most beautiful coastline in the world. Islam being the most practiced religion in Malaysia, the Malay citizens made up one of the largest Muslim populations in the world.

Again, I was picked up by a skiff that took a turn around the ships in harbor, ferrying those travelers wishing to go ashore into the passenger wharf. A bus ride into town dropped me near the center of the city.

Malaysia's capital, a large metropolitan city, was full of the hustle and bustle of activity that big cities thrive on. Located a distance inland from the coast, I was pleased to see that it was a great deal cleaner and more inviting than Penang.

Walking around the downtown area, I slowly passed a row of buildings with a bank residing in the middle of the block. I found it interesting to see one of the bank's security guards parading outside the building with a double barrel shotgun resting on his shoulder. The man was massive, having a circumference similar to a tree trunk. The guard looked like he could handle most felons without the shotgun. After seeing the bank's security, I couldn't image anyone wanting to rob a bank in Malaysia; it simply would have been suicidal.

Continuing on my tour along the main street, I stopped for a meal in an interesting looking restaurant around the corner from the bank. I was asked by the waiter if I needed anything, with an emphasis on *anything*. Being the innocent young traveler that I was, at first the question confused me, but after a few minutes of thought, I wondered what there might be that I could bring away with me from this fair city.

Being greatly impressed with the elephant tusks I had seen at Benji's house in Ceylon, I thought about asking if tusks were available. After the words had escaped my mouth, I realized that even if they were available, I couldn't carry them, nor could I afford them. In place of the tusks, I asked if I could buy a pair of ivory chop sticks. The waiter suggested ivory colored, plastic chop sticks in place of a pair made from the tusks of an elephant, but I was adamant about having the real thing. However, upon further reflection, I didn't think that was what the waiter was trying to sell.

During an excellent meal of noodles and sautéed shrimp, I contemplated my request. I realized that a beautiful animal, like an elephant, should not have to die to make me a pair of chop sticks. Appreciating the error I had made, I readily cancelled my order. That delighted the waiter, who then repeated his question, "Is there anything else you would like?" Not interested in pursuing this line of questioning I replied, "No thanks."

Wandering around the capitol after lunch allowed me to see some of the local architecture, strongly influenced by the country's large Muslim population. There were large, gold covered domes marking the shrines and mosques of the Muslim faithful, intricately carved as they represented the hopes and aspirations of a large pastoral population mired in poverty. Octagonal minarets vaulted skyward, their spires peaking above the surrounding structures like lighted buoys guiding the Muslim faithful to prayers.

On the coast were the fishing boats used to ply the local waters for the shrimp, tuna, squid, sturgeon and mackerel that swam north of the straits between the islands of Indonesia and Malaysia. Again, the poverty of third world countries was all too evident, where homes were fashioned from native materials and little of the modern world was seen. Electricity was scarce; outhouses were the common toilet, fishing boats were stored on shore to avoid the invasive shipworm..

After a short respite, the *Asian Princess* completed her business in port, then headed southeast through the Malacca Straits towards Singapore, my destination. Steaming for a couple of days, she tied up at the ship docks in Singapore in the latter half of February, 1966. The entire voyage had taken fourteen days.

✳✳✳✳✳

It has been said that the world can be a scary place, but Marshall saw only an ongoing adventure of new places, new people, and ever more interesting experiences. He possessed an open mind that allowed this unparalleled adventure of serendipity to cautiously continue.

During the past November in Ceylon, Marshall had celebrated his nineteenth birthday. Guided by an unseen hand, he was becoming a man of the world. The experiences of the past year and a half had made an overwhelming impression on him. Now at his ripe young age, he was intrepidly traveling unfamiliar parts of the world on his own.

The larva was developing nicely within its cocoon.

＊＊＊＊＊

Having docked in Singapore, I grabbed my few belongings and headed for the gangway. Saying goodbye to the ship's officers that had befriended me on the *Asian Princess*, I headed for shore with a twinkle in my eye. As I stepped ashore I allowed the excitement of exploring a new land to escape my throat, "Awesome," I whispered to myself.

After disembarking the ship, I realized I could count less than a hundred dollars in my pocket; I sought out an inexpensive place to sleep in town. I correctly surmised that I would need the majority of my money for transport to my final destination, Darwin; more than two thousand miles distant. I had a visa that allowed me to remain in this Asian pearl for fourteen days and having never visited this particular island nation, I was not sure how to go about finding my way. On board *Paisano*, we had grown accustomed to our well-educated leader making all the arrangements and finding directions to wherever our next destination might be. Now that I was on my own and doing my own navigating, I accepted that I needed to be a little more focused.

＊＊＊＊＊

My first stop was the Chinese YMCA; residents there looked at me like I was an alien from another planet. They questioned, "What was an American doing at the Chinese Y?" It never occurred to me that there might be a Y for Europeans; after all, this is Asia. Two Y's would be redundant, wouldn't they?

When I first entered the building I ran into a friendly young man named Chin, who, surprised at seeing a non-Asian face, asked why I was there. I explained that I needed a place to stay until I could find passage to Australia. We became instant friends; then Chin walked me through the registration process. He helped me find a cot to sleep on. The Y was *very* Chinese, rooms were not available, but a large dormitory with cots, separated by a cloth barrier, was offered to travelers in transit. It was both inexpensive and different.

Being the odd man there, I received looks from most of the other guests, some hello's, some growls. When someone looked like they wanted to end my stay on the planet Earth, Chin stepped in and defused the situation. While China and America were not at war in the sixties, China was very poor and jealous of wealthy Americans, apparently even poor ones, as in my case.

I represented a democratic republic that was politically maligned against China and their communist ideology. And there was a war that was beginning to rage in Vietnam whose northern border touched on Guangxi Autonomous Region and Yunnan Province, in the southern reaches of China. With that ongoing conflict, the Asian communist regimes viewed America as an aggressive bully with future thoughts of occupation, perhaps domination; a future the communists found unpalatable. Fortunately, I had the advantage of height and weight in most encounters, but encounters of this type were not what were on my itinerary. I did my best to be away from the Y, except to sleep at night.

Interested in exploring this new land, I began to visit the downtown area of Singapore and was delighted how clean and quiet it was for a large modern city. It felt good to be there; it was safe. I found the famous Raffles hotel, had a beer in the large wood paneled bar and ran into a past acquaintance. I had first met Phil Lowry in Brisbane when maintenance was being done on both *Paisano* and *Destiny.*

Both boats were docked at Norm Wright's repair yard on the Brisbane River in the early months of 1965, almost a year earlier. A retired engineer, Phil was pursuing his retirement single handed sailing around the world while visiting satellite offices of his company. He was an exceptionally bright, taciturn individual who possessed the unique personality that is required to tolerate days on end sailing a boat alone across vast expanses of sometimes tranquil, sometimes heaving and sometimes tempestuous ocean.

There are inherent dangers in single handed transits. After enduring an extended time at sea, solo sailors often begin talking to the boat, then the sails, then the ocean. A time of solitude, some may find God out there; others, entering sailing's dark side, may find delusion, dementia, or death.

The ocean is a place of immense beauty, full of prancing porpoise, massive cetaceans and bountiful schools of fish under the guidance of Proteus, the shepherd who oversees Neptune's realm; it will sometimes turn to be the meanest of mistresses. Many ships have foundered during the centuries of sea trade and the ocean can be whipped up into a ferocious maelstrom of huge waves and horrific winds that can sink the stoutest ship. Circumnavigating the planet alone in a forty foot boat can be a fool's quest.

But with luck, storms can be avoided, shoals skirted and sand bars rounded. One obstacle that can be daunting is the few areas that still exist where pirates patrol; preying on passing ships. Thinking of pirates as an anachronism of the 18th century, many are surprised to find that pirates still ply the waters in under-policed areas. The first recorded act of piracy was in 75 B.C. when a young Julius Caesar was held for ransom. The Barbary Wars on the east coast of the fledging United States were fought in the early nineteenth century in an attempt to control privateers and the British needed five years to clear brigands from the Persian Gulf. True, they've left behind the Jolly Roger mascot and no longer wear eye patches or tricorn hats; today they employ machine guns and speed boats to capture their unsuspecting, unarmed and innocent prey.

Phil recounted his adventure of sailing *Destiny*, after much internal debate, through the infamous Malacca Straits. The narrow passageway is formed by the proximity of the main-land of the Malay Peninsula and the Indonesian island of Sumatra. Spanning thirty miles in width, numerous small islands provide safe haven to those wishing to be invisible.

As Phil was sailing his small sloop on a northwesterly course, having just slipped over the north side of the Equator, he was approached by a fast moving gunboat manned by a crew of well-armed pirates. Unfortunately, Phil was a sitting duck for the hooligans. Sailboats have no remedy against anything with a motor; Phil's sloop sailed at six knots, he couldn't outrun a bicycle.

The unsavory pirates came alongside his boat and ordered him to heave to, drop his sails and prepare to be boarded. Phil tried his best to ignore the ruffians, but when they fired a few rounds from a machine gun through his sails, his attention became thoroughly fixed on their demands. He rapidly complied before things degenerated into a more lethal clash.

Steering into the wind and dropping *Destiny's* sails, Phil waited to be boarded. Observing the sleazy characters that came aboard his boat, Phil became fearful for his life. Seeing the reckless abandon with which he was attacked and taken prisoner, he thought this might just be the end of his years' long voyage.

His apparent carelessness to sail into a waterway known for roving pirates was tempered with the belief that they wouldn't bother a solo sailor who had little worth stealing. Phil's thoughts and actions provided powerful evidence against any possible correlation between advancing age and wisdom.

Regrettably, he didn't factor into his thoughts that pirates might be interested in killing him and taking his boat, or holding him for ransom. That's exactly what they did, putting a hefty price on his head for his release. Phil's boat was taken in tow while he was guarded on board by an armed goon. The pirates took him to a small island and put him under house arrest. After extracting personal information from him, they sent word to his family in the states; he would only be released upon the payment of a ransom of one hundred thousand dollars.

Thoughtfully, his family turned this threat over to the United States government. A warship cruising in the area was dispatched for a rescue. A message was sent to the Malay government to contact the culprits, and let them know that if Mr. Lowry wasn't immediately freed, the warship, with a brigade of Marines, would secure his release. When word of the U. S. government's response reached the lawless rogue's hideout, the incarcerated sailor was quickly liberated by his captors, put aboard his boat and hastened to depart. The pirates wanted no quarrel with a U.S. warship.

Having survived his surreal experience, Phil then motored *Destiny* to Singapore where he safely tied up at a boatyard in the island's Marina District; he made arrangements for the damage from his encounter with the bandits to be repaired. Satisfied that his boat was secure, Phil headed to the international airport; jumping on the next flight home, he returned to Connecticut to spend time with his family. Surrounding himself with familiar faces helped shake off the horror of the pirates' most unexpected and unwelcome intrusion into his previously peaceful voyage. He had recently returned to Singapore and with his boat repairs completed, was making ready to continue on his single handed journey westward when we met.

After hearing about Phil's adventure I realized, once again, that not all was well in the world. What I was also about to find, was that not everyone functioned in a manner that made any sense, at least not to me.

I recounted staying at the Chinese Y and the negative vibes that resulted from my residence there. Phil told me about an ashram run by a local Hindu priest he had met. He suggested visiting the ashram, thinking I would find more peaceful, and safe, lodging there.

Taking Phil's advice, I traveled a short distance through town, arriving at the Hindu enclave. Entering a walled compound, I met some men conversing in the courtyard in their native tongue; I asked about a place to stay, using my now highly refined hand signals.

I was shown a room in the compound; it was about eight by eight feet, had a dirt floor and was empty inside. Water for washing was offered in another area of the compound. The building was a simple one story square with a main temple for prayers and meditation in the center of the structure.

Small rooms encircled the outer rim of the building; one of them was where I was invited to sleep. There was a large courtyard that surrounded the building where activities could take place; the faithful could debate world affairs or play chess. The entire compound was within an outer wall that stood six feet high and had a metal gate that marked the entrance. The gate could be closed and locked at night to safeguard the grounds and its inhabitants.

Finding this sort of accommodation intriguing, I decided to

stay for a while. I offered to pay the person who led me to the room, but the devotee wouldn't accept any money. After dropping off my gear, I went to see if I could communicate with some of the other men standing about the courtyard. As my gaze swept the men dispersed throughout the area, I glimpsed what looked like another foreign visitor on the far side of the yard, near the wall. I approached him, introduced myself and questioned his presence at the Ashram.

My new friend introduced himself as Steve. He was a tall, brown haired Aussie who had just arrived; he was heading north, farther into Asia. We both admitted that this was our first time visiting an ashram of this sort; we thought it kinda cool. I now understood the term *ashram*, adding it to my continually expanding vocabulary. We hoped that by staying at the temple we could learn more about the Hindu religion, its practice and its history, both of which were currently a mystery to us.

The two of us strolled over to a group of bearded men standing in the courtyard. We began to communicate, again employing a pantomime of universal hand signals I had gleaned during the past twenty months of travel. They were an odd bunch. Long hair with dirty cloth raps covered their heads while untrimmed beards flowed from their faces. The Hindu's explained that their religion forbade the cutting of hair except on special occasions. They did look like a motley group.

Unfortunately, Steve wasn't totally aware of the strict rules that these people adhered to in their places of religious worship. Our first and our last mistake was when Steve pulled out a pack of cigarettes from his pant pocket. He managed to get his cigarette lit before some of the Hindu faithful loitering in the courtyard stormed over, gesturing wildly at the cigarettes while pointing toward the heavens, perhaps invoking God's wrath on us. They made some pretty nasty grunts; lots of arm waving and yelling. Apparently, this was an egregious act that desecrated the sacred grounds of their temple.

Steve realized he had made a major blunder and stubbed out the cigarette. However, that didn't seem to placate the locals. They demanded we leave, pointing towards the outside of the compound walls while making a sign like they were sweeping us out the door while shrieking something in unintelligible Hindi. It seemed Steve had defiled their holy place and the infidels were no longer welcome at the ashram. We grabbed our belongings and headed out the gate before the growing hostility reached a violent level.

I later learned that this was a Sikh temple. Wishing to follow a monotheistic philosophy, the Sikh's had broken away from the main Hindu religion in the 16th century. They were an orthodox group that had no sympathy for anyone who didn't follow their rules in their house; another lesson for us novice travelers.

The two us found a small, inexpensive hotel where we could spend the night, renting a room with two twin beds for a few dollars. The next morning, we had breakfast together while Steve explained that he was going to head northwest up the Malay Peninsula into Thailand and eventually onward to Europe.

I responded that I was headed in the opposite direction, hoping to find a ride back to Australia, where I had so many great experiences. After finishing breakfast, we separated, each heading off in his respective direction and wishing each other "Safe travels."

✳✳✳✳✳

I returned to my search for transport to Australia, a fair distance from Singapore. Parsing the distance between the two points on a map, it was much farther than I had first appreciated. Airfare was beyond my means; I decided to look for a ship that I could join as crew, or to pay for passage. Unfortunately, there were very few ships heading for Darwin. Actually, there were none.

I wandered the harbor's docks inquiring into the destination of ships that I was invited to board. They were all going in the wrong direction. Then one day I went aboard a ship where I heard English being spoken. Listening to the crewmen conversing, they sounded very much like me, a Californian.

The crew was American, but the ship flew a foreign flag. I asked to speak with the officers, inquiring about their next port of call, while hoping they were heading east.

I was invited onto the ship and given directions to the officers' lounge. The ship's officers invited me into the small space, pointing to a seat. It being lunch time, and food being placed on the table, they encouraged me to help myself. During the meal, one of the officers inquired into what I was doing by myself in Singapore. I explained how I had arrived, about my recent travels aboard *Paisano*, and how I was searching the docks in an attempt to reach my next destination.

Intrigued with my story, the crewmen sat, listened and chatted. One of my hosts requested to see my passport; he noticed that my visa expired on that same day. With my focus on finding a way off this small island, I gave no thought to the expiring visa. But by the time we had finished lunch, an immigration officer representing the Singaporean government was at the door. He stepped into the small room and looked at me.

The officer's face showed his surprise at my young age and innocent appearance. He stepped outside with one of the men eating lunch, and they spoke in hushed tones for a short time. The immigration officer reentered the room and asked to see my passport. He reviewed the paperwork, then the visa; he asked me to come with him. While the officer asked politely, I understood that it was more of an order. I asked where we were going and why?

The officer explained that when my visa expired it made me an illegal in his country. I explained, "I was trying to leave Singapore and if you hindered my search, I would get nowhere." The officer responded, "He had to hold me in custody until I could get a valid visitor's visa from his government's office." I asked "How can I leave the country if you hold me in custody?" He replied, "That doesn't matter, the important thing is to have a valid visa."

He told me; once I had the proper paperwork I would be free to roam the country at will, allowing my exit strategy to achieve fruition. This exchange took place on a Friday afternoon and by the time we arrived at the police station, both the government's offices and the American Consulate had closed for the weekend; there would be no help until Monday.

I was stunned; I was doing my best to leave their country, they wanted me to be out of their country, so they put me in jail where I couldn't go anyplace. This seemed criminally senseless to me; I began to become agitated, but fortunately realized getting irritated would be of little help and could possibly make things far worse.

The chamber that was used for overnight guests was somewhat less stylish than the hotels, ships and yachts to which I had grown accustomed. I tried my best to be a gracious detainee; I bit my tongue in an effort not to yell at anyone. But I really wanted to.

While lacking the lush amenities of a first class hotel, the room was spacious. A large, twenty by twenty-five foot raised concrete platform filled the room with a three foot wide aisle surrounding it. I had the spacious lodging all to myself; there were no other guests in jail for the weekend. While the concrete slab was hard and uncomfortable, I was not truly apprised of its lack of conviviality until early in the morning when I came to understand the term *stone cold*.

There were no blankets, no pillow, no padding on the obdurate concrete; I speculated; one was supposed to form a cocoon and gently wrap the concrete around oneself? Unfortunately, I could not quite figure out how to mold the rock hard slab around my thin frame.

When I awoke in the early morning, the stone was freezing. Being in the shade and having cooled overnight the slab felt glacial. I rose quickly and began to move about to get both blood circulating and heat rising. I thanked God I was in the warm tropics rather than some frigid climate where that cold slab might have been a great deal less hospitable.

My feathers ruffled, I complained to the guard in charge that I needed to have a warm meal to keep me healthy after a night in their tomb. The guard could see that I was obviously not a criminal and should not have been spending the weekend in the company of my jailers. The guard agreed to take me out into the city for a meal at a nearby restaurant.

The guard paid for the meal and, after finishing a plate of steak and eggs, I was momentarily consoled. Returning to the jail found me contemplating a return to the slab; I began a conversation with the guard that lasted through the afternoon and half the night; anything not to re-enter the tomb.

The guards were well dressed in clean, crisp police uniforms. They were bright young men with good attitudes and were very respectful towards me. That really helped to prevent me from becoming enraged whenever my thoughts turned to the idiocy of my current incarceration. They were simply following the rules; in their eyes, I was the interloper. It appeared the guards understood that my imprisonment was more a matter of a bureaucratic blunder, or simply bad timing, than any criminal act.

When it was time for the guard to retire, he urged me to return to my accommodations, so he himself could slip off to bed. In an effort at placating my bruised ego, the young officer showed me where he slept, a small room with a metal spring bed; no mattress. Another night on the concrete slab found me cranky and wanting as I stiffly arose in the cool morning hours.

There were no showers, no soap to wash with; one insult seemed to be piled upon another. A small barred window broke the continuity of the wall, allowing fresh air to enter; an uncovered light bulb hung from the ceiling. I now understood why few people break the law in Singapore, a country known for caning its unruly citizens. But I was a young traveler, had not knowingly broken any laws; I felt maltreated by the government's inflexible rules.

I whiled away the hours Sunday, again conversing with my jailers in their office, attempting to stay out of the inmate quarters for as long as possible. One of the guards was thoughtful enough to bring me some magazines written in English, allowing me to expend a number of hours reading. As the darkness of nightfall enveloped the jail, I reentered my cold, foreboding quarters for my last night in concrete captivity.

Monday morning found me eagerly awaiting my freedom. Personnel from the American Consulate came and escorted me to their offices. My passport was sent to the local government office to have the visa renewed. By mid-day I was freed and with a new fourteen day visa had gained an extended timeline to find transport out of the country.

My feathers still ruffled, I asked the consulate's officer why I had to spend the weekend incarcerated like a criminal while awaiting a new visa? Were the authorities afraid I might try to make a break for it; escape the island without the proper paperwork? But didn't they want me to leave? And wasn't I trying to arrange passage out of their country when I was so rudely interrupted and detained? So what did sitting imprisoned in their tomb accomplish? I offered, "The same result could have been achieved if I had stayed the weekend in my hotel."

Shrugged shoulders answered my questions; I was dumbfounded by, what I felt, was this episode of incredible stupidity. What really confused me was that this whole unpleasant affair was initiated by my own countrymen aboard the American ship where I had felt so *at home* only a few days ago. For the life of me, I couldn't figure out why my compatriots had turned me in to the authorities. Were they trying to teach this nineteen year old nomad a lesson?

I had come to understand that life is an ongoing educational experience; however, I failed to entertain any illusion of learning from this most unpleasant of weekends. Perhaps one gem did enter my intracranial sanctum; *always obey the laws in a foreign country.* Governments seemed to have their own agendas and weren't especially concerned with the wellbeing of travelers. Only their paperwork was essential to them, even if it made no sense in how it was handled. As for my American brothers, I didn't know what to make of their very inhospitable and unsolicited actions.

✻✻✻✻✻

After parting company with my weekend captors, I ran into a young man who worked for the Christian Church in Asia. The two of us were eating at a local seafood restaurant where we exchanged greetings and began to converse. Allan

245

explained he had been in Asia for two years; he was trying to spread knowledge of contraceptives into the minds and sexual practices of the rapidly expanding populace of the region. Actually, it was the use of contraceptives that was their goal and they seemed to be failing miserably.

Aside from Muslims, Hindu and Buddhists, the region was inhabited with God fearing men and women of the Christian faith, and if the Pope said not to use contraceptives, then they wouldn't. It didn't matter that they couldn't grow enough food to feed their people or that their country couldn't employ their burgeoning populations; if God said to procreate, then by God they would…and, of course, they did.

Fortunately, they made up a very small segment of that country's population. But the question of overpopulation in Asia wasn't one limited to any particular faith, culture or nationality. The fact was: most families simply couldn't afford any type of contraceptive device. And so the population of the region continued to grow…

Finishing my meal, I wished Allan good luck and headed off to find transport out of Singapore. As I was walking away, thinking of the insurmountable challenges of Allan's quest, I whispered softly to myself, "Are you kidding?"

✶✶✶✶✶

The next day, after finishing breakfast and departing my hotel, I headed to the harbor where I again began to explore the docks. New ships had entered port while others had departed; creating some fresh opportunities for my ongoing pursuit of transport to Australia. But none could be found. I did board a ship, however, that was headed to New York. "Hmm," I mumbled aloud. My mind drifted to Yonkers, New York, the place of my birth. A place I hadn't seen for more than nine years and then only as a skinny ten year old, grade-school kid, with his parents on summer vacation. While I didn't really wish to head in that direction, I did have family on the east coast and at this moment in my travels, returning to my homeland seemed to be the course of least resistance.

*****

An American built Liberty Class ship, given that name by F.D.R. as he promised that these ships would liberate Europe; she was used to carry troops and equipment east during the assault on the Continental theater. Originally built as a utilitarian vessel, the Liberty ships could be fitted out either as a troop carrier, a cargo ship, a hospital ship or a tanker. In concert with a massive flotilla, she helped deliver the strength to overpower the iron grip of the Nazis, putting an end to the Second World War. Having achieved her intended purpose and having no further use, she was put into mothballs on the European coast. Later, the ship was purchased by a Hindu freight company based in Bombay. The ship was renamed the *Indian Trader*, the crew was completely Hindu; the ship, fitted out as a freighter, was employed in carrying general cargo to various countries around the world.

*****

I was invited to speak to the Captain, a well-educated Hindu gent who spoke English with a British accent; his accent providing a clue to where he received his education. He explained that the ship was heading to New York via Malaysia, India, and other exotic locales. The crew was short one officer and a cabin was not in use, "If you want to head home?" While home had taken on a completely new meaning for me during the past twenty months, the home he was speaking of wasn't the direction that I had intended to travel.

*****

However, it seemed that fate was once again furtively directing my travel. Not being able to find any other form of transport out of Singapore, I accepted the Captain's offer of the vacant cabin. A verbal agreement to pay for my food was reached, payment being delayed until reaching my parents' home in California. The passage was to be free as the ship was contracted to carry its load of cargo to New York City. Having received word from the company office giving permission for me to sail with the ship, the Captain explained that they would charge me three dollars per day for the food I consumed; a very fair deal.

The most beautiful bay in the world-Galle

XVI
Heading Home

I retrieved my belongings from the hotel where I had been staying; threading my way through town I returned to the docks. Once on board, I settled into the vacant cabin made ready for me on the *Indian Trader*. The cabin, located on the ship's upper deck, fit the definition of a ship's cabin; label it spacious and you'd be accused of exaggeration; it measured a meager seven by ten feet. It did have a small sink against one wall and a single bunk with three drawers underneath. A small writing desk was attached to the far wall which was interrupted by a porthole that allowed light and air to enter in warm weather. Sparse yes, but clean and private, it was definitely an upgrade from my recent custodial lodgings in Singapore.

Having stowed my gear, I checked in with the Captain; informing him that I was on board with my belongings and looking forward to the voyage. I took a turn around the numerous decks, checking out the ship and introduced myself to the officers whom I bumped into. Many were occupied with getting the ship ready to sail; leaving or entering port was always a busy time for the crew.

The *Indian Trader* departed Singapore as I raised a digital salute to the authoritarian government of the island. I stood outside the pilot house watching as the city slowly faded away behind me. Due to the rigidity of their rules and their lack of sensitivity, I had attained a profound displeasure for the small nation during my short stay on their island. Truthfully, I could not fathom the inhospitable means with which they treat youthful travelers. My vitriol was barely contained when I thought about my recent confinement in their most unpleasant accommodations.

The tropical sun had reached high in the sky as the ship moved slowly out of the harbor and into the open ocean; seagulls, petrels and fulmars flew noisily overhead, squawking

249

as they sang out their unfulfilled desires for their next meal. The engine was put ahead to standard speed as she headed northwest towards our first port of call, Kuala Lumpur. It turned out that I was about to retrace my recent journey through Malaysia before turning north and steaming towards India's west coast, a voyage of almost two thousand miles.

The ship anchored on the coast, a ways from Kuala Lumpur; for two days she loaded cargo and then headed northwest towards Penang, where she also loaded general cargo bound for the States. I again traveled into town in Kuala Lumpur, feasting my eyes on the intricate architecture of the mosques and temples of the capital. Admiring the sophistication of the work that created these buildings, I felt these people must be very interesting; I was disappointed when I had so little time to interact with the Malay citizens. In all my travels, the only other place where I had seen such fine detail work on buildings and furniture was Ceylon. Woodworking of the quality I viewed in these countries greatly interested me and would became a craft that I pursued in later years.

Our work done, the *Indian Trader* headed north for what I hoped would be an especially interesting visit to India. Much of the youth of America had become fascinated with the mysticism and spirituality of that distant land. I was thrilled to have the opportunity to visit this part of the world; I eagerly looked forward to hearing more of this uniquely cultured country and learning of its recently introduced Gurus.

Meals were taken with the ship's officers in the main dining room. The meals were mostly Indian, which I especially enjoyed, it bringing a distinctive taste to my palate. Only this time, there was no need to request a decrease in the strength of the curry, as the ship's chef was familiar with non-Asian tastes. On different days, I was introduced to various native dishes: Dal, a lentil soup; Roti, an Indian flatbread and Dosas, a type of crepe. On Thursday, Puris, a disc of fried wheat was served with Chaval, a native rice. The Indian foods were so tasty that I eagerly looked forward to mealtime. With the same thought in mind, the Indian crew looked forward to Fridays, when Cheeseburgers and other American style food was served; a nice change for their curry saturated palates.

Discussions ensued with the junior officers who, although juniors, were actually older than me. They were interested in my travels; some curious about me as a human being; from a world very distinct from their own.

Others were disdainful of me, due to my current style of travel; they were the children of wealthy Hindu families that would never allow their children to travel in this less than first class manner. However, I did manage to connect with one of the junior officers named Jamie. He was very open-minded, eager to make friends and although very young, he presented himself with an unexpected air of elegance and dignity that belied his young age. During meals, the two of us shared thought-provoking conversations that helped develop a brotherly bond between us.

Another of the junior officers was Tashid, a somewhat jealous young man. He seemed to be irritated that he was not the center of attention among the crew. Somehow, along the way, he had become a very spoiled young man. I seemed to be an innocent, unwitting, yet irksome thorn in his side. Like any resentful miscreant, Tashid seized every opportunity to let it be known that there was both resentment and distrust in the air. I did my best to ignore his occasional jab.

The officers had, what was considered in their country, advanced educations; they had traveled some and were now settling into a mariner's life that would carry them up the professional ladder of success, something that was much more difficult at home. They agreed with Magellan who stated, "The Sea is a dangerous place and its storms terrible, but these obstacles have never been sufficient reason to stay at home." Besides, there was a life to be lived.

The sea offered them the opportunity of seeing the world, earning a superior living, and improving their personal stores of knowledge and experience. There was also a downside to the peripatetic lifestyle of merchant mariners, they rarely saw their families.

My new friends all had specific responsibilities in the running of the *Indian Trader*. The Captain was in charge of the ship and made final decisions that were required to be made while at sea. He was also responsible for the ship's paperwork, as well as communications with the company offices in Bombay.

The Chief Officer, also known as the 1st Mate, was in charge of the deck crew that loaded and unloaded cargo and supplies. He was responsible for the deck equipment: cranes, electric winches, anchors and the below deck gear that was employed in the stowing of cargo being carried to distant ports. The 2nd Officer was in charge of the ship's safety, navigation and radio communications. He was also charged with equipment maintenance and repair. On larger ships, there was also a 3rd Officer who assisted the 2nd with shipboard tasks.

The Chief Engineer was in charge of the ship's electrical and mechanical needs. He would often have a 2nd and 3rd engineer as assistants. The engineer pointed out that while at sea, the engine ran twenty four hours a day; there was always an engineer on duty ensuring the engines were well oiled, fueled and functioning properly.

There was a cook on board who was acquainted with both Hindu and Western cuisine. He was responsible for three meals a day for both the ship's officers and the forty odd crew members. He, and his helpers, were busy guys.

✳✳✳✳✳

Having a young American who had traveled the world during the past twenty months on board, was indeed a chance for the ship's officers to exchange ideas and to learn of places they hadn't yet visited. We had mealtime discussions on our teenage years, the difference between dating in America and India and the differences in our educational opportunities.

Interestingly, while I started going to dances, chaperoned by my parents, at the tender age of twelve, my Hindu companions had little, if any, interaction with the gentle gender in their country. Marriages were commonly arranged by the parents in India; it was not unique for a groom to never have met his bride before their wedding; dowries were an important ingredient of the marriage compact. It was difficult for me to understand their way of life; it seemed they still lived in the 15th century while much of the world was enjoying the swiftly changing dynamics of the 20th century.

Education in India was similar to Ceylon, where those that could afford to pay for an advanced education, received one. Since ninety eight percent of the Indian population was mired in poverty, any education past the primary years was rarely attained. The officers working on the *Indian Trader* had the advantage of coming from well-to-do families that could afford the tuition of a Mariner's College.

✶✶✶✶✶

I was looking forward to learning more about India as the dwelling place of eastern spirituality; it was a country with a strong disdain for the capitalist nature of my homeland, a philosophy I didn't completely understand. Unfortunately, that disdain created a country of mass poverty; a nation with too many people, not enough food to feed them and too few jobs to employ them.

At the same time, India was the origin of a new spiritual awakening in America, one that was spreading across the North American continent creating a migration of pilgrims traveling to India in search of their own spiritual liberation.

I eagerly scanned the horizon for a landfall. I was not disappointed as the southwest coast of India first became a ghostly outline and then a firm reflection of the vast Indian sub-continent.

The *Indian Trader* anchored in the shallow opaque waters off the coast of Cochin, a small trading port on the southwest coast. Unfortunately, the ship was only to spend less than one full day at anchor in the murky brown water of the near shore; I was told that there was not enough time for me to go into town and investigate the riches of this coastal community.

Greatly disappointed, I spent the day on deck gazing at the coastline. How could I be so close to this great land of mysticism, ornate temples and spiritual gurus, and not actually touch its shores? With these thoughts, I began to notice a nascent yearning within myself; I hungered to know more about the magical ways of the east. At this time in my young life, I had little to no knowledge of religious ideas, lacked totally in religious instruction of any kind, and was bordering on moral bankruptcy--all the more reason for me, like many others, to find a moral compass. At the same time I questioned the intense focus on spirituality that existed in India while the country had difficulty feeding and employing its people. It seemed that something was out of balance there.

I was brought up with ideas of right and wrong, yet it seemed that many of the places I visited had no guide to lead their citizens on a path to righteous living. Certainly, every place had civil codes or laws to guide the community towards an honest existence, yet theft, adultery, and ethical lapses were condoned in more places than not. Can you hear my youthful idealism speaking? It appeared that India was not to answer any of those questions for me, at least not at this time. Disappointedly, I watched as India's west coast became a ghostly silhouette shrouded in the purple haze that hung over its littoral outline.

A rapid evening departure from Cochin put the *Indian Trader* on a westerly course across the serenely calm waters of the Indian Ocean. Aden, a small port on the south coast of Yemen, was to be our last stop in that tranquil ocean before entering the Red Sea.

During the transit across the Indian Ocean, bored with inactivity, I asked if I could do some work on the ship. The captain replied that if I was given work, it would remove one of the Indian crewmen from his job, an unacceptable proposition. I understood; the crew were poor and needed the income derived from their on board employment.

A few days later, with the confidence gleaned from steering two boats half way around the world, I requested permission to steer the ship. I was given permission and took the wheel. Five minutes later, I found steering the *Indian Trader* to be much more difficult than the ketch or the dilapidated old copra carrier. Although the steering mechanism was hydraulic, making the wheel turn with ease, the ship reacted very slowly to changes in rudder position. By the time the ship moved two degrees to port, it then kept going five degrees past the intended course. Steering back in the opposite direction only created the same response to starboard. Looking behind the ship I could clearly see the zigzag pattern the ship had created from my unpolished steering skills.

In slight embarrassment, I returned the helm to the Indian crewman who put the ship on a straight course once again, creating a perfectly straight wake that streamed out behind the ship. I observed the crewman's skill with a great deal of respect, realizing that steering a ten thousand ton ship was significantly different from steering a small boat; another lesson learned.

✳✳✳✳✳

The *Indian Trader* listlessly cruised across the calm ocean; reaching the southwestern shore of the Arab Peninsula, she was pushed into her berth by waiting tugs. She tied her docking lines to the cleats lining the freight docks in Aden.

The Yemeni people were part of the Arab world that was, unbeknownst to me, in turmoil during the 40's, 50's, 60's … Not being exposed to television, nor reading newspapers for over a year left me happily ignorant of the world's woes and the plight of the people of that desert nation.

Once the ship was docked, I made ready to head into town. Always eager to meet new people, enjoy a unique type of architecture, try some different foods and discover exotic points of interest in unknown places, I rapidly walked into the port city. From the docks, it was a short distance into town where I could fill my inquiring mind with information on a community that had adopted a totally dissimilar culture than any I had previously visited.

I had read that Arabia was known in the 19th century for its colorful people, its exuberant lifestyles and its decadent luxuries. With thoughts of Omar Khayyam and the stories of A Thousand and One Nights swirling in my head, I knew that Aden was going to be different.

It had been some time since my hair was last trimmed; I was hoping to take care of that periodic task while in port. I intended to search out a place where I might find a barber shop. As I came into the main street, I came to a rapid stop; I encountered British soldiers carrying carbines at the ready, as they patrolled the town's main street. There was no gunfire taking place and I was puzzled at the presence of the military in town. There were no pedestrians ambulating along the city's principal avenue; an eerie silence pervaded the community.

The soldiers, in full battle dress, had donned combat helmets, carried loaded guns held high as they patrolled the street with twenty feet separating them. I felt a little out of place as I walked the street in shorts and sandals. I was the anomaly there, but looking around the street I saw no evidence of danger. Wanting to get my hair trimmed, I stopped to ask a soldier if he knew where I could get a haircut. The soldier looked at me like I was crazy.

Another, less abrasive, soldier pointed out a place that cut hair and said, in a deep cockney accent, "Not to get your throat cut along the way, mate." Somewhat puzzled by the response, I continued a few doors down the street and entered the barber shop that had been pointed out. The shop was devoid of customers; the proprietor stood in the back of the shop, leaning against a counter, daydreaming while waiting for something to do. I asked if he would cut my hair. I began my pantomime, creating a two fingered scissors and held out my hair, a message the barber easily understood. The nonverbal communication continued when the proprietor responded with a vertical head shake and pointed to an empty chair.

I followed the invitation by sliding onto the thickly padded leather chair and speaking slowly in English. "I only want my hair trimmed." When the barber began to take out his razor to give me a shave, a soldier standing at the doorway, yelled out, "Cut only his hair, no razor!" He waved his hand back and forth in a, *don't do that*, admonishment. After having my sun bleached locks trimmed, I thanked the barber, paid for his services and exited the shop with a soldier walking behind me.

I was completely unconscious of the fact that I appeared to be the eternal *wandering Jew;* not a welcome sight in an Arab dominated community. I would have been an easy target for the armed inhabitants of that community, had the soldiers not been there to protect me. In my youthful ignorance, I was unaware of the hatred that existed between the Jews and the Arabs in that region; with the incredible journey I was on, there was really not any time to harbor hatred against anyone, nor the desire. With my trusting mind-set, I was completely unmindful to the danger I had just walked through. The entire episode bewildered me. However, the soldiers, in their gruff manner, recommended that I "Beat it," as the streets of Aden were not a hospitable place for a young American wanderer.

I later found there was an armed insurgency challenging British dominion in that country; the Brits were maintaining control of their colony with a strong show of force. This conflict went on until they decided to quit the region, giving the Yemenis their independence in the late sixties.

Disappointed, I sauntered back to the ship; making myself comfortable on board; except for short walks on the docks. Confined on a ship at sea for days or weeks at a time creates a need to find Terra Firma. Stretching one's legs, ambulating as long as possible before again being restricted to the ship, is the only way to get some exercise on an extended crossing.

Since ships don't get paid to stay in port, they spend as little time there as necessary; solely to load and unload cargo. Then, it's to sea again where they sail on to the next port, where they do get paid for delivering cargo. A cargo ship will spend ninety percent of its life at sea, constantly moving from one port to the next. A difficult existence for roving mariners who routinely see little of their land based families.

The captain of the *Indian Trader* explained that his wife would accompany him on a voyage at least once a year, but mostly was shore bound, where she was raising their teenage children. However, it was only the captain that had sufficiently large quarters to accommodate his wife. Fortunately, for the captain and crew, their ship made port somewhere in Indian waters at least once a year. At those times, the crew would abandon ship, doing their best to escape the physical confines of the craft while embracing their waiting families.

Having taken on cargo, we made ready to depart this unsettled area of the southern Arabian Peninsula. The ship rounded the southwest tip of Yemen, heading into the Red Sea, bearing north towards the Suez Canal. Fully loaded, quite a few days were required to traverse the fifteen hundred mile long Red Sea. I had to admit my disappointment when I found the water to be a cobalt blue; I questioned the origins of the Red Sea's name. One theory suggests the sea was named for seasonal booms of algae that turned the shallow waters red; another states the sea was named for the *red lands* of the Arab peninsula that surround it.

The narrow entrance to the channel, at the Bab el Mandeb Sound--translates as, "The Gate of Tears," for all the mariners that have perished in the strong storms that episodically visit these waters; it separates the Arab peninsula from northeast Africa; its slim channel providing shelter to the ships that cruised there. In ancient times, this waterway was a treacherous place to sail due to a shifting bottom, fierce winds and surging currents. The elders: Edrisi, Arrian, and Artendorus detested this long, narrow body of water that destroyed many of their primitive sailing vessels while causing a large loss of life.

However, modern ships had no complaint with the now cleared waterway, the land mass fell off to both the east and west, making the sea more like an ocean of almost two hundred miles in width. Farther to the north, in the Gulf of Aqaba, the channel narrowed to eighty miles before ending at the southern entrance to the canal. The air was still warm, the wind mild and the passage tranquil. No hint of the disruptive nature of the surrounding area could be discerned from the placid sea.

The canal, actually the second that was burrowed through the isthmus, was dug with the help of hundreds of thousands of forced laborers from surrounding countries. Completed in 1869, it was the work of the visionary Frenchman, Lesseps, who promoted and initiated the massive project. The first canal, the Canal of the Pharaohs, was built by Senusret II around 2000 B.C. It joined the Nile to the Red Sea. An active waterway for six hundred years, it eventually fell into disuse. With the constantly shifting sands of the desert, the canal soon silted up, disappearing from the local topography.

In short time, we arrived at the port of Suez and the small town that marked the southern entrance to the manmade canal. The narrow waterway was only wide enough for ships to traverse in single file. Traffic sailed in convoys, either south or north, mandating that ships wait their turn until traffic was heading in the desired direction.

The *Indian Trader* was fortunate to arrive at a time when we could enter the ninety eight mile canal after only a brief wait at Suez. Southerly traffic had cleared the inland waterway and northbound ships began their slow journey towards the Mediterranean. The canal itself was lined with concrete on both sides, bisecting the middle of the barren desert whose inexorable sands stretched as far as one could see. Surrounded by blazing sun and scorching winds, one was smart to stay in the shade of the ship's upper decks or inside the air-conditioned passage ways of the freighter.

No hint existed of the Bedouin tribes that inhabited this desolate area for the past two millennia. Only their spirits rode here today. No longer did those preferring the freedom of a nomadic existence gallop over these sterile sands. Unsaddled by the restraints of permanent communities, restrictive rules, and authoritarian leaders, the *desert dwellers* roamed the barren and inhospitable regions of the desert while being melded to the demands of the land. They lived a harsh life that, after centuries of endurance, the roving tribes had become quite comfortable with. Time passes, people change, cultures evolve and new ways flourish.

Nor could we view the pimpernel and sorrel of winter that the tribesmen used to fatten their famous Arabian mounts and laboring dromedaries. One could only wonder at the richness of desert life that T.E. Lawrence wrote of in his <u>Seven Pillars of Wisdom</u>; a life that no longer exists today.

✳✳✳✳✳

With nothing to see but sand, or water while crossing the ocean, a great deal of reading took place on board. I had devoured a good portion of the ship's library by this time and was happy when we had completed the ship's journey through the southern half of the canal into a large inland body of water, known as Lake Timsah, renamed today the Great Bitter Lake. The lake separated the man-made canal's two segments, providing a resting place for ships to lay-over.

The *Indian Trader* was instructed to wait at anchor while ships heading south were allowed to complete their passage, clearing the northern half of the canal. When given the signal to weigh anchor, the ship joined the procession heading north. We began the second half of the voyage through the canal terminating at Port Said on the water-way's northern boundary. Reaching our destination, we were now at the entrance to the much larger Mediterranean Sea.

At Port Said--pronounced Saa ide--land trailed off to both the west and east, showing the sandy coastline of Africa on the left and the Arab lands on the right. The Mediterranean, measures approximately eighteen hundred miles in length with a width of anywhere from eight miles, at its western entrance near Gibraltar, to four hundred miles at the Ionian Sea, and separates North Africa from Southern Europe. It looked more like the oceans I was familiar with, than a small sea. Travel through the Mediterranean took more than a week due to the navigational hazards and increased shipping that interfered with full speed travel.

Thankfully, in entering the Mediterranean, we had left behind the tropics; we experienced seasonal cool weather. It was the first time in almost two years that I had felt the refreshing caress of springtime. We still experienced full-sun days but finally, finally, life in the brick oven of the earth's tropical zones had been happily left behind.

I enthusiastically looked forward to the ship's next port of call and was excited to discover that our next stop would be on the north coast of Africa. While I had touched on a few small African ports while passing through the canal, Africa was a continent mostly unknown to this enterprising traveler. A small Spanish port on the north coast of Morocco, Ceuta was another brief stop on our westward journey.

The whole feel of my trip had undertaken a rapid metamorphosis as the cargo ship I currently traveled on was on a schedule; it did not dilly-dally for months on end at any one place. Gone were the halcyon days of endless surfing, carefree partying and incessant drinking. I had entered the world of efficiency, punctuality, and industry. Everyone had a job to do; they did their work, ate and slept.

Not being involved in the running of the ship, I was only allowed to watch as life was enacted by those around me. I filled my time with reading, sun bathing, eating and sleeping, and began to wonder what I would encounter when returning to the country of my birth.

Arriving at Ceuta, the most westerly seaport on the south side of the Mediterranean, we again stopped to load general cargo. Ceuta, known throughout history as a military stronghold, was to be our last landfall before crossing the mighty Atlantic. This small coastal village was known as a jumping off point for those wishing to veer north into Europe and a gateway for Europeans heading south to explore the deep, dark jungles of central Africa. The small Spanish enclave was a mere twenty kilometers from mainland Spain; its location made the smuggling of goods into Europe a short, somewhat daring, relatively unchallenged pursuit.

A two day port call allowed me to amble into town and again visit with people from another country. A different style of architecture greeted me as I entered the foreign community. A Spanish influence was melded with North African to create a mixture of old and neglected. Simple churches with their spires that reached up to the heavens drew my eye. Hungry from my walk, I ate a meal of beef and rice at a Spanish restaurant, and then ambled around viewing the facades of the centuries old churches.

Graced with a 15th century cathedral, this small community was a place that both Spain and Morocco claimed as their sovereign territory; it allowed the two countries to have something to fight over, and for centuries they did.

Cruising down the main street, I gazed in shop windows without being terribly impressed or interested by what they displayed. Unpredictably, in some places, the best thing to do was to simply stay onboard, curl up with a good book and read. It was difficult to learn much about a place when the ship only stayed one or two days in port. Nor did I have the advantage of travel brochures or any other method of learning about where we were going or what to expect.

With my recently acquired knowledge of the sea, I gave some thought to our upcoming excursion into the Atlantic Ocean. I was aware of the fierce nature of the Atlantic in winter; my mind was curious to learn more about the storms that might harass mariners this time of year. I was put at ease by the ship's officers, who passed on the knowledge that during the month of April few severe storms stalk the North Atlantic. They said, "Not to worry."

I had become immersed in a temporarily boring existence which was about to come to a screaming halt, as all hell would break lose as we sailed through the North Atlantic. Apparently, the ship's officers had not done their due diligence in confirming the weather outlook prior to our crossing.

This last and most lengthy leg of my adventure couldn't be found in any brochure, it wasn't on any itinerary for travelers; but travel was about to become very, very interesting!

XVII

You Needn't Worry, Unless the Bucket Falls Over

The captain, having received a weather report that suggested caution, ordered the boat ship-shape, the hatches battened and the mooring lines hauled. The *Indian Trader* turned westward once again, commencing the last leg of her twelve thousand mile voyage. Excited about our transit across the Atlantic, I hastily wandered up to the ship's bridge, searching the horizon longingly as though I expected to find something. But my effort was premature as we had thousands of miles of sea to cross before we would again sight land. The ship's officers informed me that we were to pass through a massive ocean that encompasses over twenty five thousand square miles.

I had learned that the vast oceans of the earth, that cover two-thirds of the blue planet, connect the land masses, the people and the diverse cultures of the planet. They create employment, nourishment, transportation and recreation to the landed populations. The ocean currents help drive the global climate, creating mini-weather environments that often dictated which areas would receive sufficient precipitation and what others might suffer drought. In later years, the El Nino effect was found to be responsible for climatic changes with a strong influence on regional rainfall in the eastern Pacific.

The seas were moderate and the winds light as the ship passed through the Straits of Gibraltar; leaving behind Cape St. Vincent, the most southern point of Spain, to starboard. She began her crossing of the unbounded ocean that separated the east coast of North America from Africa. I was both excited about returning home to America and somewhat sad, knowing that this journey through paradise would soon come to an end.

Viewed from a distance, you could see that I had a bit of

trepidation about returning to the home that I left almost two years before. I had long forgotten high school life; living at home with the parents was a distant memory. I had undergone a significant transformation during this extended time in Shangri-La. I wondered if my parents would recognize me. One time, when I had telephoned the parents from Australia, they weren't sure it was me, saying I spoke with an Australia accent. Their response made me question if they were really my parents?

As this fantastic voyage was slowly reaching its end, I found within myself an even greater appreciation for the sea. I had long been stung with Neptune's barbed trident; I had acquired a great fondness for the oceans and everything that lived in them; I felt as though the vast waters of the sea flowed through my veins. My mind cleared for a moment as I reflected back on my years as a junior lifeguard, the summers swimming in the ocean at Venice Beach, and the years spent surfing on the California coast. I loved the smell of the water, found incredible solace in the tranquility that surrounded me in the middle of the ocean, and felt a oneness with the sea that I had never before experienced in my short life. However, that tranquility that I had become so accustomed to, and prized so greatly, was soon broken by increasingly stormy weather.

✳✳✳✳✳

Four days out of Ceuta and the winds buffeting the ship began to increase until they approached forty miles per hour. The gale force winds kicked up waves ten to fifteen feet in height. Having experienced a cyclone in Australia, I was undaunted by this recent change in the ocean's temperament, becoming energized upon viewing the large waves; I wished I could jump overboard and ride them on my surfboard. But I had left my surfboard behind in Ceylon. Not to mention the ocean temperature was significantly cooler here than that to which I had become accustomed. Where I was used to surfing the bath tub temperature water of the tropics, the Atlantic was a great deal less hospitable with its fifty degree water, a temperature that would be more easily appreciated in a wet-suit.

Being an eyewitness to the unbridled sea in all its fury is a majestic sight not viewed by many. During the next two days the wind continued to increase in intensity; the waves grew in height; the storm petrel flew in bounding circles above the pilot house. The ship heaved and rolled in the incredibly howling winds, and I began to suspect that we were in for more than a late winter gale.

The *Indian Trader* held her position steady in the raging seas. The ship's anemometer measured the wind at ninety knots; she creaked and groaned while struggling to maintain herself in the sea's wicked grasp. For her safety, the ship was steered directly into the wind and waves. If she began to turn away from the waves and was hit by a large swell she could broach.

If she were to heel over too far to one side, her fuel and water might shift in their tanks, her cargo could break loose from its tie downs and the weight of her massive superstructure could cause her to roll completely onto her side, rendering the ship helpless. She would sink and with a storm raging as it was outside, all hands would be lost. But the *Indian Trader* had a skilled helmsman who kept her bow directly into the wind and waves. All was well onboard the steel hulled ship, at least for the moment.

During that night, the storm's winds intensified, the ocean's powerful waves that pounded the ship's bow grew much larger, larger than I had ever seen before. The waves were cresting above twenty five feet and the storm driven winds were blowing the tops off the swells causing a horizontal rain that was coming from the sea rather than the sky.

On the following day, the seas became lethal, with twenty five to forty foot waves and winds reaching well over one hundred miles per hour. Curiosity overcame my innate caution as I stepped through a doorway from the ship's safe, heated, dry interior to an outside deck. I was standing on an upper perch behind the shelter of the ship's superstructure, high above the heaving surface of the sea. From there I could view the fury of the storm from relative safety. With wind and rain pounding the ship, huge waves crashed over the bow sending blue water cascading along the deck as spray whipped at the windows of the bridge, seventy feet above the ocean.

I had never seen a sea so troubled, so turbulent, so petulant as this. I began to feel a bit uncomfortable with the intensity of the storm. I looked out to the fugitive shades of gray that surrounded us, wondering how anyone could survive in this hysterical sea. I realized at that moment that sinking was definitely not an option.

I used the interior passageways to lead myself to the bridge to get a position report on the ship. Considering the weather outside, I wondered how many miles the ship had traveled in the past twenty four hours. My thought was, "By now we should have steamed our way out of the storm." But we seemed to be suffering the same malignant weather as the previous day. The report from the navigator was, "during the past twenty four hours the ship should have traveled two hundred miles, yet we are in the same spot that she occupied yesterday."

In response to my query, the navigator remarked, "The captain has ordered the ship's engine throttled back." He went on to elucidate, "Reducing ship's speed during a raging storm prevents the bow from being driven under swells that were rolling towards us, the less water driven across the bow the less damage resulting from tons of water raking the deck and ship's equipment." And so, we hadn't moved in a twenty four hour period.

The wind, the waves and the ocean currents had conspired to prevent the ship from advancing even one mile, the *Indian Trader* was caught in the midst of an increasingly violent storm without any avenue of escape. The lack of progress concerned me, especially because the elements of the storm seemed to be *increasing.*

That was the bad news, the good news was that the decades old ship was doing fine, she was not taking on water and all systems were functioning properly. I did take solace from the fact that I was standing on a three hundred foot long steel ship that was built specifically for crossing the Atlantic Ocean.

The navigator speculated that the misery of our current situation may have been exacerbated by the powerful flow of the Gulf Stream, which drives north offshore of the east coast of the states and then makes a sharp right turn into the north Atlantic. When the warm waters from the southern gulf collide with the cool air of the northern latitudes, all hell can, and was, breaking loose.

The next afternoon, the radio operator heard an S.O.S., an international distress signal that by its nature requested any able bodied ships in the area to come to the aid of the signaling vessel. The distress call came from a Greek freighter three hundred miles to our northwest; the violent seas had caused cargo to break loose in one of her holds and she was taking on water. The careening cargo had impacted the inside of the hull, creating a crack in the ship's steel plates. The distance of the Greek ship from our position gave those hearing the call an idea of just how massive this storm was.

In these chaotic seas, with the ship twisting and rolling in the huge waves, the captain of the Greek vessel was fearful that the crack in his ship's hull would continue to increase causing the ship's structure to weaken and eventually to break in half. The Greek Captain's thoughts were rational considering the circumstances. And while the Captain of the *Indian Trader* understood the fears of his Greek colleague, we were both held captive in the grip of the same pernicious storm, making any type of rescue attempt too dangerous to contemplate.

Having heard the call for help, it was maritime law that any ships in the area immediately respond. However, changing course in this weather could be a fatal mistake. The only acceptable reason for not coming to the aid of a stricken vessel was if it put your own ship in danger. The captain was not required to put the safety of another ship and crew before his own.

The skipper of the *Indian Trader*, after factoring the dynamics of a rescue, decided it was too dangerous to change course and make an attempt to reach the stricken freighter. Helping with the captain's decision, radio communication alerted surrounding vessels that other ships were in the vicinity and could provide assistance to the

Greeks. The ship held her course, maintaining the safety of both ship and crew.

My thoughts turned to the wooden hulled *Paisano*; I wondered what would have happened if I had been sailing on her today, in these frenzied seas. An older, smaller boat built in the early 20th century; she had a sturdy construction, but not to withstand weather of this magnitude. I had no doubt that if *Paisano* had sailed into a storm of this vicious nature, she would have lost her sails and been dismasted, her hull would have broken up and no longer being seaworthy, sunk. There would be no survivors of a shipwreck in these riotous seas.

I returned to the safety of the ship's lower decks and made my way to the dining room to have some tea. There, I encountered others from the crew seeking solace in the camaraderie of their shipmates. Looking around, I could see the fear in some faces, concern in others. It was like looking into a mirror. Having had some sea experience and been in some good blows, most mariners understood the capabilities of their ship. Things were just getting to the upper levels of safety on the old freighter; it was reflected in the faces of all on board. Gone was the laughter and jovial atmosphere of the crew during calm weather and sunny days. It was definitely *crunch time*.

During the night, as the storm was reaching its zenith, I lay reading in my cabin when a crewman knocked on the door. Surprised by the unexpected visit, I was glad to have some company, if only momentarily. Never having had a night visitor in the cabin, I was curious as to the interloper's business. I became even more curious when a young man from the crew entered the room with a metal bucket two thirds full of water.

To my knowledge the ship's plumbing was functioning normally, so I inquired, "What's the bucket for?" The crewman replied with his pleasant Indian accent while his head rotated in his colloquial lateral head shake, "You needn't worry unless the bucket falls over." He then placed the bucket in a corner on the cabin floor and without any further explanation exited the small room.

I thought it might be nice if the crewman had left some

instruction on what to do if the bucket did fall over. Perhaps it didn't matter, as there would be no recourse. A ship as big as the *Indian Trader* usually only rolls a few degrees in any direction, but with the immense forces of the storm raging outside, the ship did pitch and roll in unusually large arcs.

Any force powerful enough to knock over the bucket would surely sink the ship, as well. Having already viewed the ocean in its increasingly malicious state during the day, I couldn't imagine being out there at night without a ten thousand ton ship around me. It was a thought I just wasn't prepared to contemplate.

✳✳✳✳✳

During my many months of travel, I had read insatiably. Many of the books traded with other cruising yachts were sea stories of the kind that can inspire bad dreams. Now it seemed as though I was in the middle of one of those books.

There were stories of giant squid that, angered by a passing ship, would ram the ship, breaking its hull timbers, causing it to begin taking on water. The squid would then encircle the ship with its giant arms and drag it down to the oceans depths, drowning all on board.

Other stories told of the adventurous sailors who tried rounding the Cape of Good Hope with disastrous results. Strong winds coupled with huge waves in a frigid climate conspired to produce an ocean floor littered with shipwrecks. In the freezing water of the far south latitudes, a man could endure only a few minutes before taking his last breath and slipping silently beneath the ocean's waves. And of course, there were the stories of a massive bull Cachalot or Sperm Whale that, in their anger, rammed whaling ships with their massive heads, smashing timbers and sinking their wooden boats. Melville's remarkable narrative of the great white whale was one of the better known accounts.

✳✳✳✳✳

I thought about my current state of affairs. I was in the middle of the Atlantic Ocean; a massive storm was raging around me in cold water and cold air, during the darkness of night. I plumbed the depths of my imagination, searching for any manner of escape mechanism to extricate myself from this seemingly disastrous situation, but, "Damn it" if nothing came to mind. I found myself in the middle of a perplexing conundrum, the resolution of which, I could not fathom.

I was, as usual, in a completely foreign place. I possessed no knowledge of how to disentangle myself from this frighteningly destructive environment. Desperately seeking something to take my thoughts away from the weather, I continued reading late into the night while hoping for a tempering of the storm's intensity.

Perusing the ship's limited library, I found a book titled, <u>The Stress of Life</u>. A medical doctor had written a tome on the ability of patients to cause their own disease: high blood pressure, heart attacks, cancer, etc. from the stress they had encountered in their daily lives. With an eye and ear bent towards the horrific storm blowing outside, and the tightness that was felt in my gut, I was strongly identifying with the doc's theories. As the night wore on, I could no longer keep my eyes open. I turned off the reading light to try and get some sleep as the ship continued its brave defense from the predatory storm raging beyond the confines of my tiny cabin.

A few hours passed and I was awakened by the sharp lurching of the ship and the cracking sounds it made as it was tossed about by the Atlantic's monstrous waves. In getting to sleep, I tried to imagine being home on board *Paisano*. I dreamt I was snug in my port bunk, in a calm bay, in one of the many paradises we had recently visited, not in the midst of a massive hurricane in the middle of the Atlantic Ocean. Didn't work!

I tried to get to sleep again. An hour later, after falling asleep for a few minutes, the sound of something dragging on the floor caused me to bolt upright in my bunk. I turned on the night light to find that the water laden bucket had shifted. "Oh shit!" This was getting serious. I never, in my wildest dreams, believed that the ship could move so sharply as to slide the water-laden bucket across the floor, but it did. However, I still didn't believe that the ship could lurch so radically as to cause the bucket to spill.

I turned off the light, again trying to get some sleep. I hoped that the storm would soon begin to decrease its destructive forces. To my dismay, the storm continued unabated, the bucket made a few short excursions around the floor of the cabin, waking me and scaring me half to death each time. Exhausted, I fell back into a deep sleep.

Within the next hour, I was awakened by a sharp bang as something heavy struck the wall of my cabin. Worn out from the sleepless night, I cautiously turned on the cabin light, cleared my sleep clogged eyes and slowly sat up in my bunk. Looking toward the floor, I was deeply troubled to find that the bucket had indeed turned over, its liquid contents rolling from wall to wall on the cabin floor. "No, no, no," I whispered in disbelief.

Having already mentally debated the options of surviving a sinking ship in this storm, I knew there was no escape, no evading the uninhibited strength of the North Atlantic during one of its terminal tantrums.

I wondered if praying would help, it wasn't something that I often practiced; I thought it wrong to ask for God's help when I didn't pay my respects at less critical times. "To hell with that," I thought, and began to ask for help from someone that might have a handle on this increasingly bleak situation.

Having made my special request and understanding the helplessness of the moment, I took a deep breath and turned off the light, pulling my pillow up over my head. As I dozed off to sleep, I hoped that when I next woke, it would not be to the sound of the frigid waters of the Atlantic lapping at the base of my bunk.

For the first time on this trip, and probably for the first time in my short life, I contemplated the thought of dying. Making this realization all the more poignant was the fact that nothing I could do would influence the outcome of this predicament. I was at the mercy of God's wrath; I could only wait and see what my fate was to be.

To be truly helpless was my sentence in this mid-ocean water world. It would be the hand that had guided me to this point that would allow me to complete this journey, or not. Perhaps it was God's will to terminate my almost completed circumnavigation at this point with a visit to a cold, deep, plutonian grave. But I did understand one thing: I innately knew, deep within my core, that at nineteen years of age, it was not yet my time to die.

Happily, the seemingly impossible feat of the bucket spilling its contents onto the cabin floor marked the storm's climax. After a fitful few hours of tossing and turning, I awoke in the early morning, fatigued from my sleepless night; my bunk still dry, the ship still afloat. I could feel the storm slightly decreasing in intensity and the movement of the ship diminishing in its tortuous writhing as the sea tossed it around like a bumble bee in a stiff wind. But float we did, and that meant that the *Indian Trader* might just complete its journey to the east coast after all.

As though by some invisible hand, the waves and wind continued to mollify themselves. Tranquility returned to the ship and the toxic fear that had made its home in my mind began to diminish. What an incredible state of helplessness and dread I had encountered. After realizing that it was fruitless to resist, I acknowledged my helplessness; I accepted my impending death and wondered at the waste it would have been. At that time, nearly the beginning of my life, I had so much to give, so many games to play, so many years of study, so many books to read and so much to contribute. Dying now certainly did not seem an acceptable conclusion to my voyage. As Nietzsche so intelligently pointed out, "That which does not kill us, makes us stronger." Suddenly, I was feeling incredibly strong.

It is not often that one has the chance to ponder our own impending death. Like a bucking bronco, the mind rails at the thought, trying to unseat it, cast it out. But I was right, there was so much more waiting, so many more places, so many more experiences, so much to learn, to give and to do; dying now was simply an unacceptable thought. And so, my days went on, some good, some not so good…

As the sea continued to calm, skies cleared and the winds fell again to gale force. The captain of the *Indian Trader* sent a team of men, headed by my young friend Jamie, to check on the condition of the windlass and other gear on the ship's foredeck. The storm's belligerent waves had washed over the bow, the deck and the forward equipment during the past three days, possibly leaving the forward gear bent, broken and dysfunctional. Difficult to believe that the force of wind-whipped water and rushing waves have the strength to tear steel plates from a bulkhead, loosen metal structures on deck and create all category of havoc on a steaming ship, but it does.

With my appetite finally returning, I made my way to the dining room to put some food into my knotted stomach; I hoped to find that lunch had been prepared.   My luck continued as the seas had calmed sufficiently to allow the cook to return to his duties in the galley.

As I entered the dining area, I noticed an eerie silence among those seated around the tables. Rather than the happy faces I expected, from the reprieve of having survived the storm, the expression on the crew's faces looked more like the ship had already sunk. No one looked up when I entered; no one offered a greeting as I passed among those present. Food was played with on its plate, rather than being consumed by ravenous seamen. A mist of melancholy pervaded the area.

I searched the room for Jamie, wanting to join my friend at his table, but didn't see him present. Feeling as though something was amiss, I queried those present, "What's wrong?"   Someone, in a quiet whisper responded, "The Captain sent Jamie and some other crew members to check equipment on the forward deck of the ship. While inspecting the gear, a rogue wave of twenty feet in height vaulted over the bow, catching the crew members unaware."

The tons of water from the errant wave struck the men, knocking them against a steel bulkhead. One man drowned, two others were twisted and broken from their collision with steel and water. The deceased was my friend, twenty-three year old Jamie. I could scarcely believe my ears. Jamie was the nicest person I had ever met: energetic, sincere, candid, intelligent; a gregarious young man with an entire life ahead of him. Like the others, I was shocked and greatly saddened by Jamie's death; I suddenly lost all interest in food; the knot in my stomach tightened a notch.

Jamie's body was secured in the ships medical facility, wrapped in a body bag and stowed in the freezer until the ship reached New York. The men that had suffered broken bones from their encounter with the steel bulkhead, had their limbs splinted and were maintained in their bunks until they could be attended by a doctor for casting.

The rest of the trip continued in a more subdued atmosphere. The gaiety was gone, the freshman antics of the young crew members were lost, as a mood of gloom and despair hung in the air. A veil of grief had fallen upon the *Indian Trader*, suddenly, everyone yearned for this trip to be over.

✶✶✶✶✶

With the calm of the ocean increasing each day, the storm battered ship increased her speed and steamed full ahead toward the east coast of the U.S. and its destination, the island of Manhattan. She arrived on a bright, sunny, brisk day in late April. Steaming under the Verrazano Bridge into New York Harbor, she humbly sailed past the Statue of Liberty, steering to port up the Hudson River. Finding her appointed docking place, the ship was gently nudged into the pier by waiting tugs. Docking lines were heaved ashore; she tied up at the freight docks reserved for cargo ships on the island's west side.

Agents from Customs and Immigration came aboard; there was an investigation into the accident that caused Jamie's death and the injuries to the other crew members. I was questioned briefly, but could offer no help; knowing only what I had heard from the others. I did express my disappointment at this most painful, unexpected and unacceptable of events.

Up to this time, my trip had been highlighted with storybook adventures and exotic locales; some down times, but much laughter and happy times. After twenty two months, completing this circumnavigation of the planet with a death was not the ending I had anticipated. At least in the movies, the good guys always win, the heroes escape almost certain calamity and life goes on. I was learning that real life was not exactly as you might expect from the movies.

For the Captain of the *Indian Trader*, the deadly accident on board his ship would probably end his career at sea. While no one could have foreseen a rogue wave cresting the ship's bow, to send the crew out into an unprotected area while the storm's winds were still howling and the seas large, was a poor decision by the person in command. And where was the Virgin Mary, the protector of mariners at sea? Does she not protect the Hindu as well as the Christian? Apportioning blame was difficult, perhaps an act of God?

True, the storm was tapering off when the Captain sent the crew forward, but there was no rush to check the gear. It was not needed in the middle of the ocean; waiting a few more days, when the sea was much more sedate, would have been a more sagacious act. There still would have been plenty of time to do any necessary repairs and the death of one young man could have been avoided. But, as you well know, hindsight is always twenty-twenty. Tears rolled down my cheeks, "Another lesson I suppose," I whispered to myself, this one more difficult to digest than most.

Before leaving the ship, I spent some time with Sagh, the ship's radio operator. Sagh spoke of another ship, paralleling our course at sea during the agonizing transit. The *Michelangelo* was a large, white, Italian cruise ship. This was her maiden voyage, her first trip across the Atlantic Ocean and she certainly picked the wrong time to make the passage. Upon docking in New York, the *Michelangelo's* captain reported being hit by a rogue wave eighty feet in height. The wave crashed over the ship's bow, clobbering the deck with tons of water from the wave's mass. Thrust forward by the full fury of the one hundred twenty five mile per hour wind and rampaging seas, nothing could withstand its destructive power. The devastating wave was responsible for the death of two passengers that were swept out to sea when the aluminum plating was ripped from the outer wall of their cabins. A crewman died a few hours later and over fifty passengers were reported injured and taken to hospital.

I viewed the ship as she sat peacefully, safely, secured to the dock; I was shocked at the condition of the nearly new giant white cruise ship. No longer a gleaming new ship, she looked as though she had been through a war zone, not quite escaping the violent assault of the enemy's weapons. Nylon tarps covered the holes in the ship's superstructure, bent metal could be seen along the deck; her paint looked worn, dull and in need of repair. Looking at her sitting safely in New York harbor, one would be shocked to learn she had just finished her maiden voyage. With the damage she had sustained in the storm, the mighty *Michelangelo* wasn't going anywhere soon.

XVIII

America the Beautiful

I gathered my few belongings into a duffel bag I had acquired during my wanderings. Sitting in my soon to be vacated cabin, I contemplated my life and the recent events of my almost completed journey.

I was both shocked and disillusioned by the recent change in the demeanor of my days. I had come to believe that people doing good works, serving their communities and their fellow man, lived under the shield of a celestial guardian. Then an accident and a death occurred that did not fit the pattern. Perhaps it was too simplistic I thought; after all, I was still learning how life worked, and it seemed to be more complex than I ever imagined. Simple answers did not seem to exist. I was beginning to entertain the idea that understanding why tragic events took place could be challenging, if at all possible.

In my limited number of years, my parents had taught me to be honest, help others and never pick on anyone smaller than me. I had become a strong, healthy young man and believed that the good deeds I had done had catapulted me on his unparalleled voyage of adventure and discovery. Then suddenly, all hell broke loose and an innocent, decent, caring young man in the spring of his life was killed through no fault of his own. Hastily, I was bombarded with existentialist questions that failed to provide acceptable answers to my inquiring mind. Like many my age, I drank from the goblet of ignorance while fiercely seeking clues to who, why, and where?

The death of my friend Jamie greatly disturbed me, it threw all I believed in out the window; making me question the correctness of my life and the virtue of following any inveterate rules. "What for?" I questioned, if in the flick of an eye your life can be extinguished in an unforeseen accident. "Do we write that off to *accidents happen* and move on?"

But then another thought began to take hold. Perhaps it was wrong to seek an extended lifespan, one that was safe, and one where accidents were continually guarded against. Like living in a bubble, that could be exceptionally boring. I then began to consider the importance of continuing to do good deeds while enjoying the quality of life's *journey*, as I had done so enthusiastically during the past two years. And if life ended tomorrow, then perhaps I should be happy knowing, "I had lived, loved and done so correctly."

✳✳✳✳✳

But for now, it was time to move on. I took a turn around the ship. I said my good-byes to the crew I had made friends with during the seven week voyage from Singapore. We shared words of condolence, as the sorrow felt from Jamie's passing and the injuries to the crew, still hung heavily in the minds and hearts of those on board.

But it was time for me to return to America and I moved off toward the gangway and on to American soil for the first time in almost two years. As I stepped onto the dock, I ran into an uncle that was sent to retrieve me. My uncle Tony, the totality of my welcoming party, didn't recognize me at first. I had grown to a height of six feet, had the build of a strong, fit, young man; I now had the countenance of someone who had seen both good and evil in the world. My uncle was shocked that I came walking along in shirt sleeves and shorts. I explained that I had no other clothing, as I had been living the past two years in the tropics, where sweaters and jackets were unnecessary garments that only gathered dust in the corners of closets.

My uncle Tony seemed somewhat confused by my nonchalant air. I seemed to be completely oblivious to the mid-fifty degree temperatures that enveloped New York in late April. Tony drove me to New Jersey, where he lived with his wife, Lily, my mom's sister and a favorite aunt of mine. She was working as a cashier in a general store that day, so Tony suggested that I get in line, hand her a ten dollar bill I had brought from Singapore, ask for change and see if she recognized me.

I entered the cashier's line, as my uncle had suggested. Funny thing, Lily didn't have a clue who I was; then she spied her husband standing in the background. Knowing that I was arriving that day, she was jarred by the reality that the young man standing before her was her nephew whom she hadn't seen since I was a scrawny, ten year old kid. My aunt hadn't seen me in nine years, during which time I had grown up, circumnavigated the world and now stood in front of her trying to change my last piece of currency, a funny looking, multicolored, Singaporean, ten dollar bill. Its value was less than four dollars in Paramus, New Jersey.

When Lily realized that it was me, she screamed in surprise, which of course got the attention of the entire store. She ran around the counter to hug me while yelling to everyone around us that her nephew had just completed two years traveling around the world and had only today arrived home in America. Shoppers from all over the store came over, said hello and, "Welcome home, son." Her tears flowed and I was moved by the heart-warming reception from relatives I hadn't seen for so many years and from new friends that I had never before met. I was truly home.

The next two weeks were occupied visiting with relatives, aunts and uncles from New York and New Jersey. I stayed with Cousin Jerry in Greenwich Village for a week, enjoying the sights of the lower east side. I walked around the community, trying to meet people, but found that most were busy working. The only ones enjoying their leisure during the day were bums and the unemployed. Suddenly, life was showing me a different side; one that was not especially pleasant, while pointing out that perhaps I, too, should be joining the ranks of the employed.

Since I was soon to return to Los Angeles, the origin of my voyage, finding gainful employment in New York was out of the question. Not to mention that at nineteen years of age, I wasn't highly qualified to do much, except perhaps to crew a sailboat. With only a few dollars in my pocket, and that advanced by my relatives, there wasn't much that I could see or do in New York. Lacking the guidance of my parents, as I had during the last foray to New York some nine years previous, I was at a loss to know what there was for me to see or do. Far from the tropical paradises I was so familiar with, I felt like a foreigner in the skyscraper- studded confines of that enormous city.

In early May, New York was a cold place. Unused to the bitterness of northeast weather and experiencing culture shock, I was somewhat baffled by the changes I was experiencing. Unaccustomed to wearing clothing except for shorts; I was very uncomfortable needing to don sweaters and long pants in the daytime while adopting the practice of layering in the evening.

With thoughts turning to my impending flight to the west coast and not knowing what type of reception awaited me there, I felt some apprehension about returning to the home of my parents, a place that I no longer considered *my* home. I had matured a great deal during this trip; I no longer felt like someone's son, but had attained the bearing of an independent adult. The cloth of my life had been woven by two years of interaction with the people of the planet; my vision of life and the world had been dramatically altered. The happenings of the previous two years, while not a didactic education, culminated in an accumulation of knowledge and experience that could not be duplicated in any university.

I was however; ready to leave the cold weather that greeted my return to my native country. Uncle Joe, my Mom's brother, was generous enough to supply me with the airline ticket that allowed my fantasy trip to end where it had begun. In early May of 1966, I returned to Los Angeles; the place I had left almost two years earlier.

My gypsy-like travels had taken me to numerous countries, many islands; I had met uncounted individuals from all walks of life; I had had some of the most incredible experiences a young man could ever imagine. During this unexpected tour de force I had met and spoken with some of the most unique people from the most unusual locations; I had seen some of the most beautiful places on earth.

Both during my multiform adventures and most recently, I had spent time questioning the existence of God and tried to understand what life on this planet was truly about. I dared to peak beneath the veneer of life in an effort to dig a little deeper, seeking its substance. Some of my questions had been answered, but each answer seemed to produce a plethora of new questions.

While I may have begun this extended journey of discovery and education as a caterpillar, it was evident that I had left the cocoon and entered the world as a butterfly.

Surely, this journey was an extraordinary change from the vagaries of my prior life on the California coast; I felt as though I was awakening from a long dream, one that was incredibly engrossing; one where I would not want to open my eyes, seeing its end. But it was true--from the dysfunctional adventures aboard the *Isabel Rose* to the pleasure of slowly crossing the earth's oceans on *Paisano*, exploring islands in the Pacific and Indian Oceans, chasing butterflies in Papua, cyclones in Australia and a near death experience in the North Atlantic--I had left Los Angeles two years ago a young boy; there was no doubt that upon my return, when my parents looked into my eyes, they could see I had returned a man.

Not Nearly the End

On the West Coast of Sri Lanka

3-   -20

80 Kava
97 12-4 everything stopped

CPSIA information can be obtained at www.ICGtesting.com
Printed in the USA
BVOW040631190413

318566BV00006B/14/P

9 781450 716536